SPY vs SPY

THE TOP SECRET FILES!

WRITTEN AND ILLUSTRATED BY

PETER KUPER

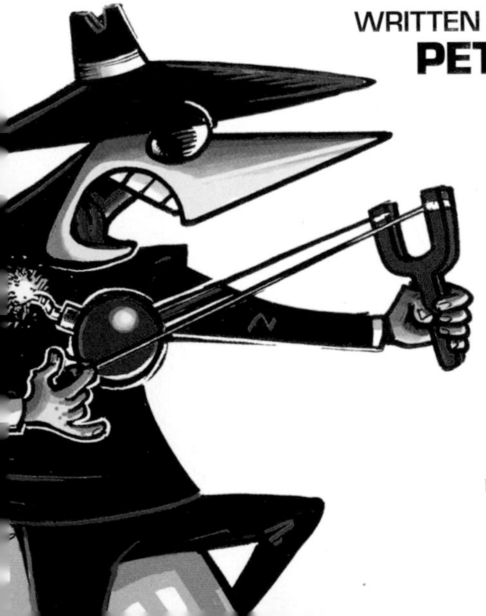

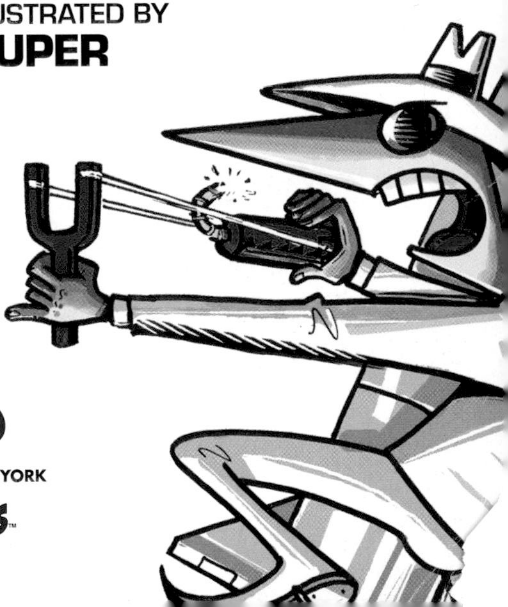

MAD
NEW YORK
BOOKS™

Compilation and new material © 2011 by E.C. Publications, Inc. All Rights Reserved.

MAD, Boy's Head Design, and all related indicia are trademarks of E.C. Publications, Inc.

Published by MAD Books. An imprint of E.C. Publications, Inc., 1700 Broadway, New York, NY 10019.
A Warner Bros. Entertainment Company.

CARTOON NETWORK and the logo TM & © Cartoon Network.

No part of this book may be reproduced in any form or by any electronic or mechanical means, including information storage and retrieval systems, without permission in writing from the publisher, except in the case of brief quotations embodied in critical articles and reviews.

The names and characters used in MAD fiction and semi-fiction are fictitious. A similarity without satiric purpose to a living person is a coincidence.

Printed by RR Donnelley, Crawfordsville, IN, USA. 10/14/11. First Printing.
ISBN: 978-1-4012-3527-7

Spy vs. Spy created by Antonio Prohias

SUSTAINABLE FORESTRY INITIATIVE
www.sfiprogram.org
Certified Chain of Custody
Promoting Sustainable
Forest Management
Fiber used in this product line meets the
sourcing requirements of the SFI program.
www.sfiprogram.org SGS-SFI/COC-US10/81072

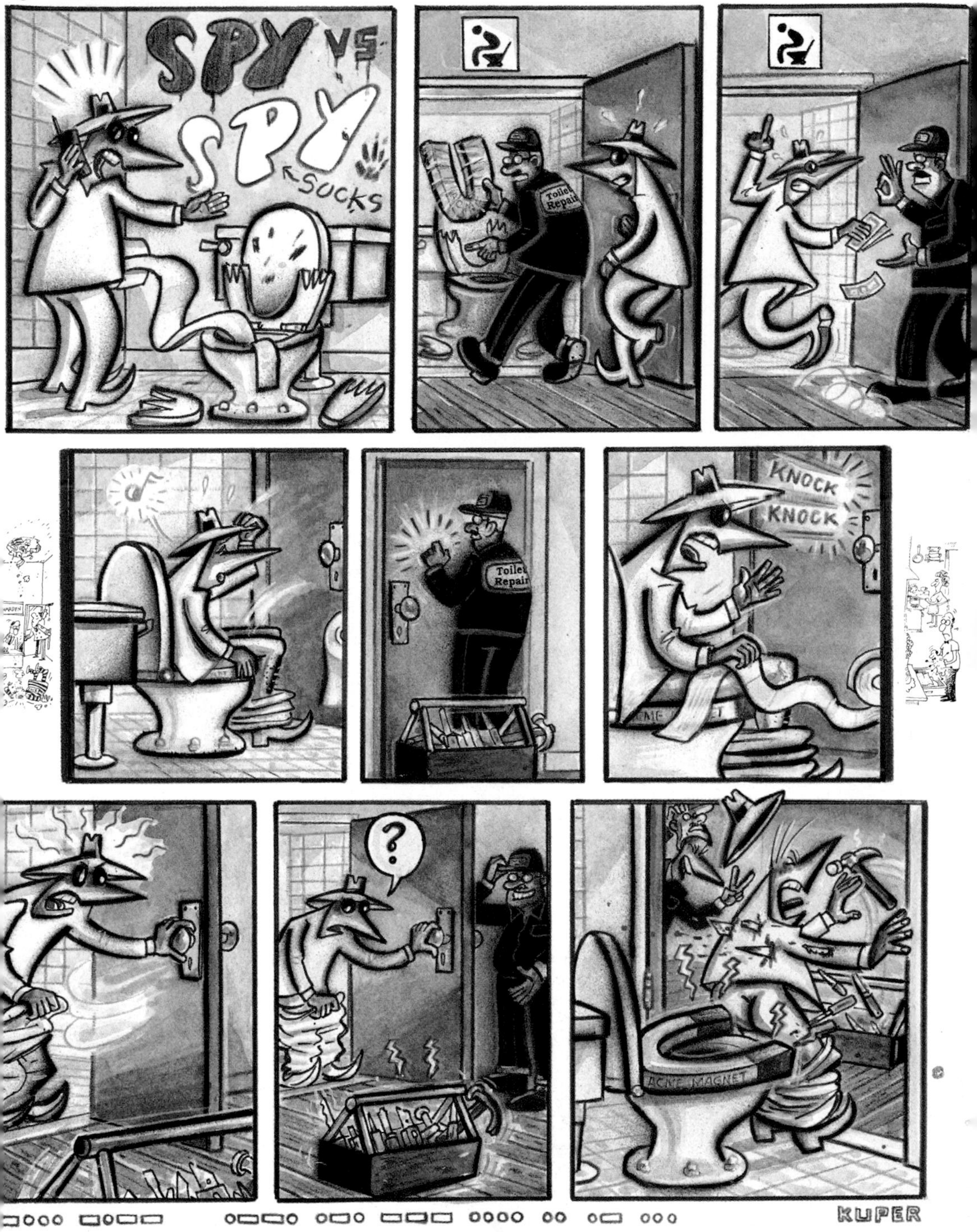
SPY VS SPY
SUCKS
Toilet Repair
Toilet Repair
KNOCK
KNOCK
?
ACME MAGNET
KUPER

JOKE AND DAGGER DEPT.

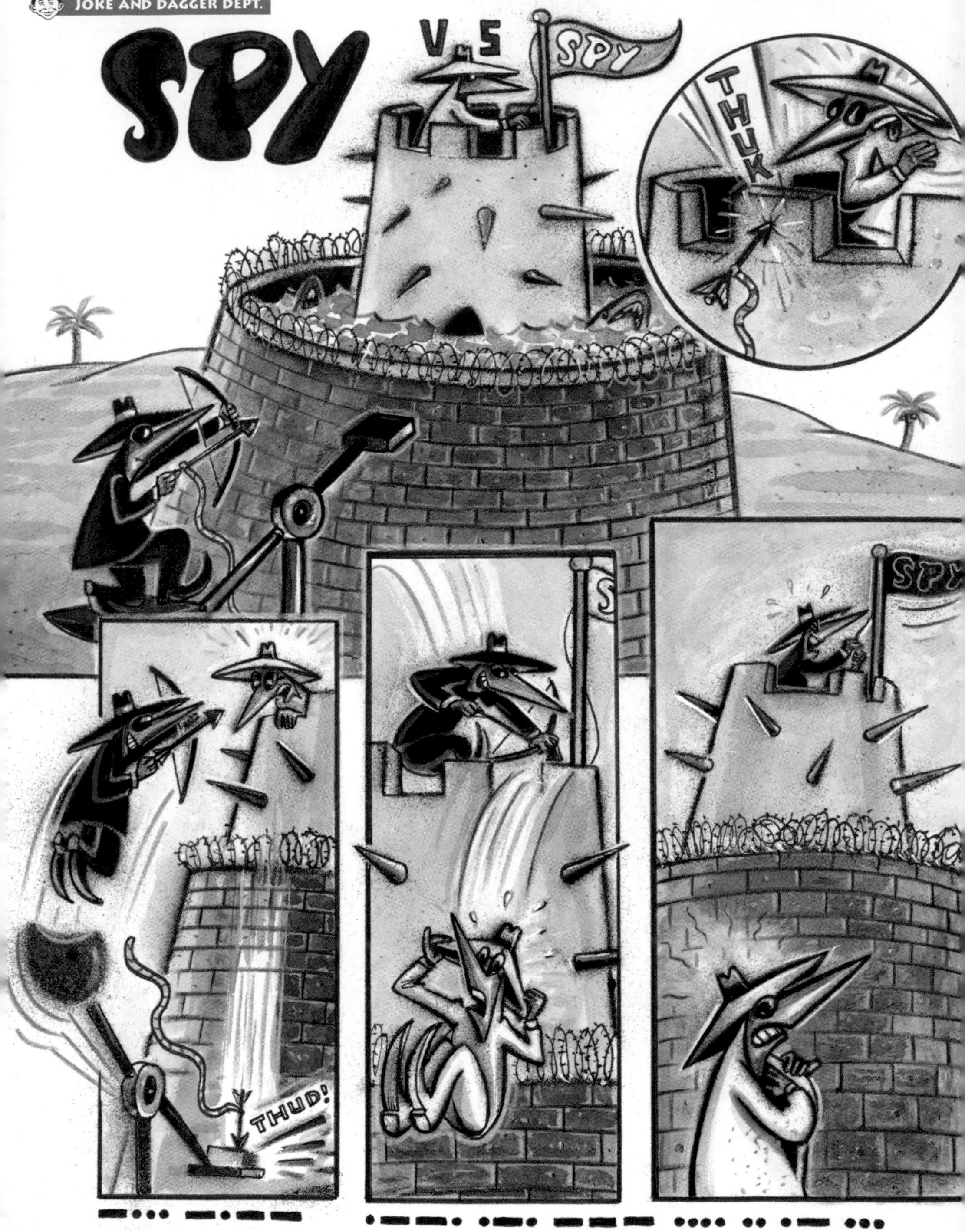
SPY
VS
SPY
THUK
THUD!
S
SPY

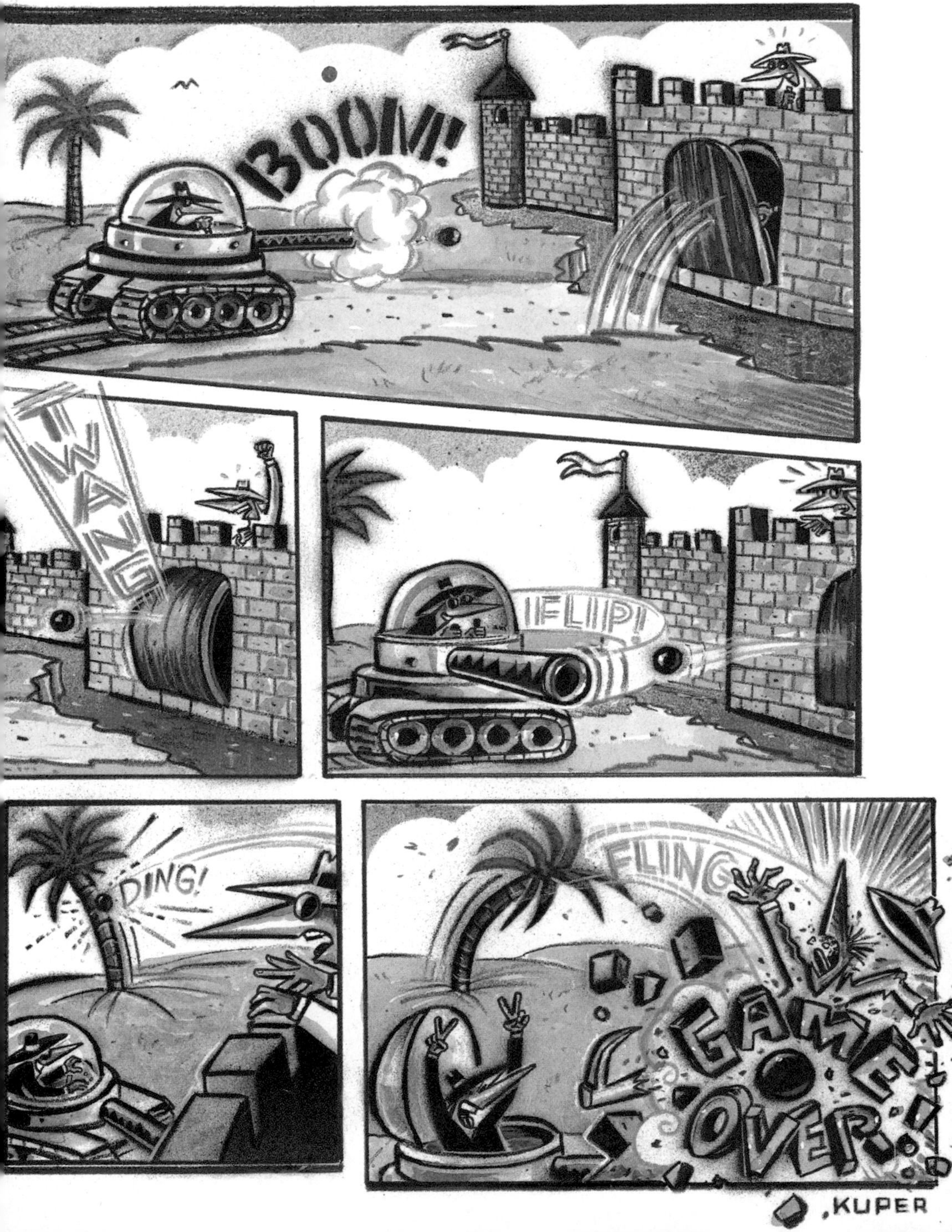
BOOM!
TWANG
FLIP!
DING!
FLING
GAME OVER!
KUPER

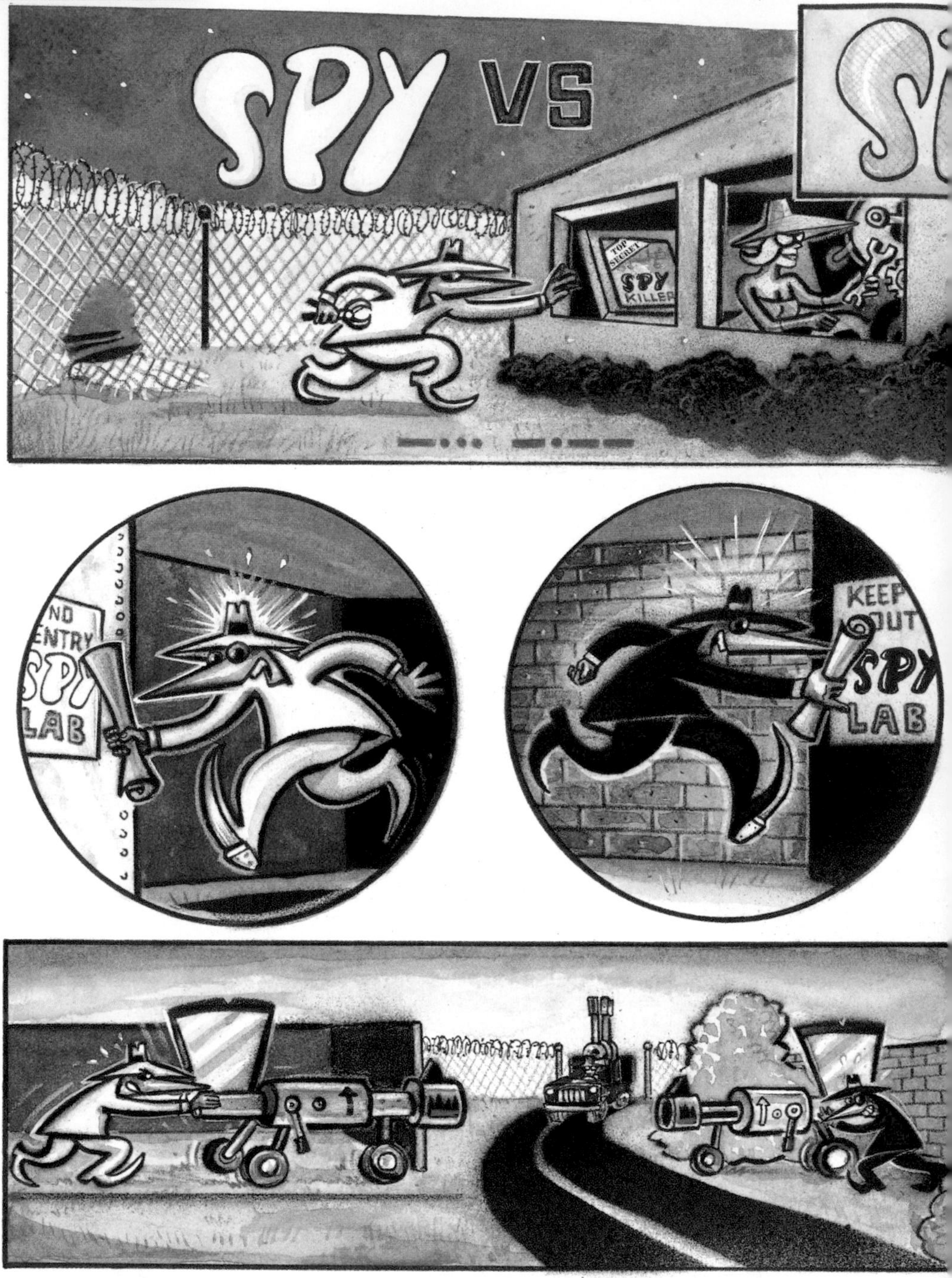
SPY VS
TOP SECRET
SPY KILLER
NO ENTRY SPY LAB
KEEP OUT SPY LAB

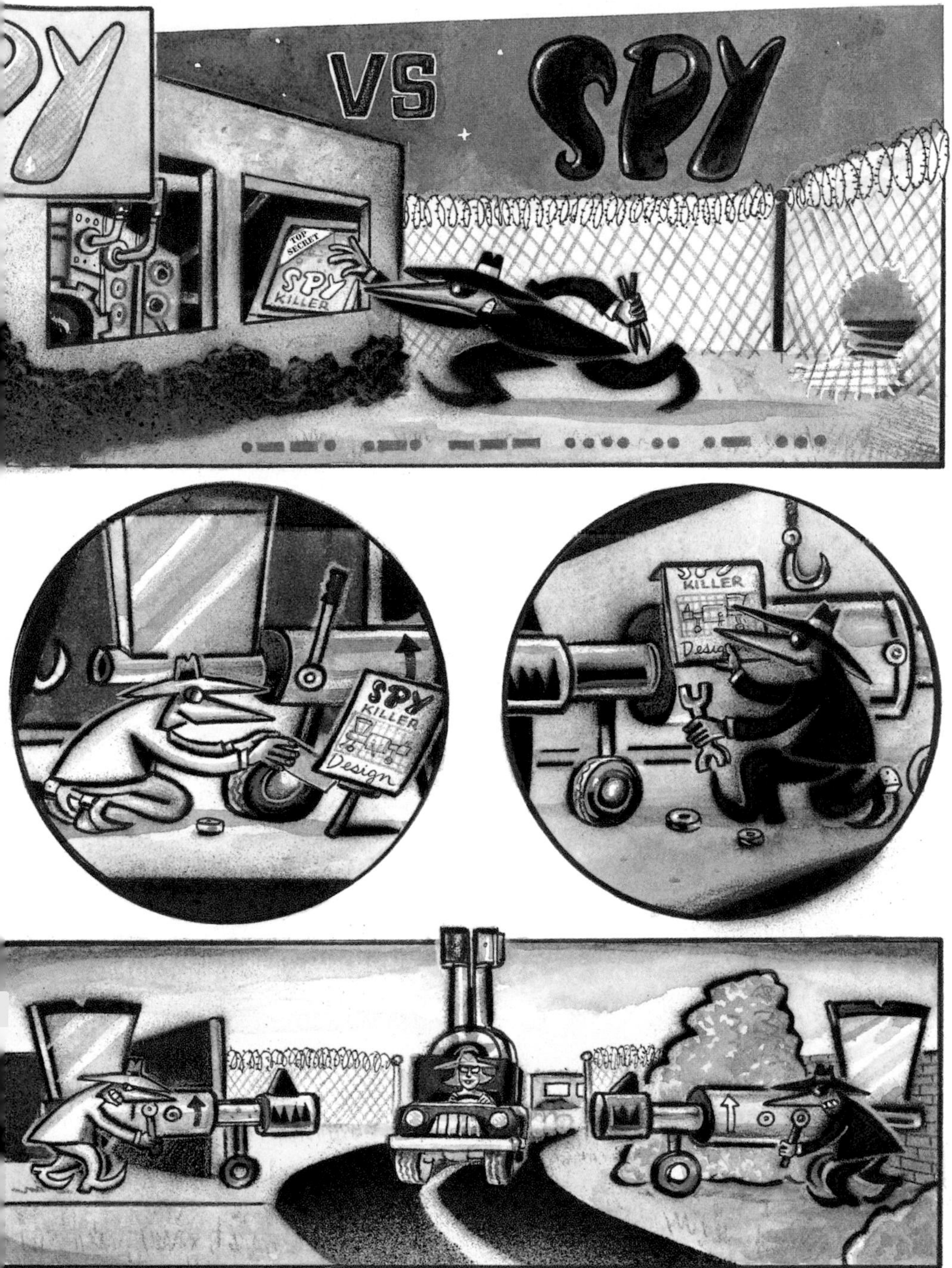
SPY VS SPY
TOP SECRET
SPY KILLER
SPY KILLER Design
KILLER Design

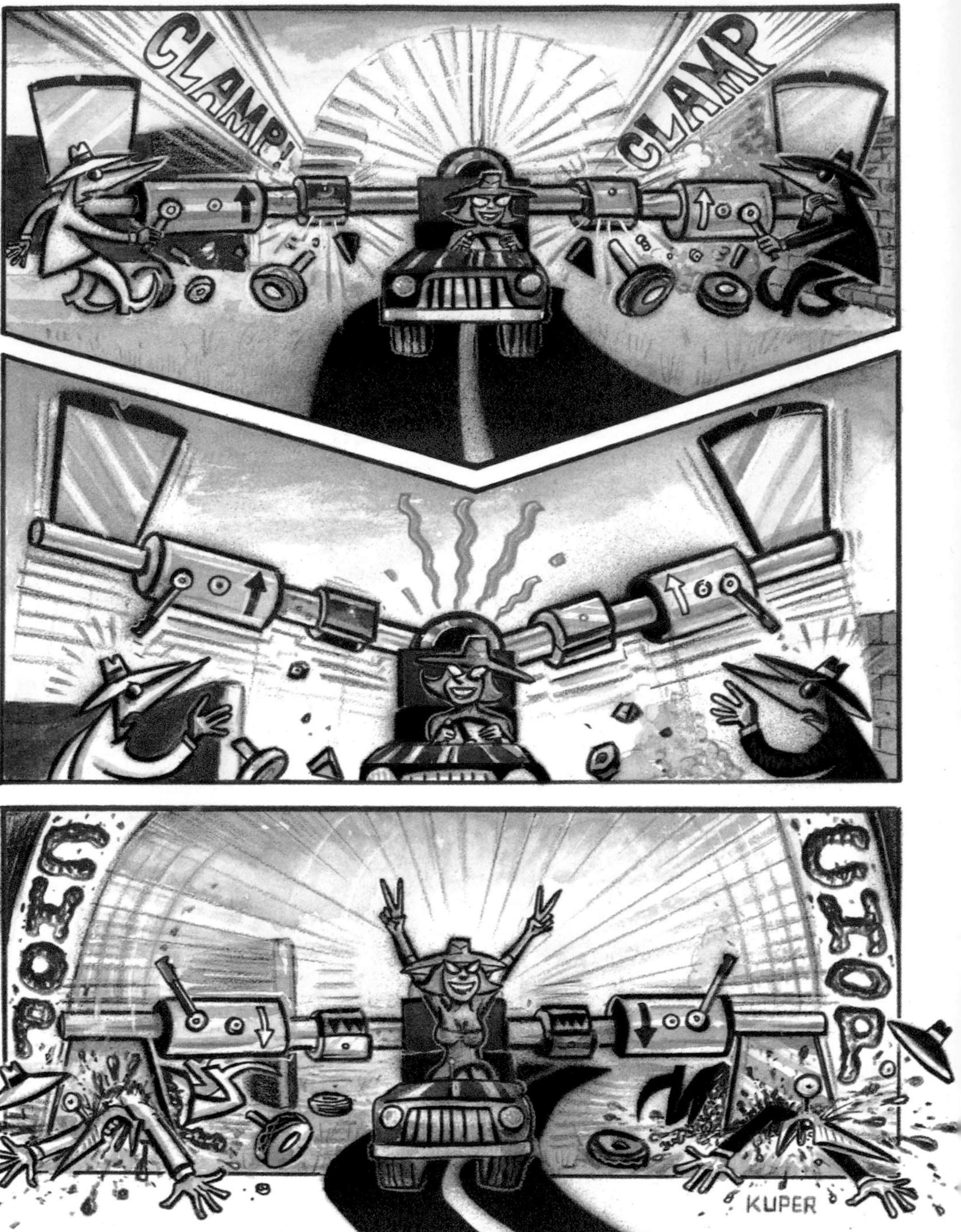
CLAMP!
CLAMP
CHOP
CHOP
KUPER

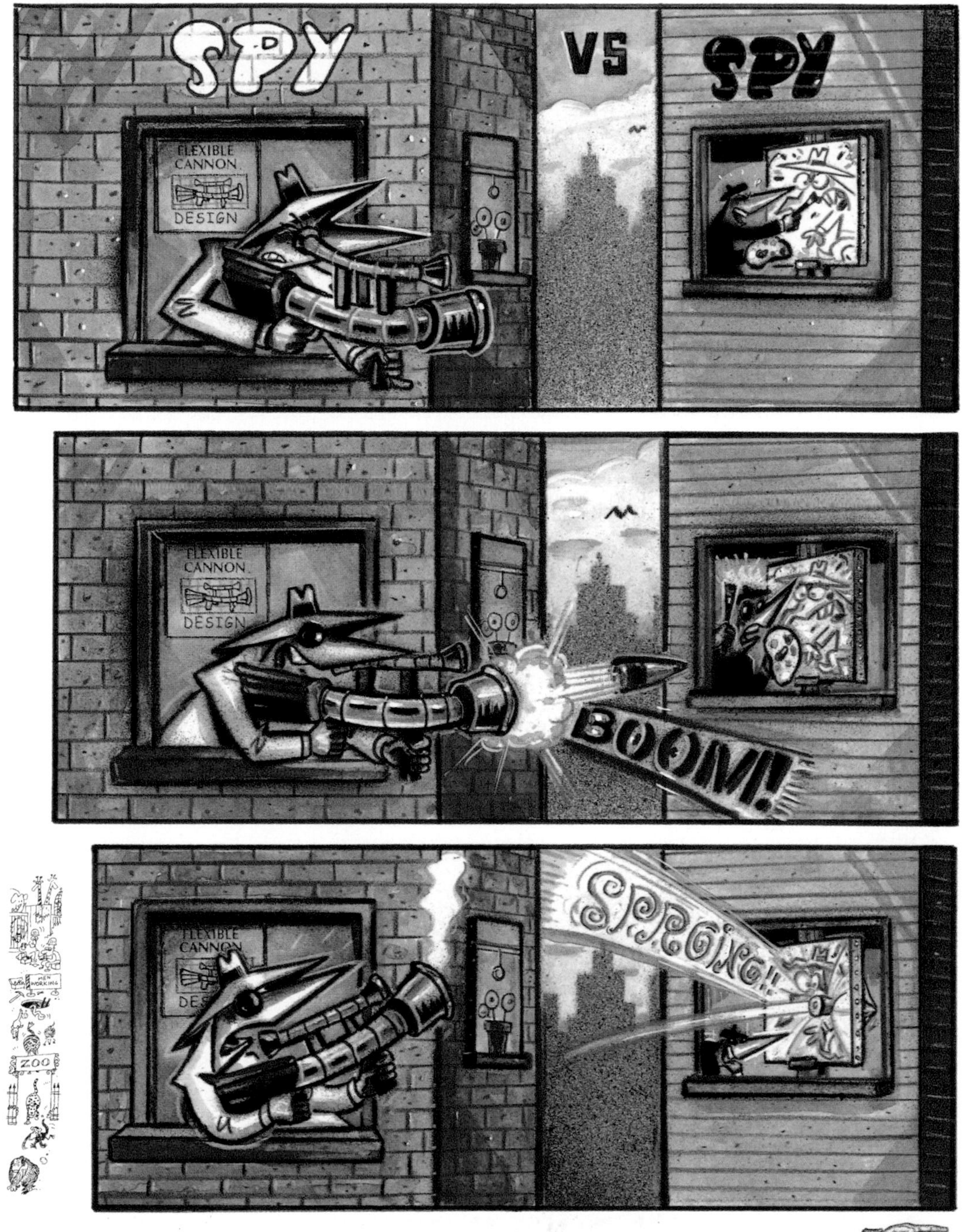
SPY VS SPY
FLEXIBLE CANNON DESIGN
FLEXIBLE CANNON DESIGN
BOOM!
FLEXIBLE CANNON
SPROING!!
MEN WORKING
ZOO

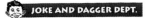

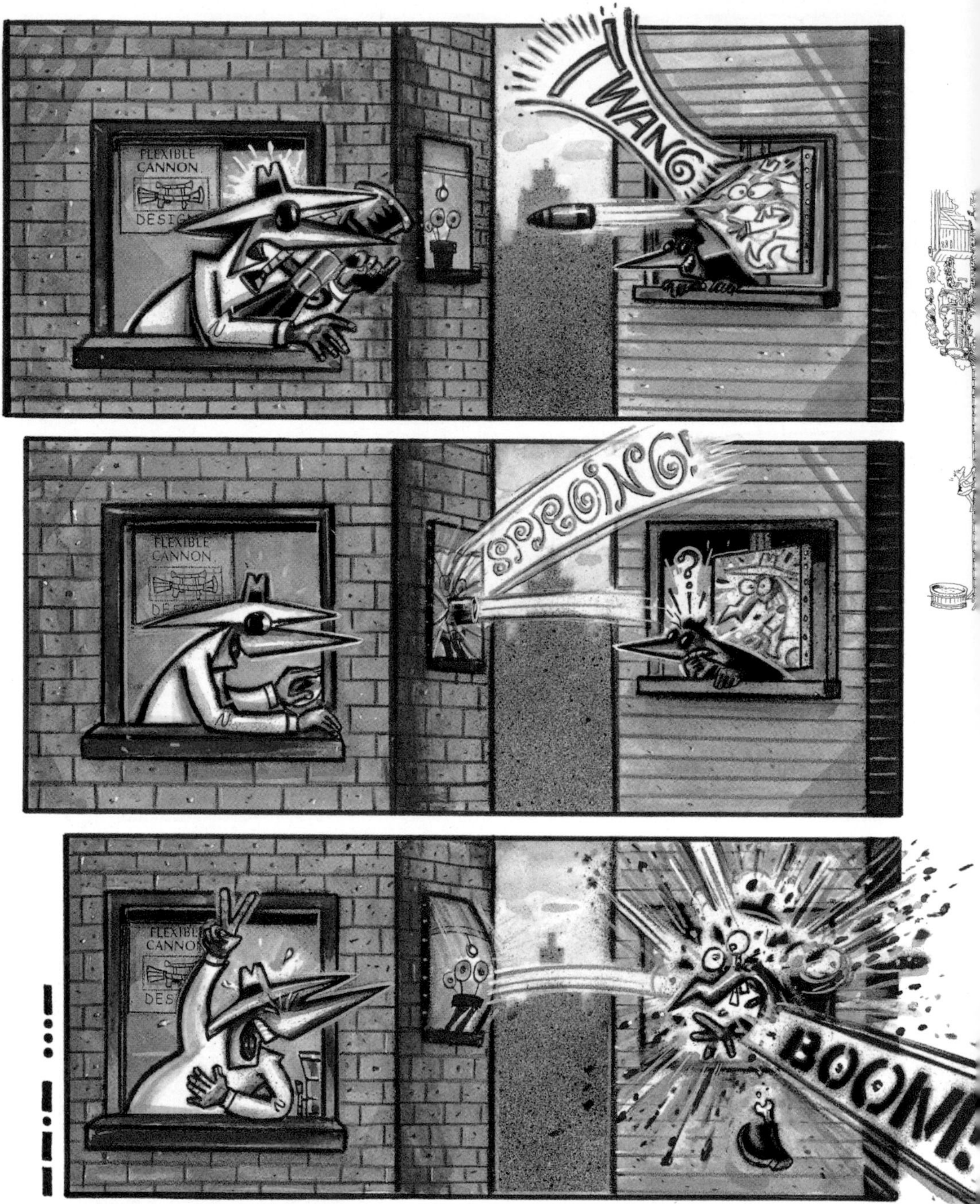
FLEXIBLE CANNON DESIGN
TWANG
SPROING!
BOOM!
KUPER

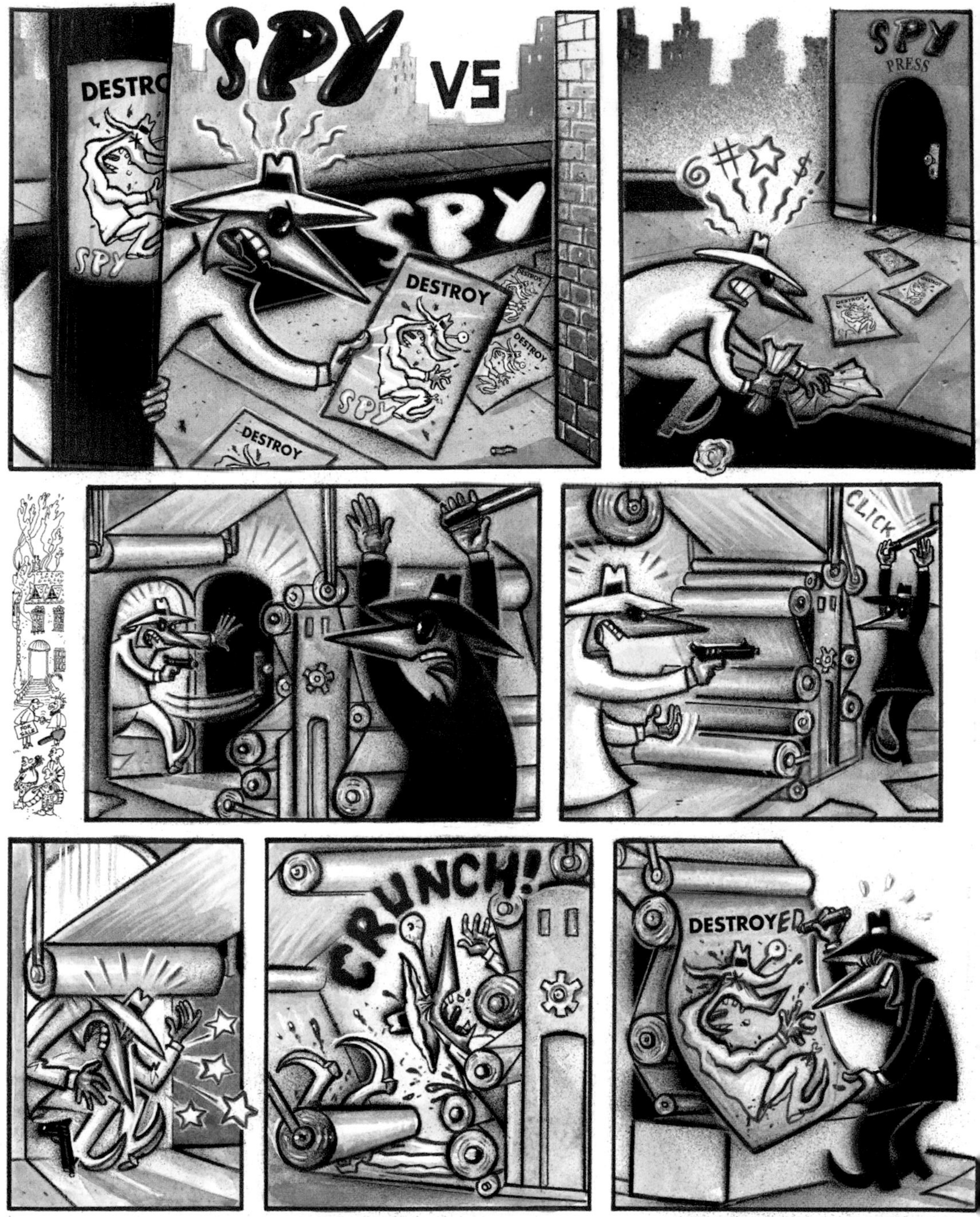
SPY VS SPY
DESTRO
SPY
DESTROY
SPY
DESTROY
DESTROY
DESTROY
SPY PRESS
CLICK
CRUNCH!
DESTROYED

KUPER

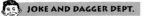

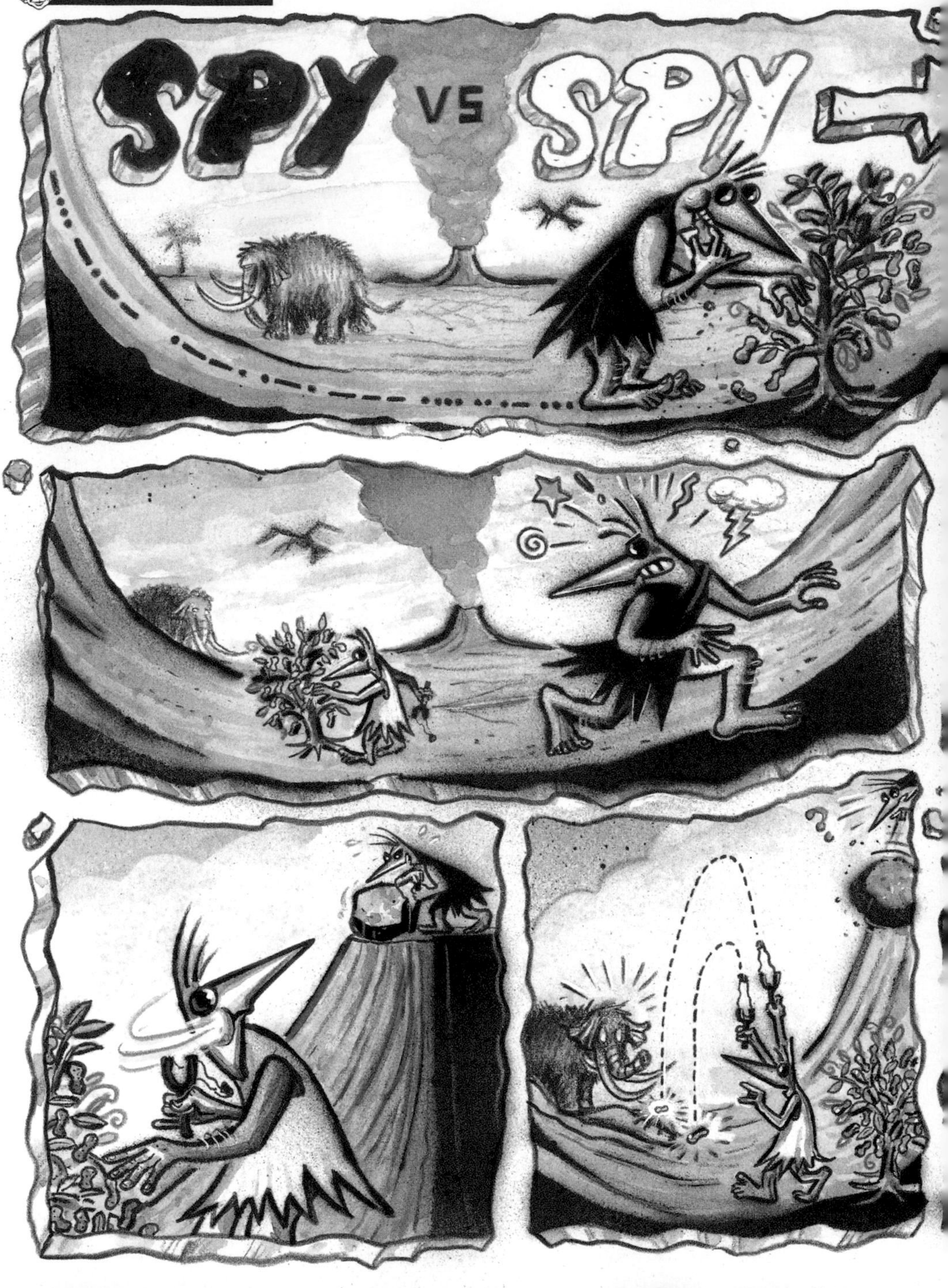
SPY VS SPY

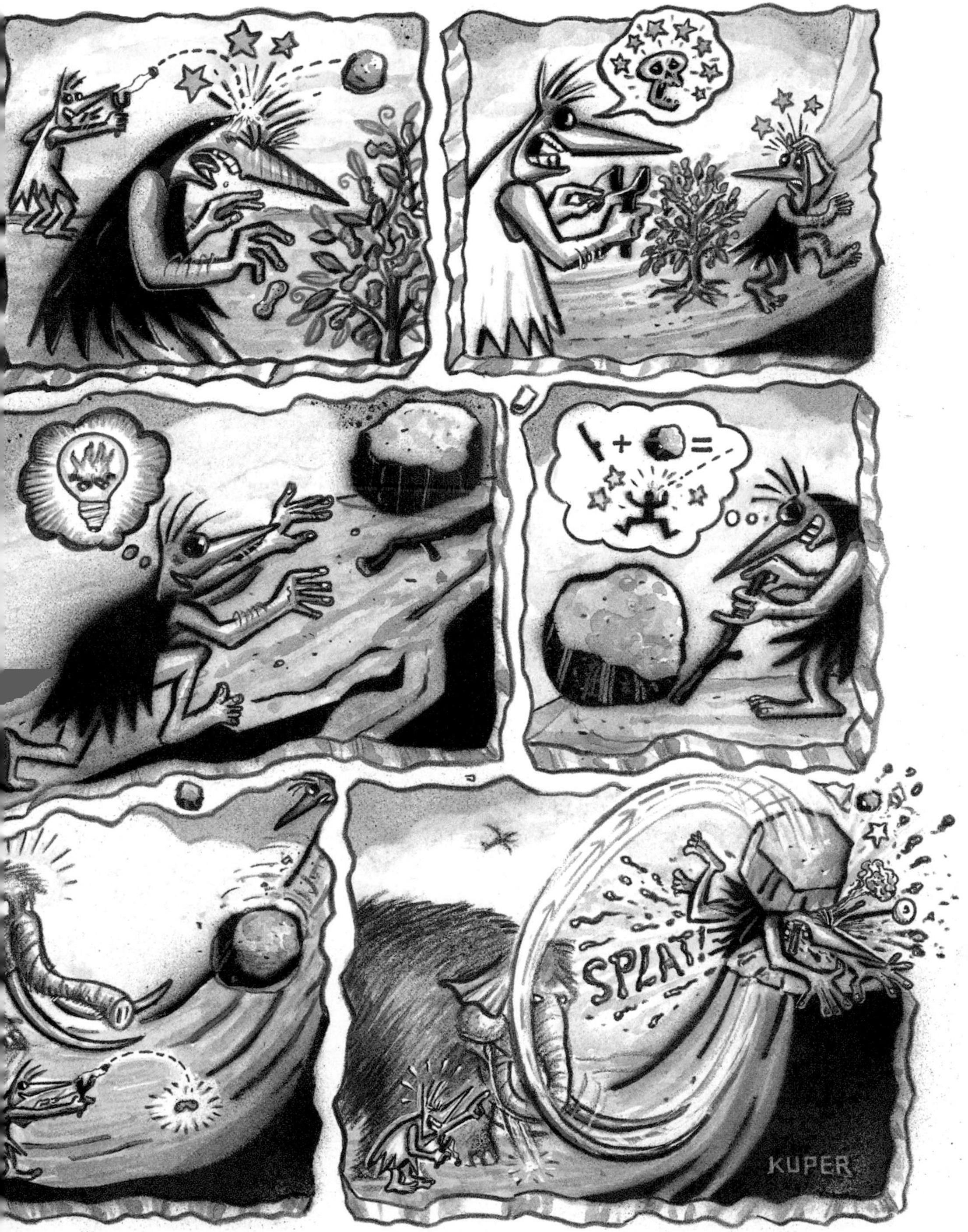
SPLAT!
KUPER

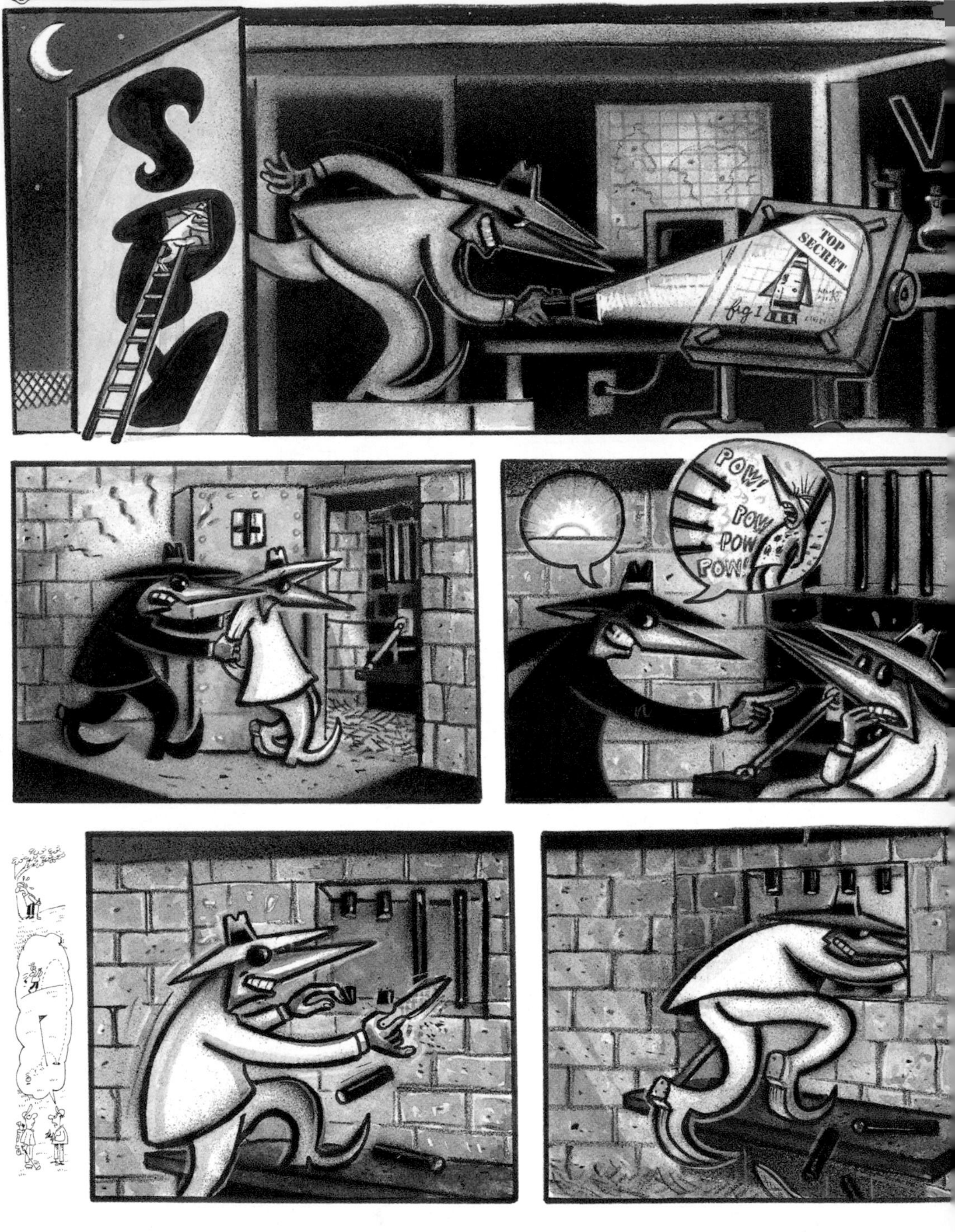
TOP SECRET
fig 1
POW!
POW
POW
POW!

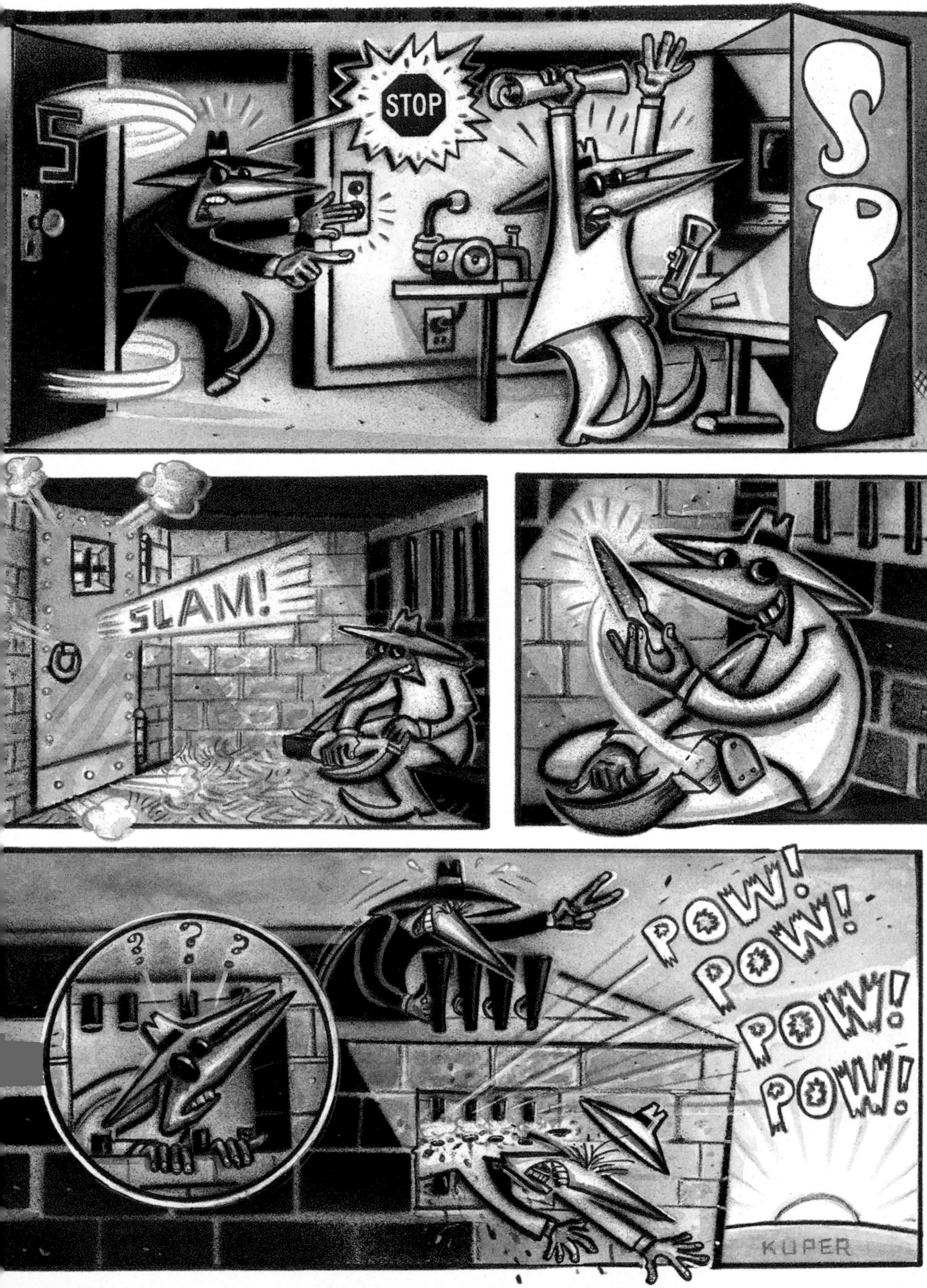

SPY
STOP
SLAM!
POW!
POW!
POW!
POW!
KUPER

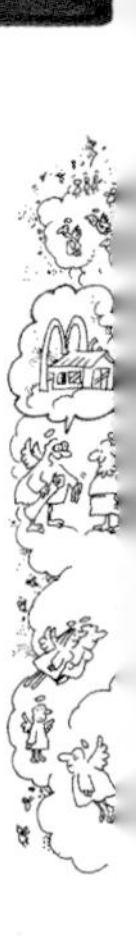

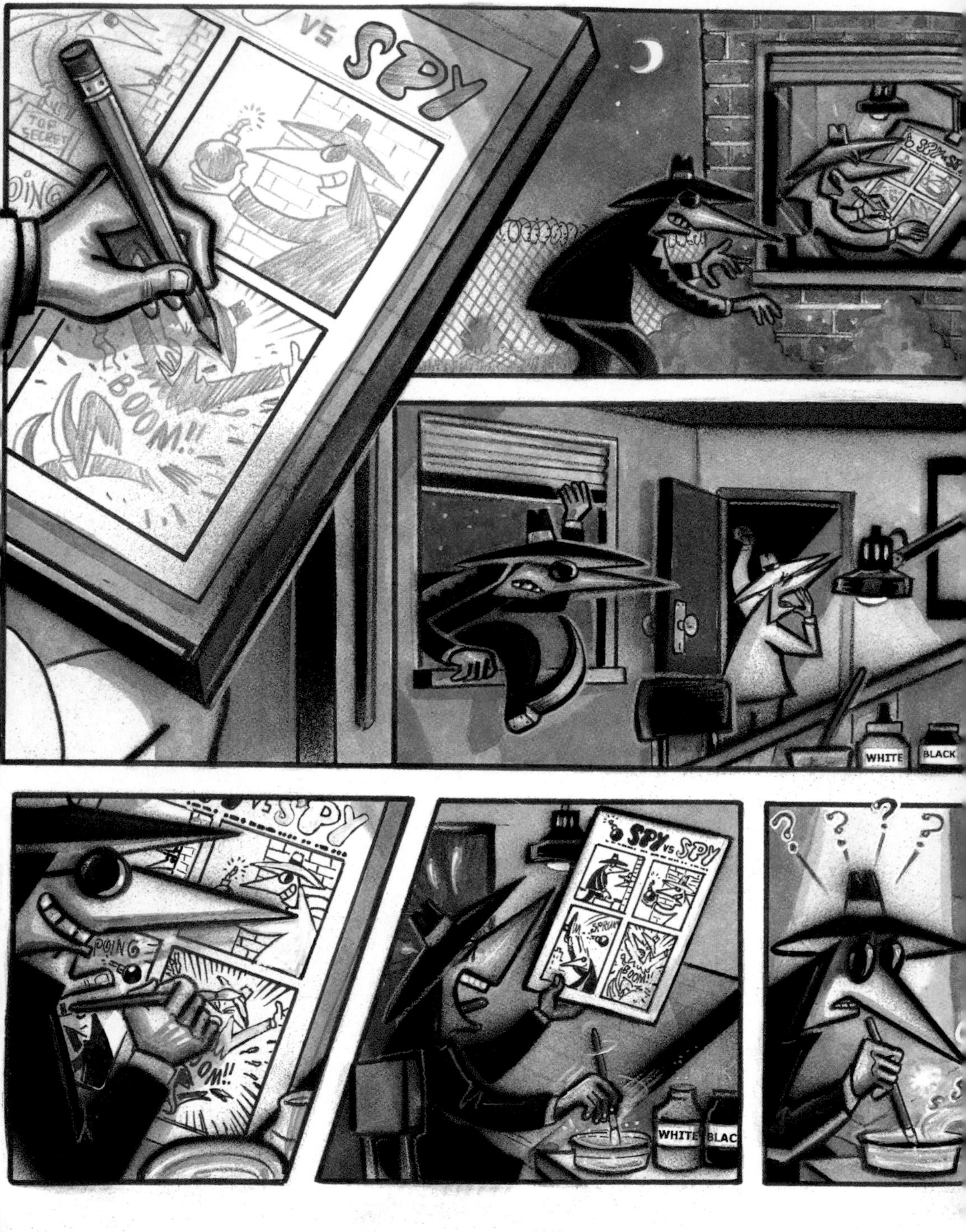
VS SPY
TOP SECRET
OING
BOOM!!
SPY VS SPY
WHITE
BLACK
SPY
POING
OOM!!
SPY VS SPY
BOOM!!
WHITE
BLAC

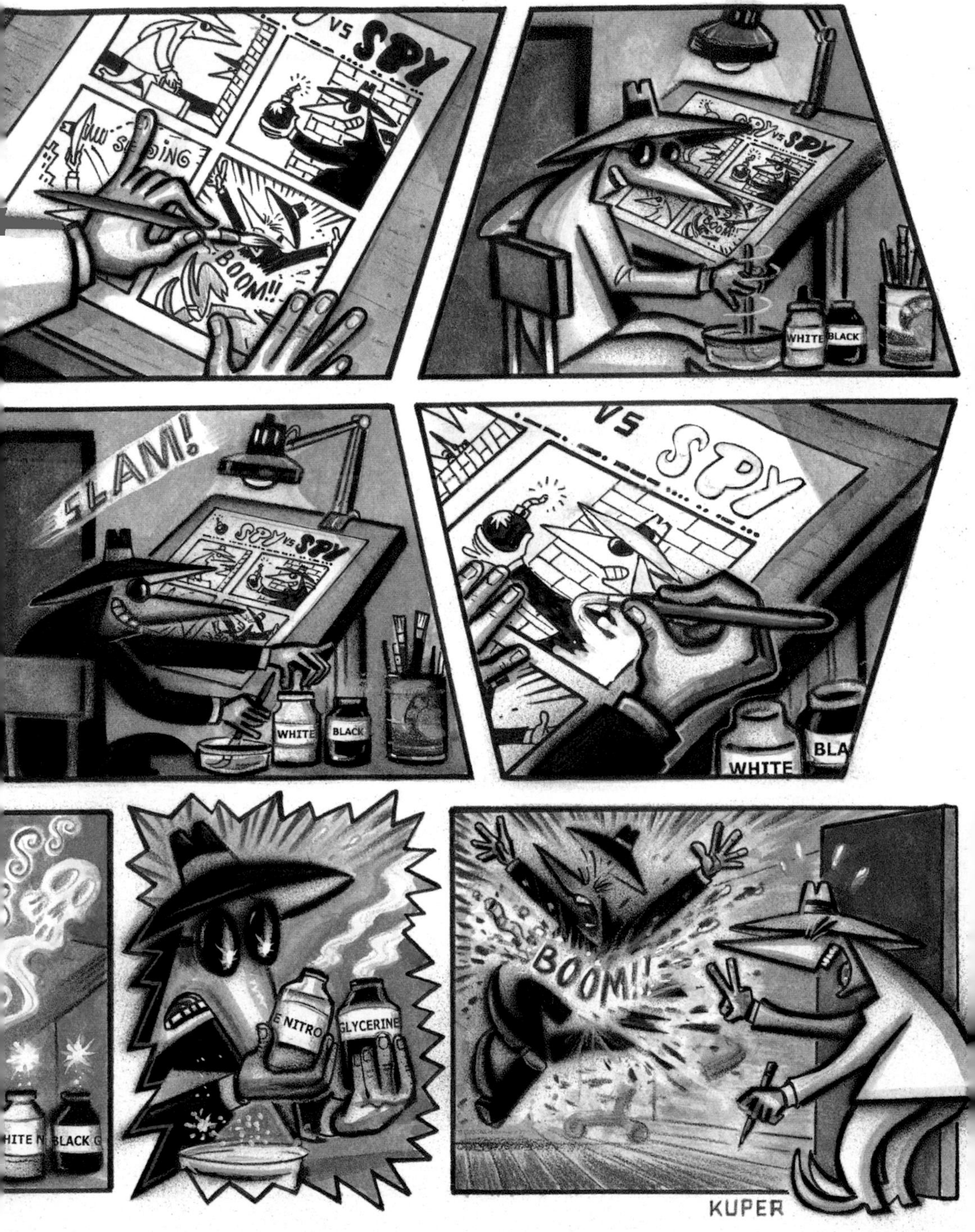
VS SPY
SENDING
BOOM!!
SPY VS SPY
WHITE
BLACK
SLAM!
SPY VS SPY
WHITE
BLACK
VS SPY
WHITE
BLA
WHITE N
BLACK G
E NITRO
GLYCERINE
BOOM!!
KUPER

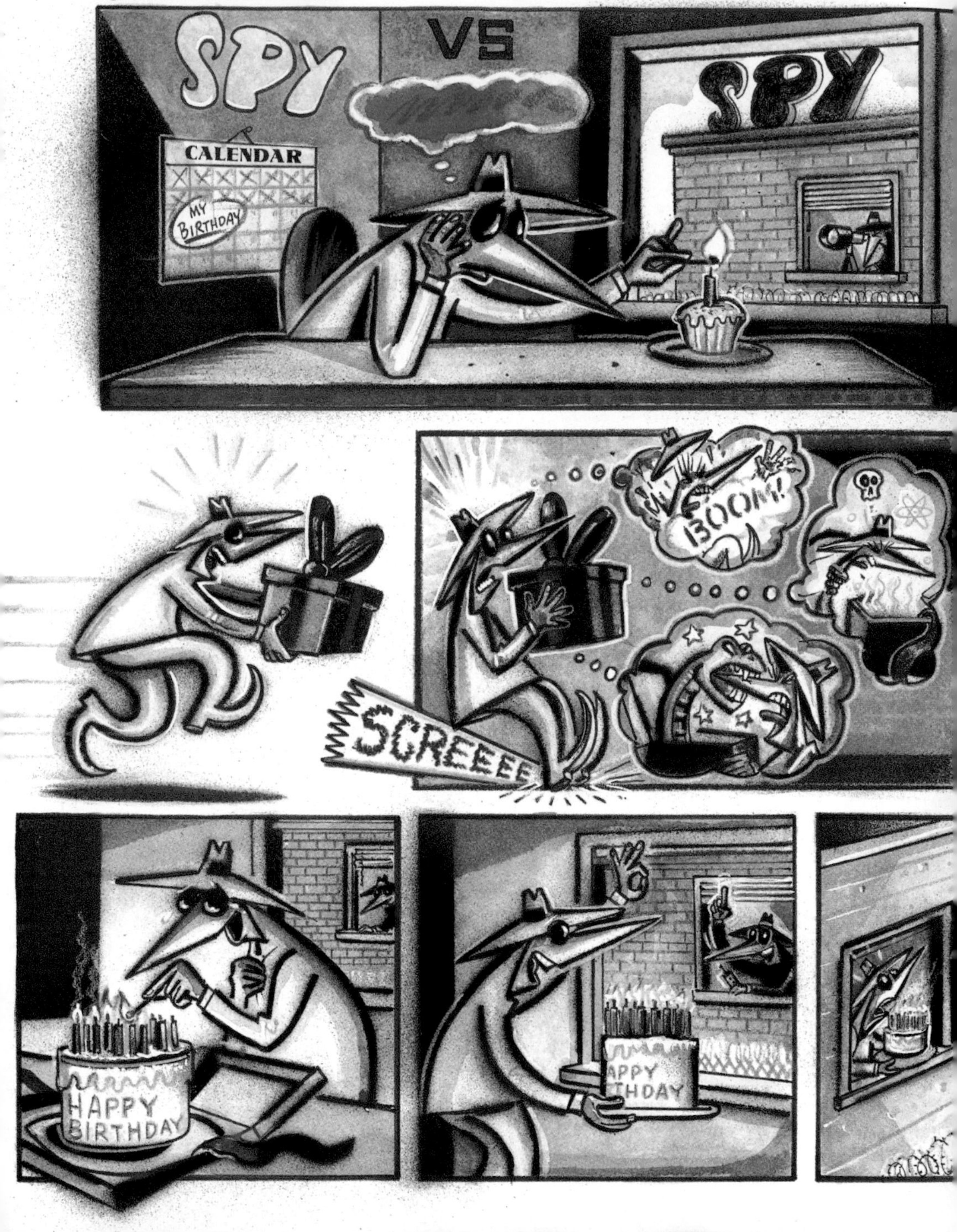
SPY VS SPY
CALENDAR
MY BIRTHDAY
BOOM!
SCREEEEE
HAPPY BIRTHDAY
APPY
THDAY

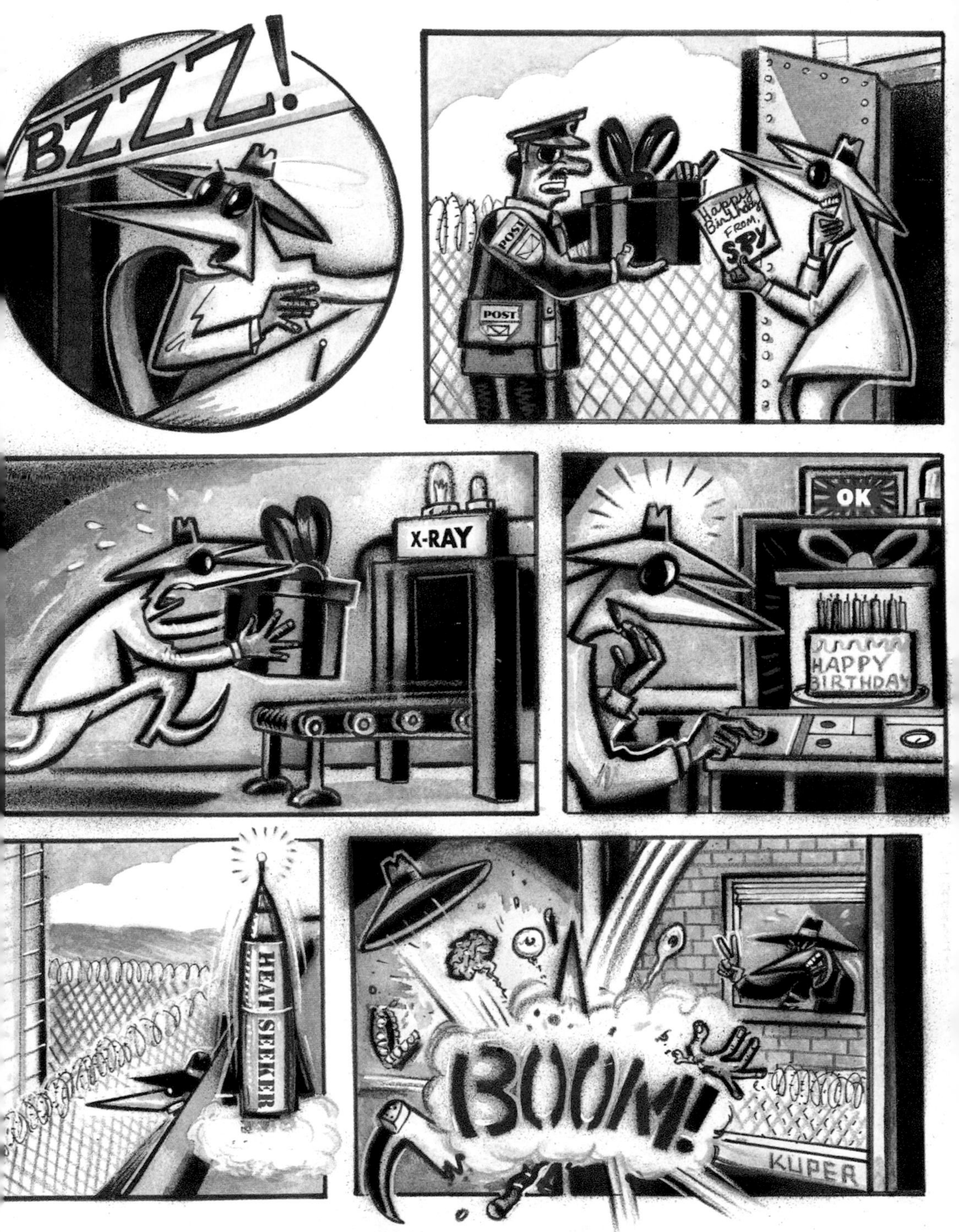
BZZZ!
POST
POST
Happy Birthday FROM, SPY
X-RAY
OK
HAPPY BIRTHDAY
HEAT SEEKER
BOOM!
KUPER

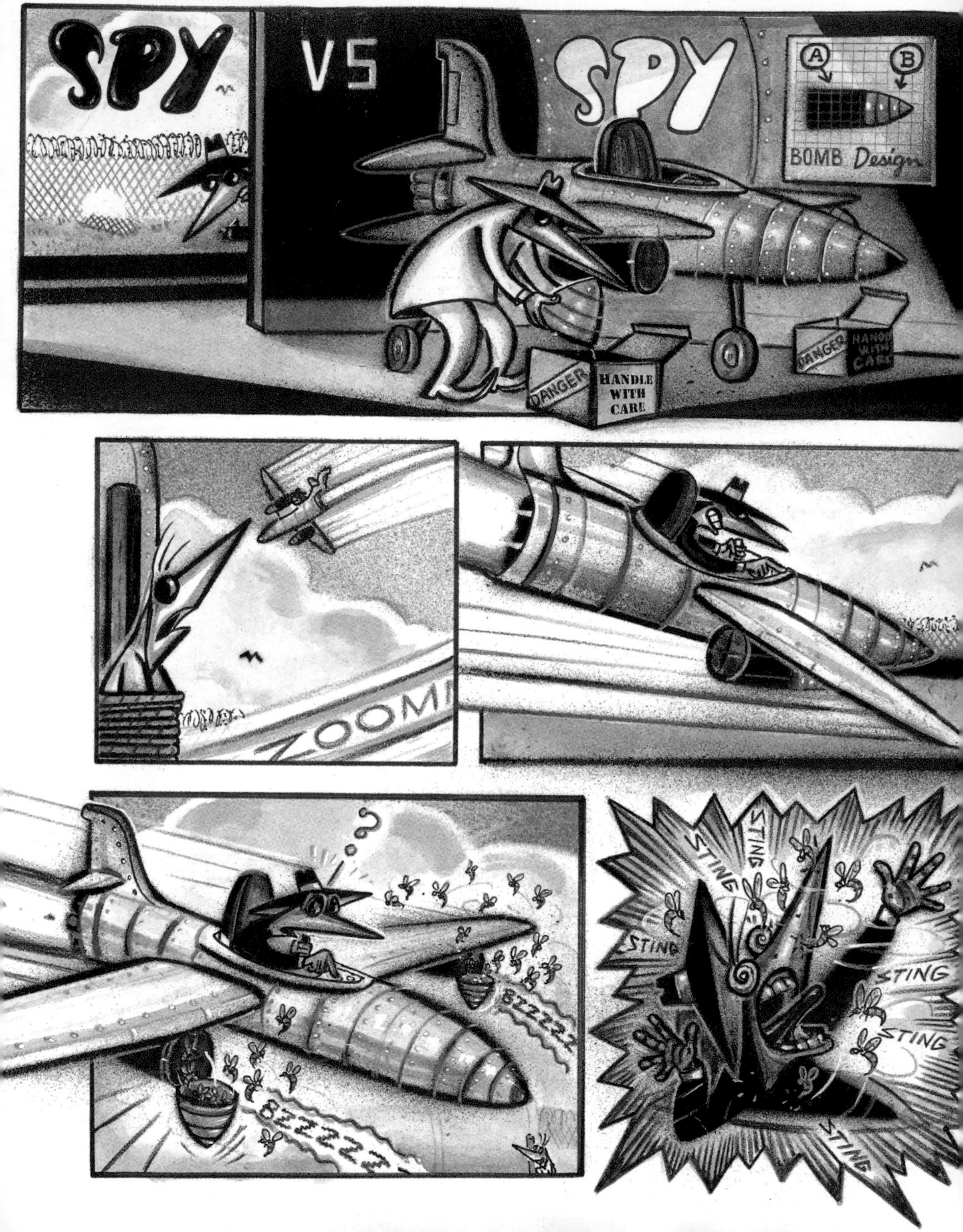
SPY
VS
SPY
A
B
BOMB Design
DANGER
HANDLE WITH CARE
DANGER
HANDLE WITH CARE
ZOOM!
?
BZZZZZ
BZZZZZ
STING
STING
STING
STING
STING
STING

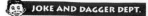

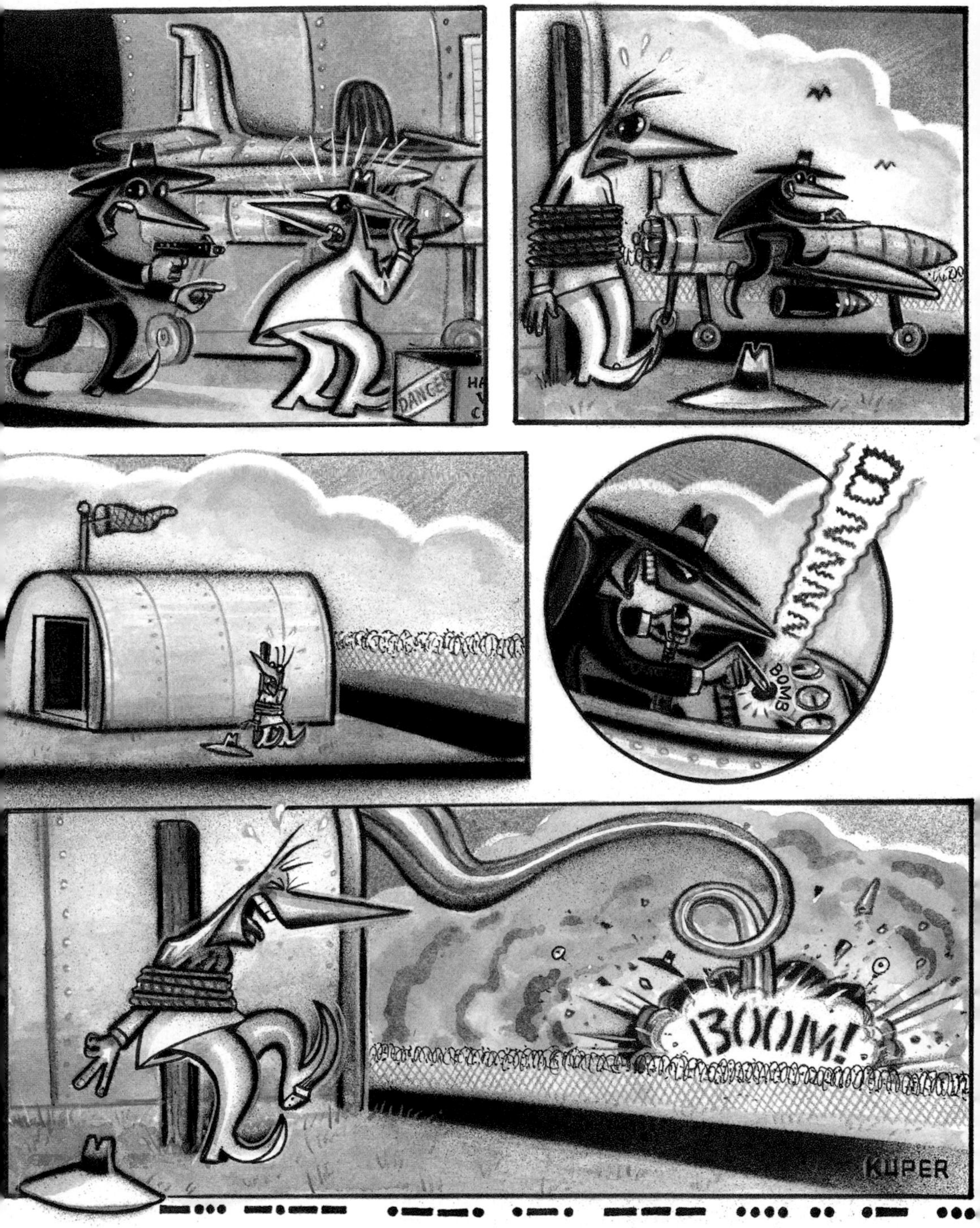
DANGER
BOMB
BOOM!
KUPER

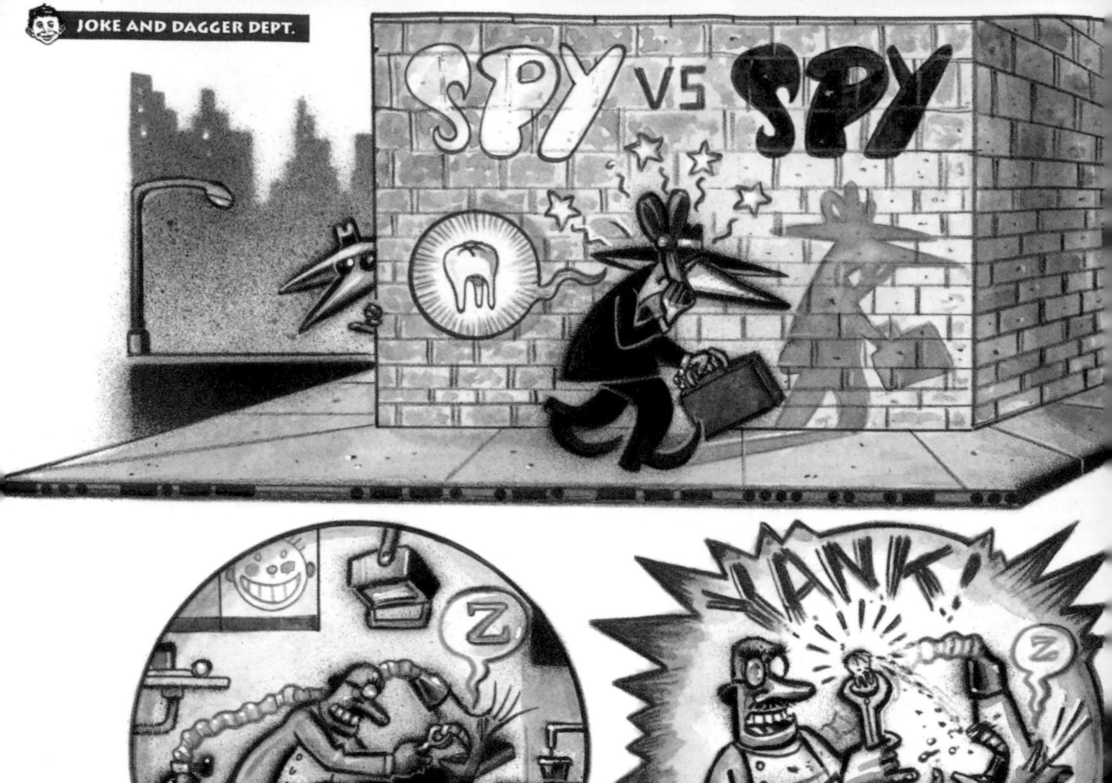
SPY VS SPY
Z
YANK!!
Z

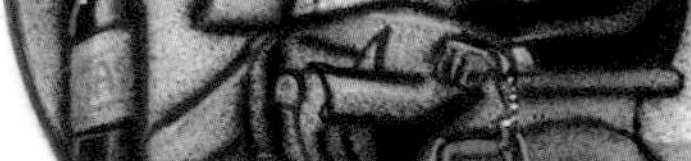
BAAA
BAAA
BAA!
BAA!!
BAA!
BAAA

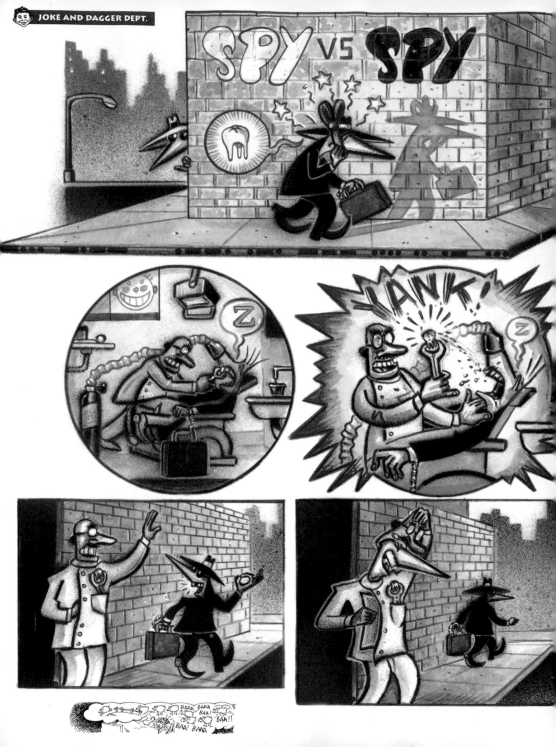

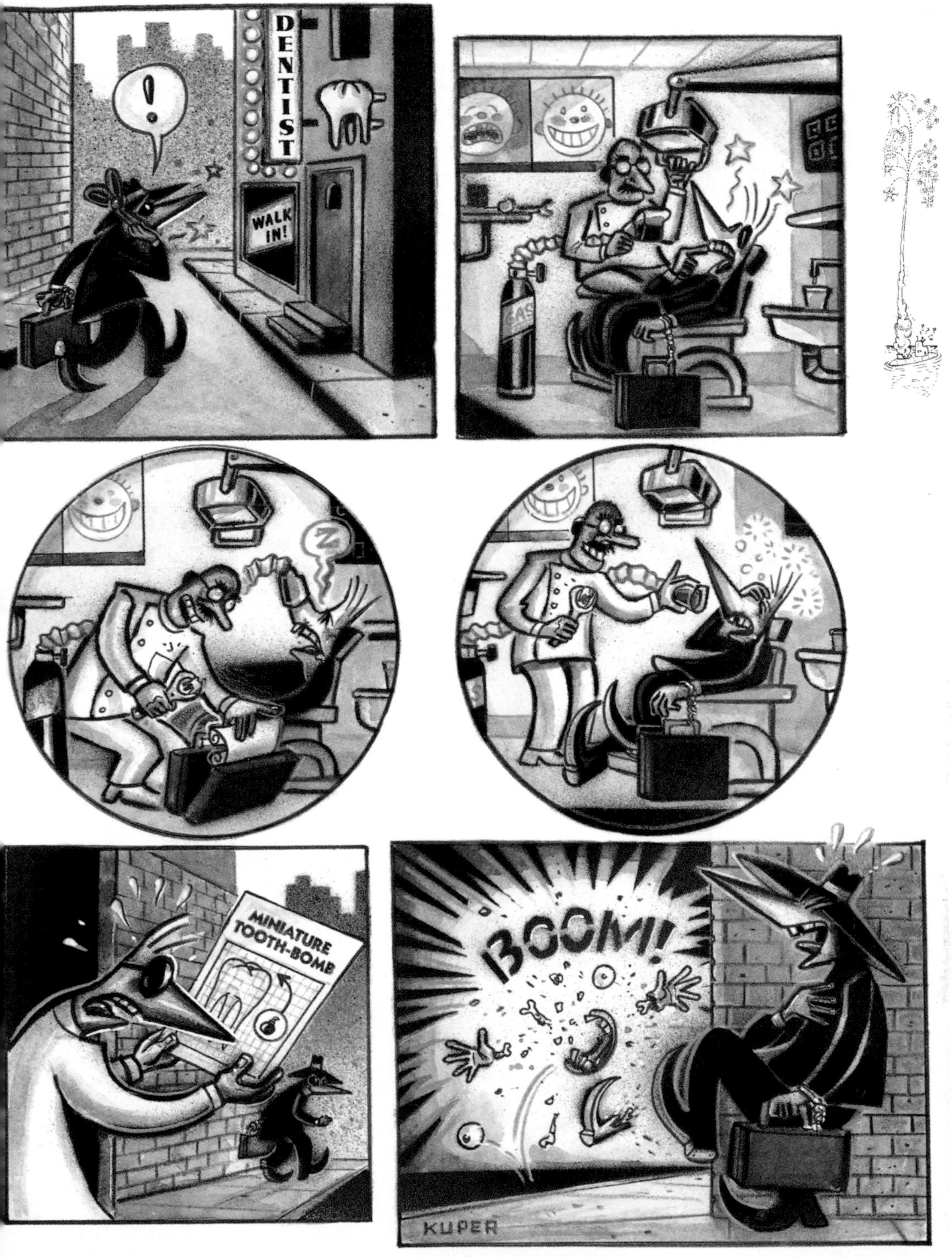
!
DENTIST
WALK IN!
GAS
Z
MINIATURE TOOTH-BOMB
BOOM!
KUPER

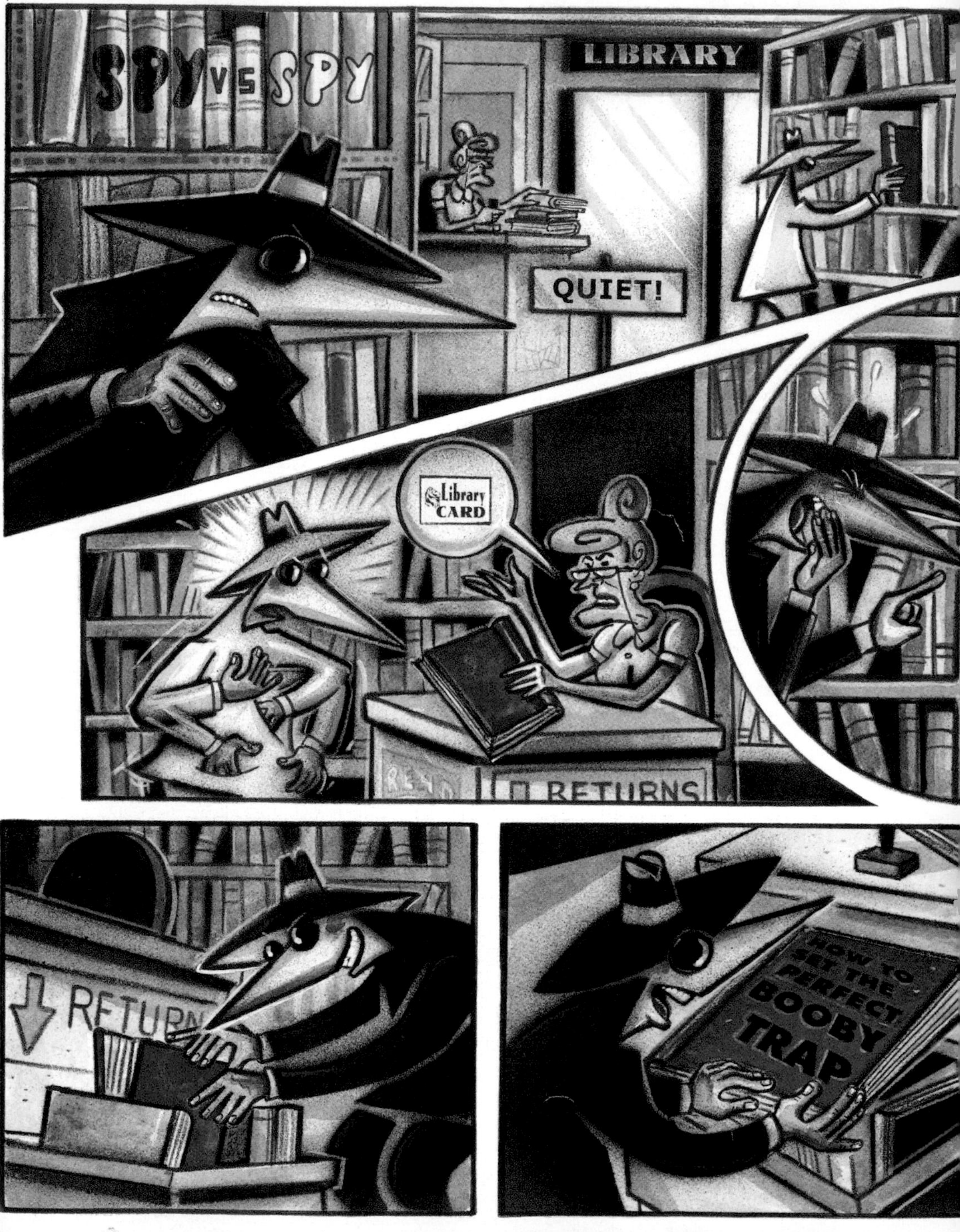
SPY vs SPY
LIBRARY
QUIET!
Library CARD
RETURNS
RETURN
HOW TO SET THE PERFECT BOOBY TRAP

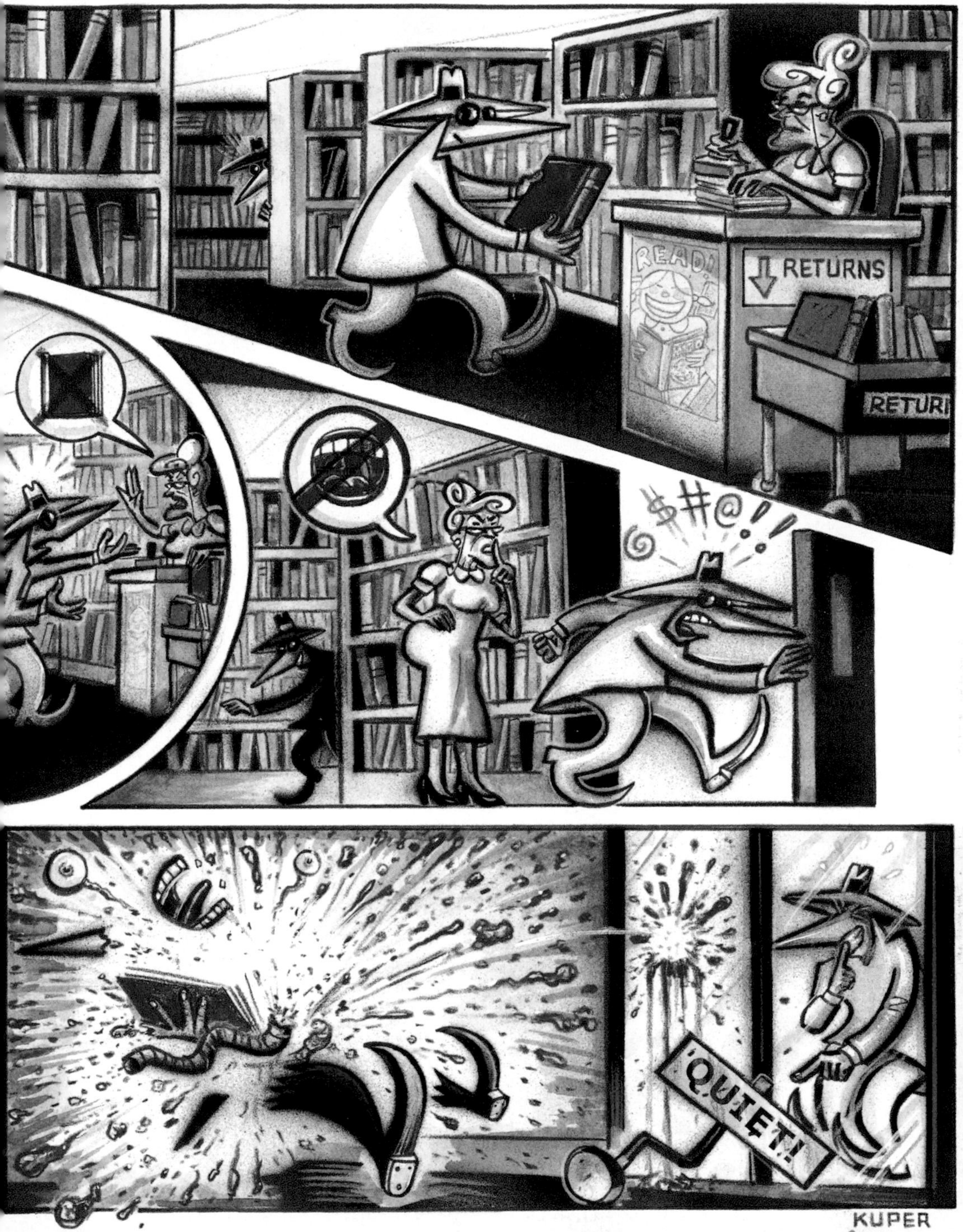

READ!
RETURNS
RETURN
$#@!!
QUIET!
KUPER

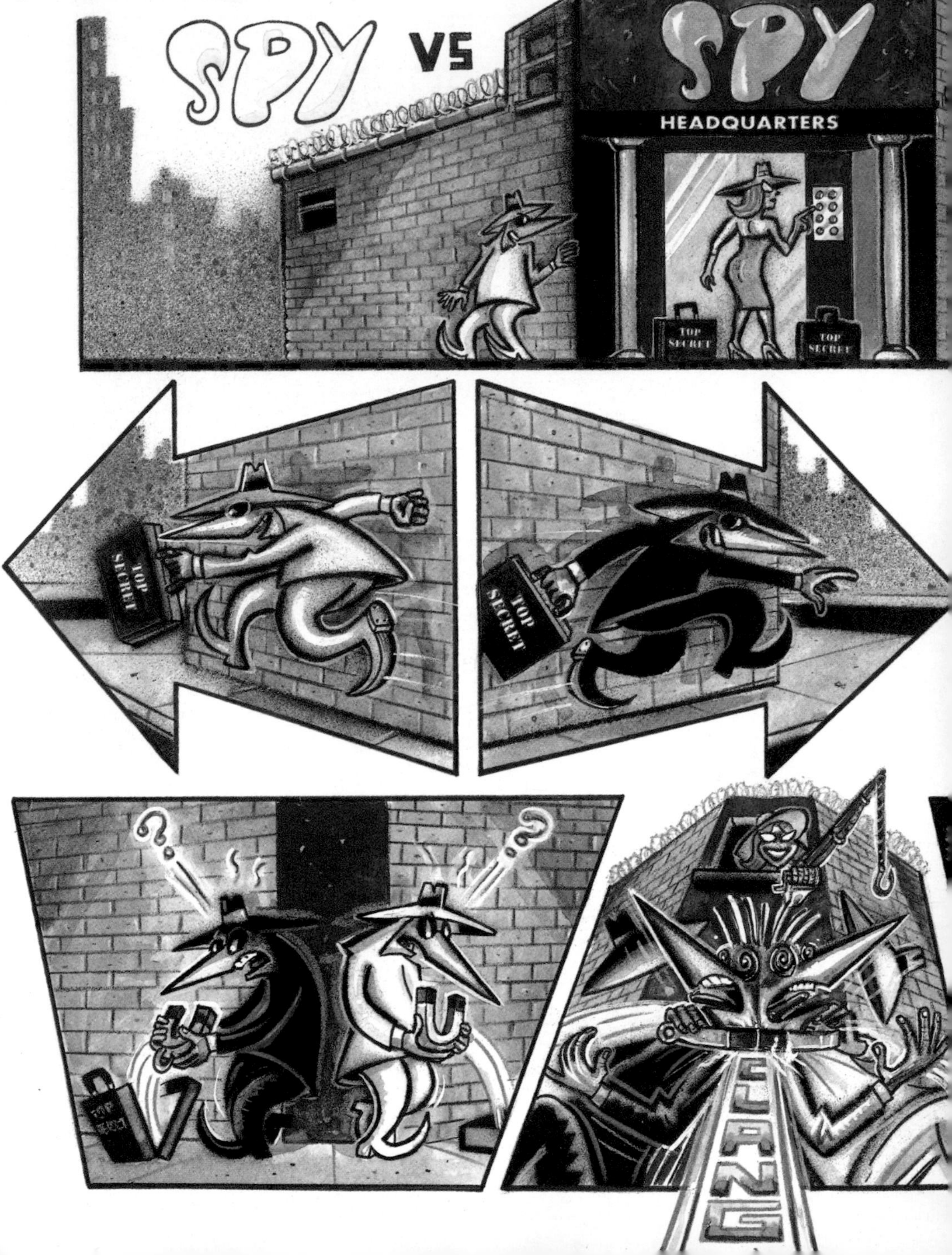
SPY VS SPY
HEADQUARTERS
TOP SECRET
TOP SECRET
TOP SECRET
TOP SECRET
CLANG

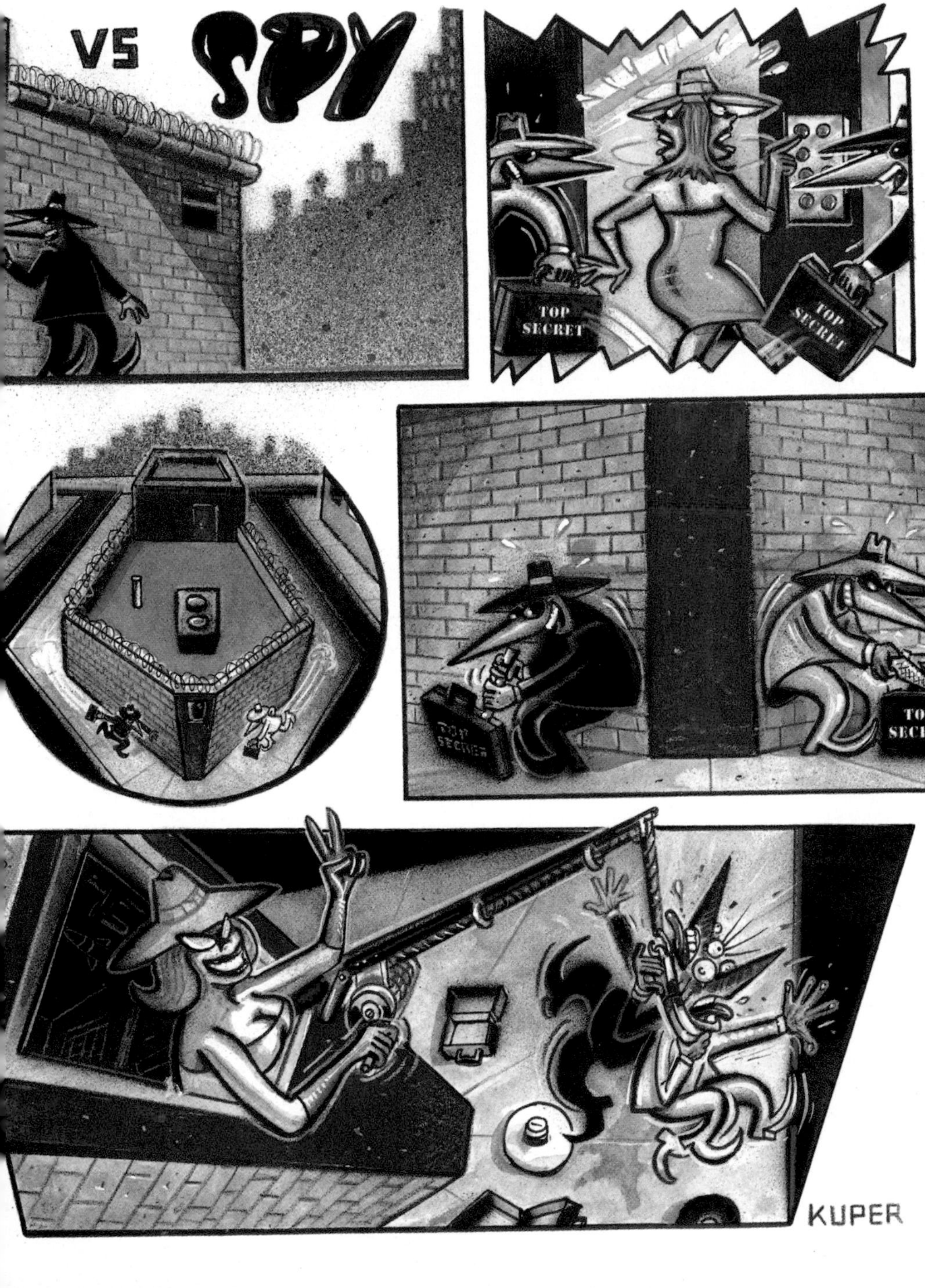
VS SPY
TOP SECRET
TOP SECRET
TOP SECRET
TOP SECRET
KUPER

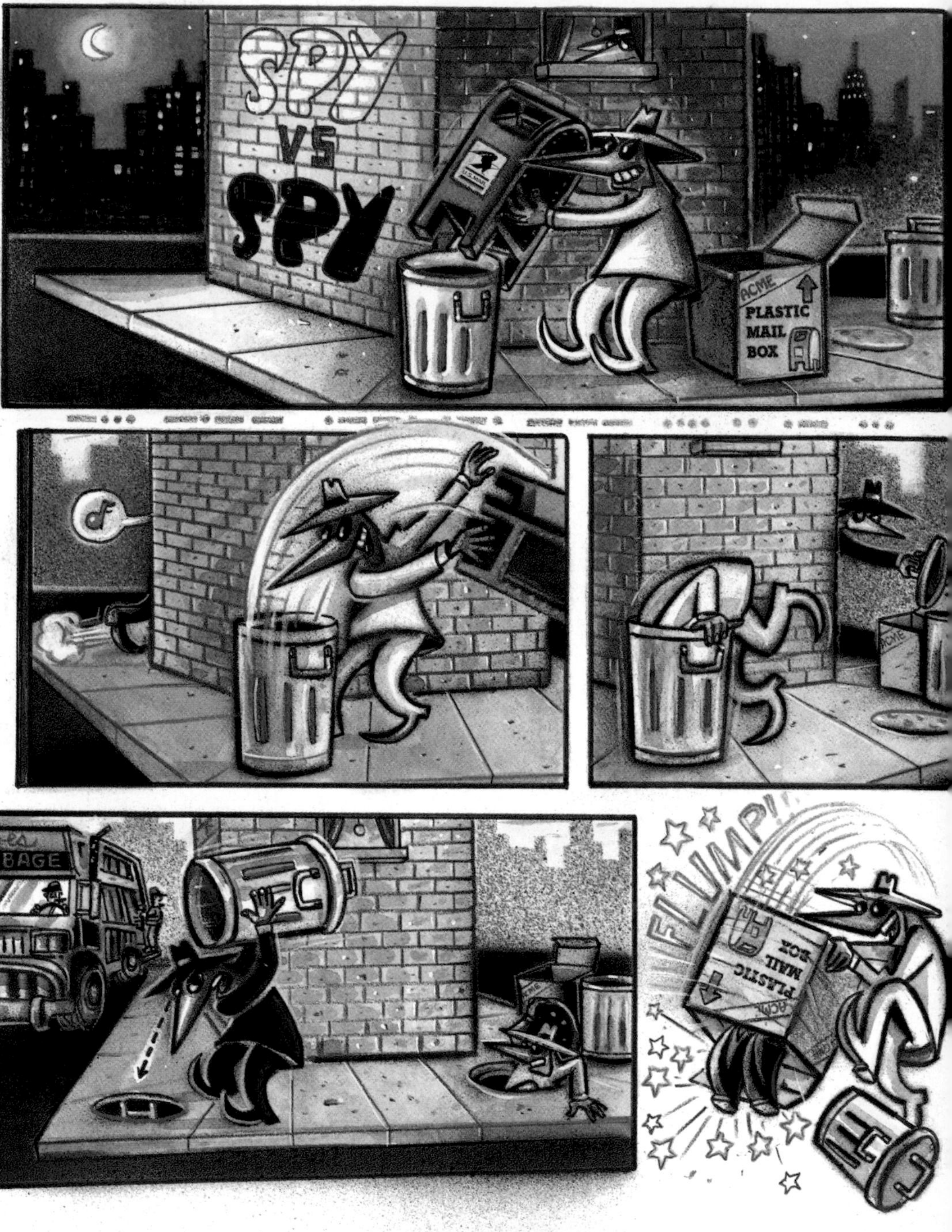
SPY
VS
SPY
ACME
PLASTIC MAIL BOX
ACME
GARBAGE
FLUMP!!
PLASTIC MAIL BOX
ACME

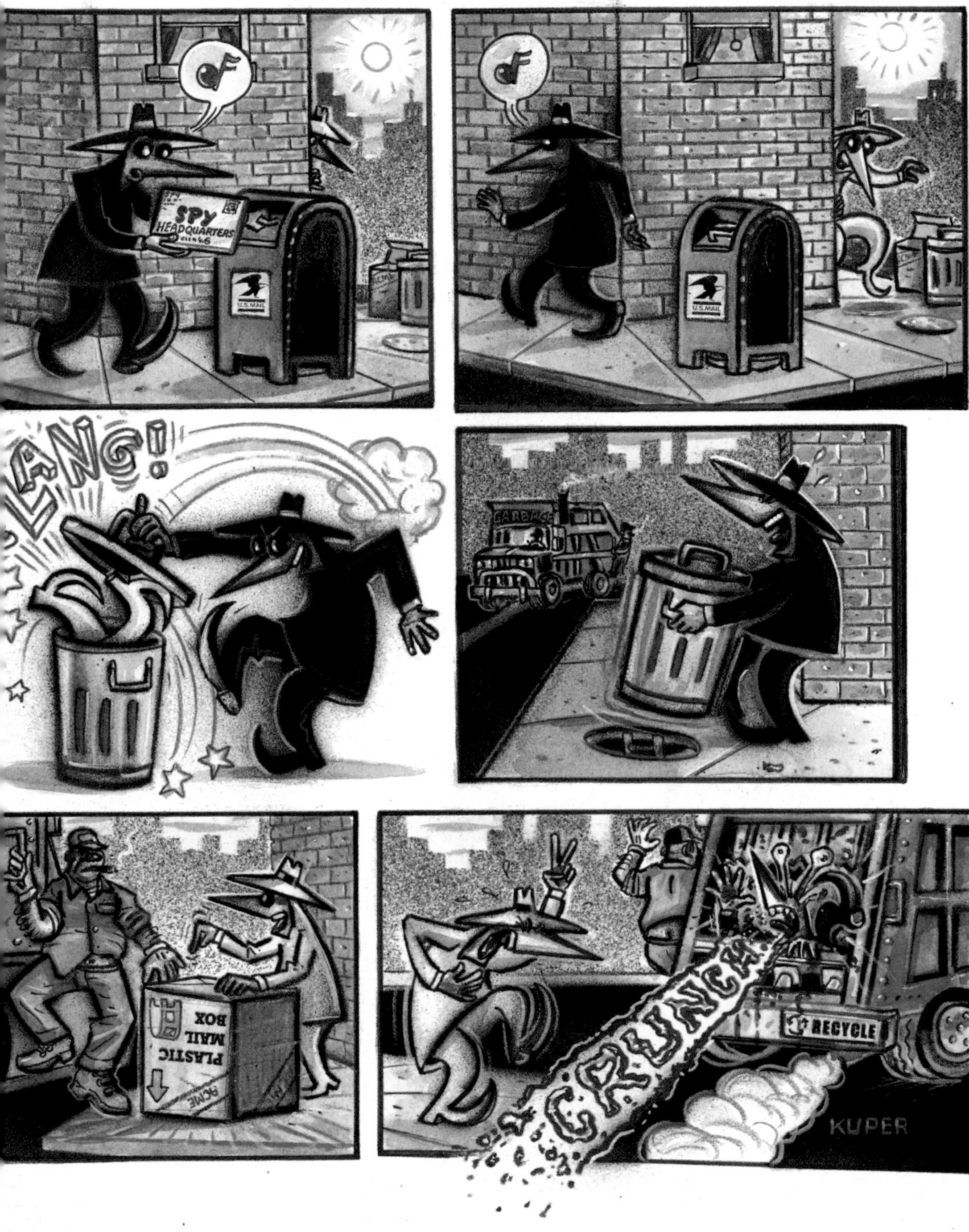

SPY HEADQUARTERS
U.S. MAIL
ACME
U.S. MAIL
LANG!
GARBAGE
PLASTIC MAIL BOX
ACME
CRUNCH
RECYCLE
KUPER

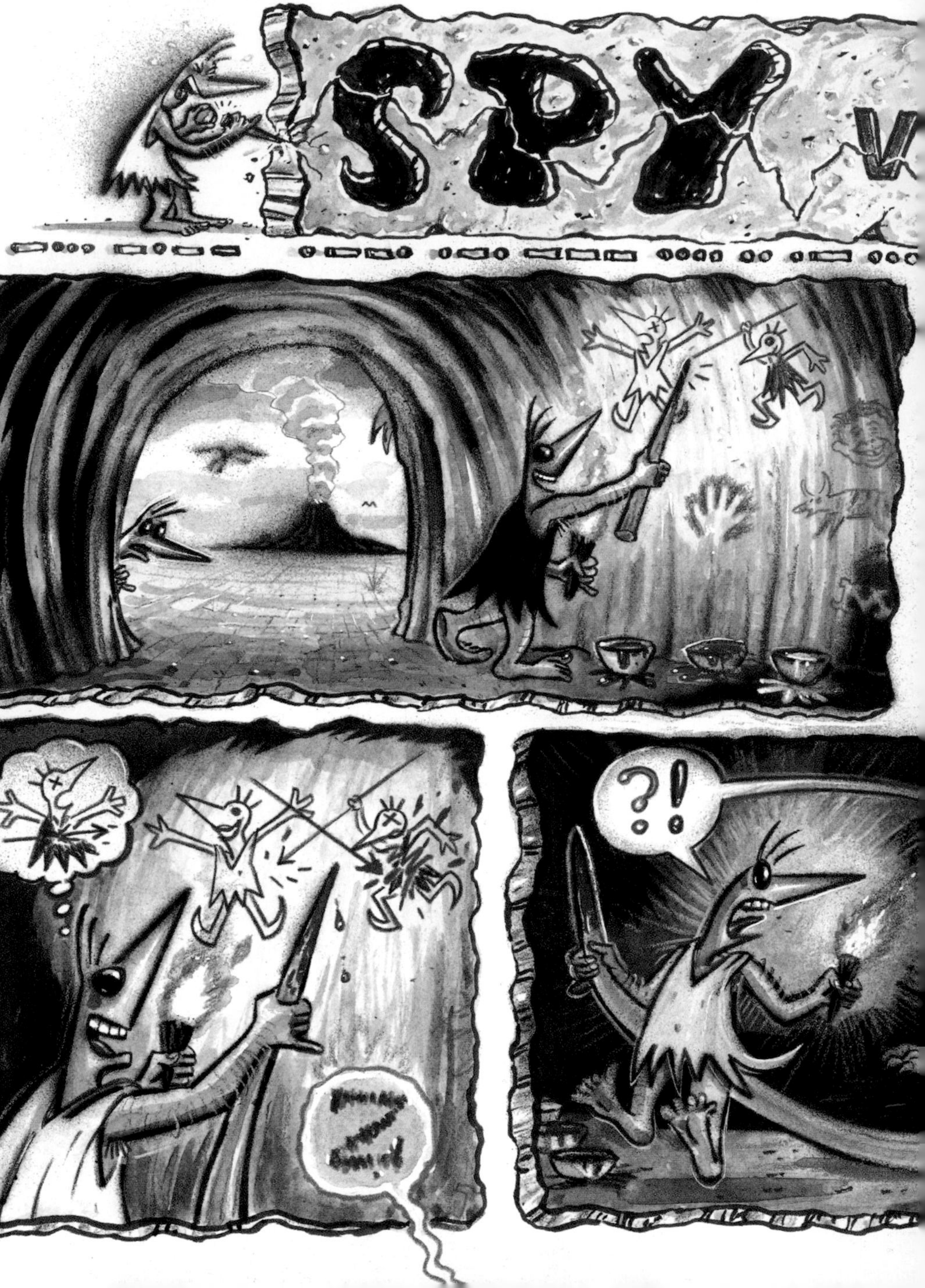
SPY
?!

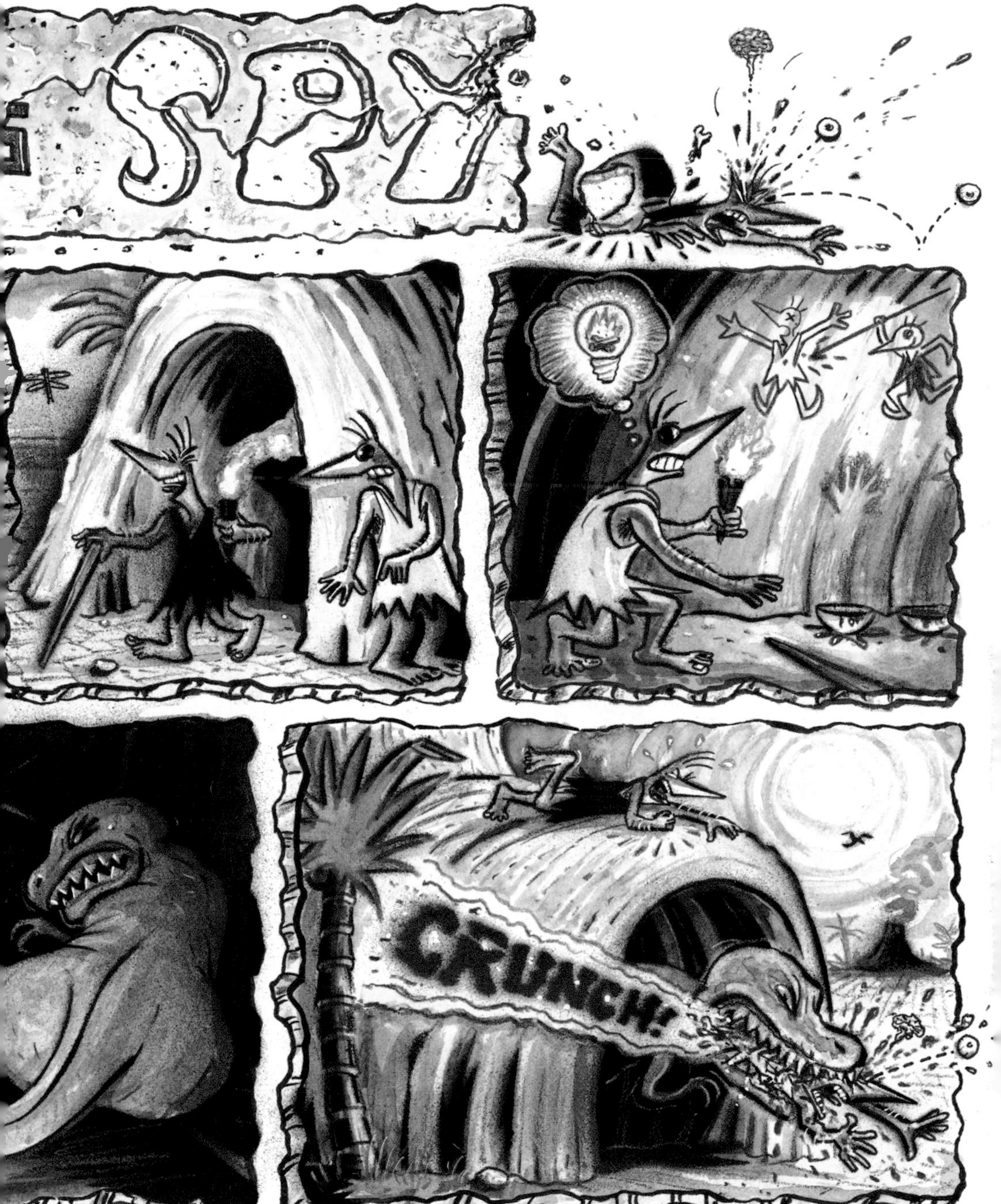
SPY
CRUNCH!
KUPER

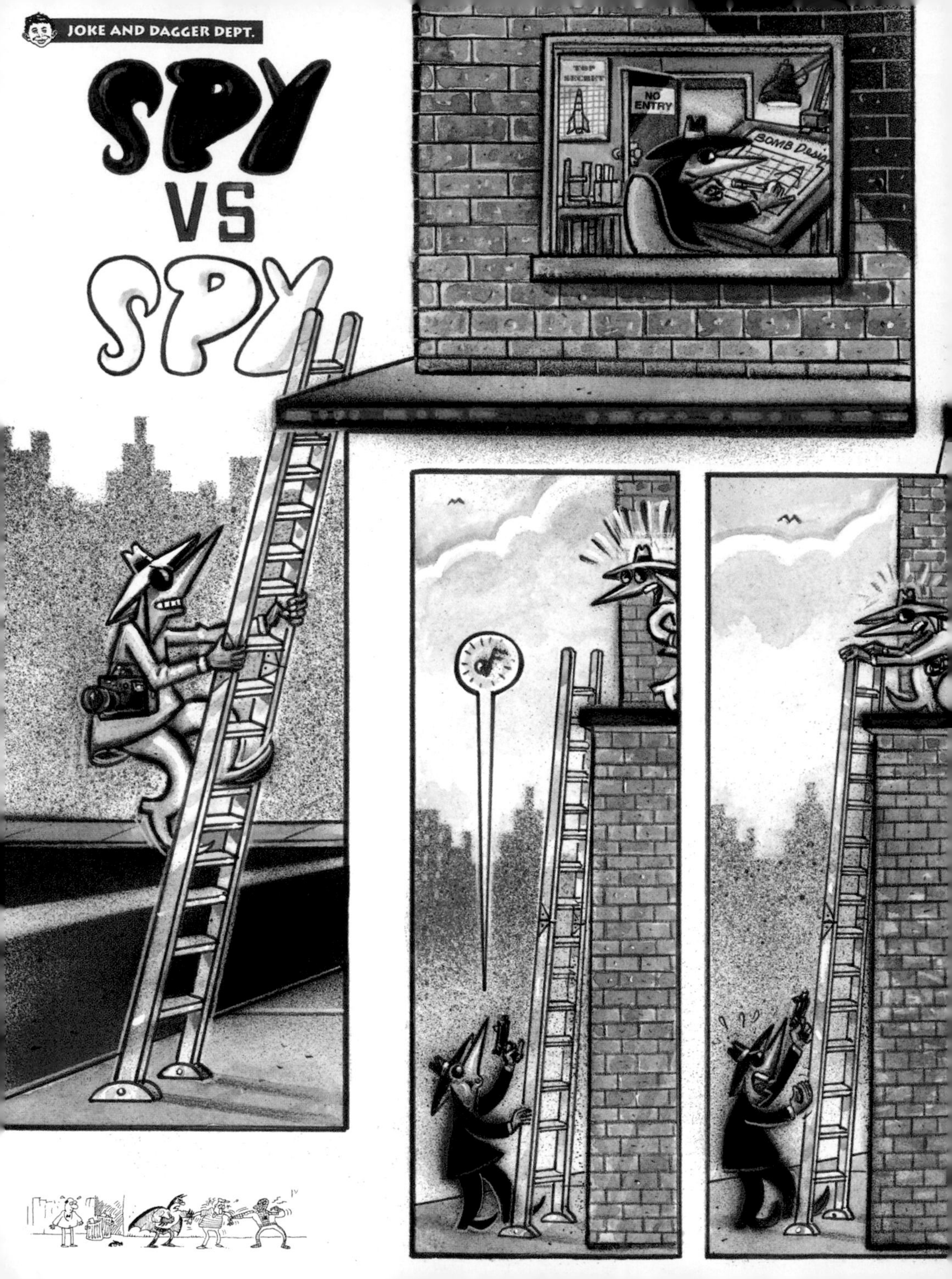
JOKE AND DAGGER DEPT.
SPY VS SPY
TOP SECRET
NO ENTRY
BOMB

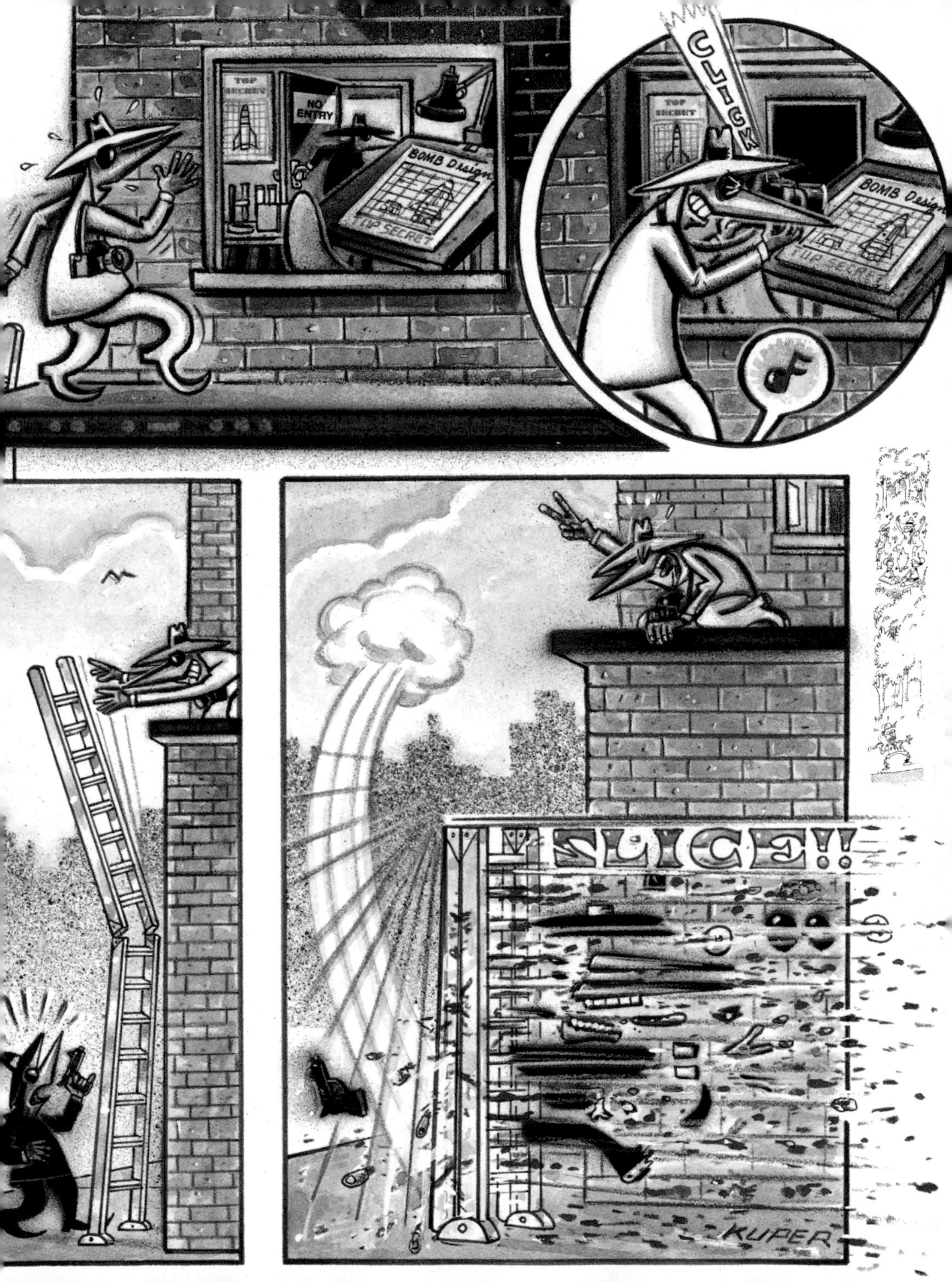
TOP SECRET
NO ENTRY
BOMB Design
TOP SECRET
CLICK
BOMB Design
TOP SECRET
SLICE!!
KUPER

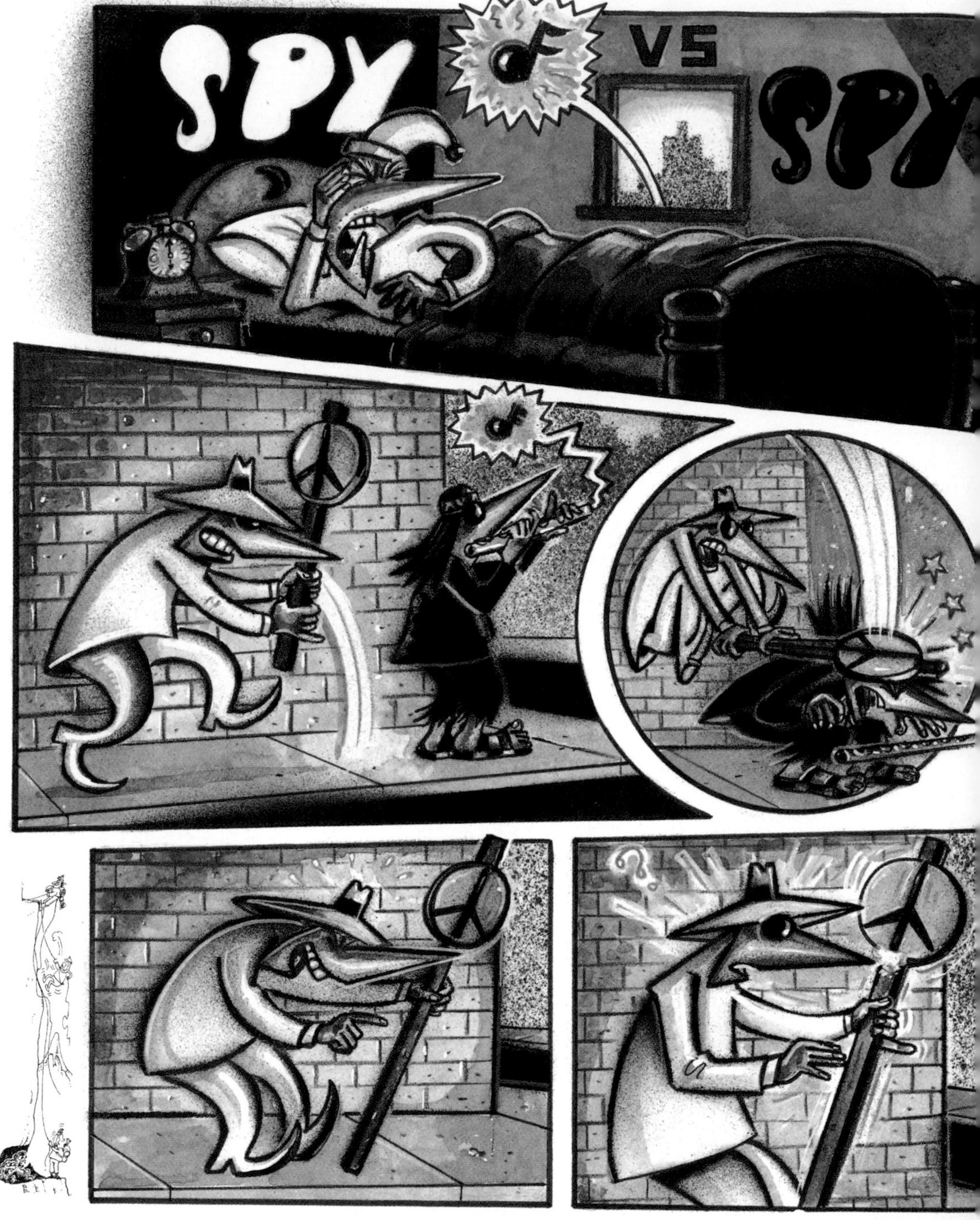
SPY VS SPY

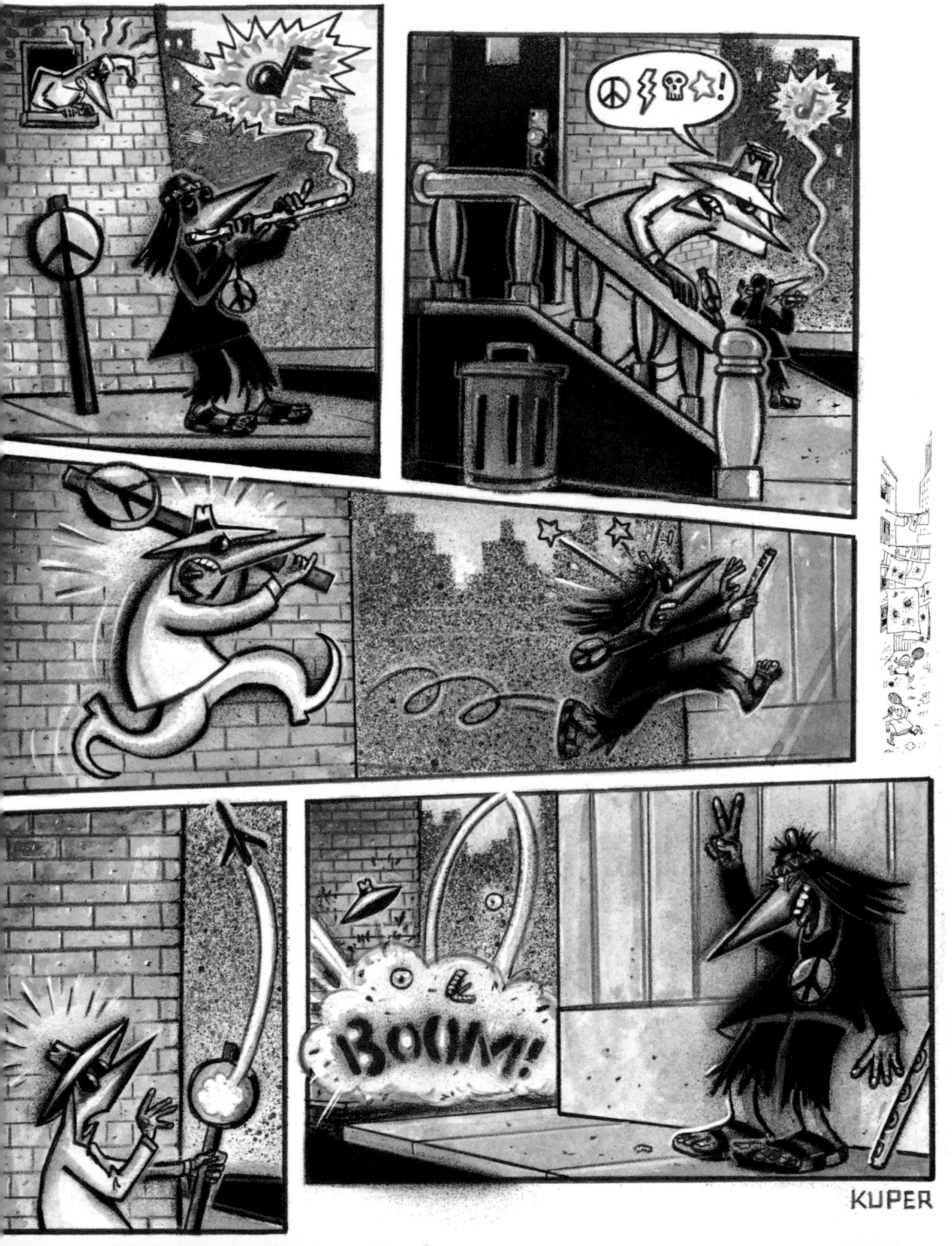
BOOM!
KUPER

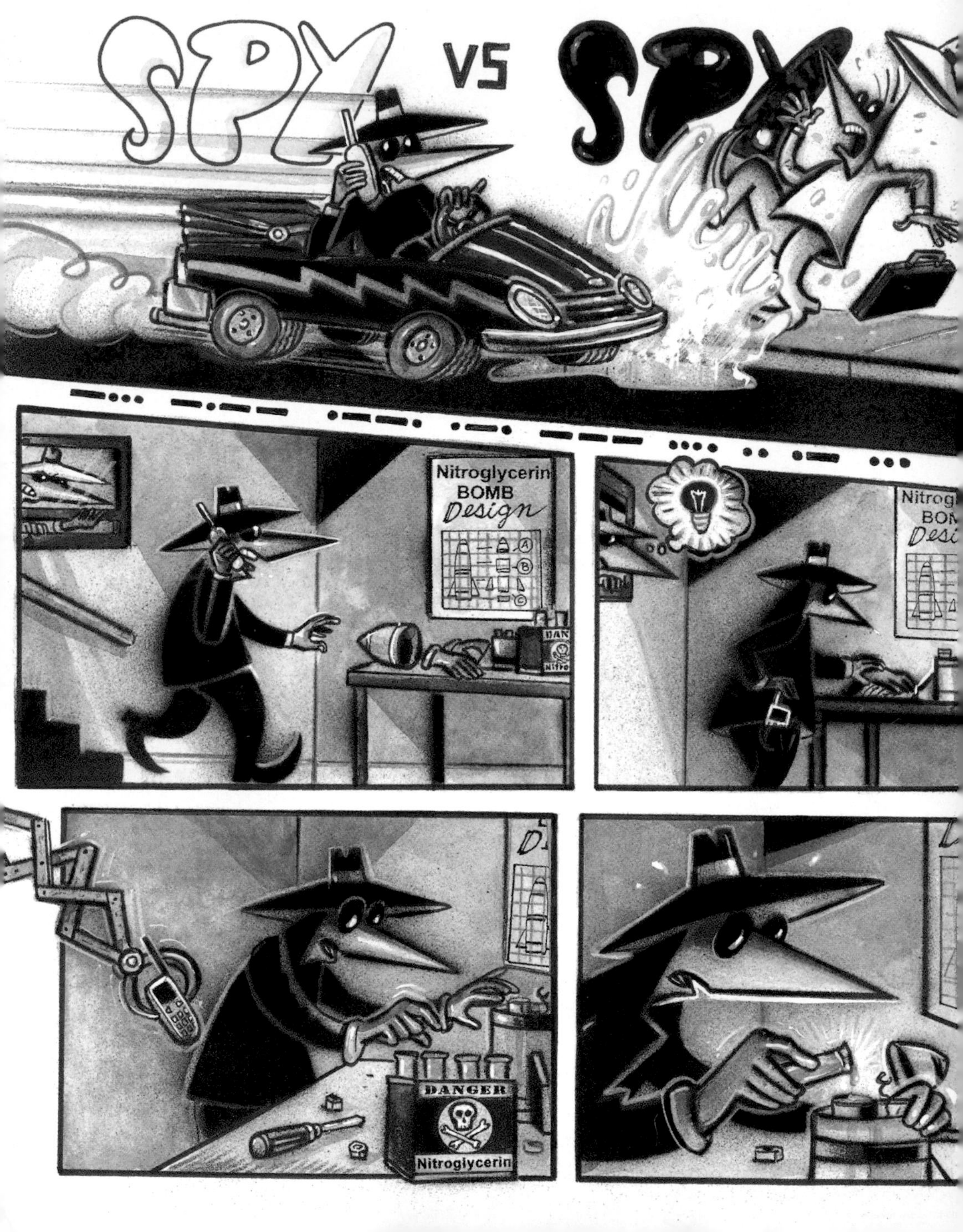
SPY VS SPY
Nitroglycerin
BOMB
Design
Nitroglycerin
DANGER
Nitroglycerin

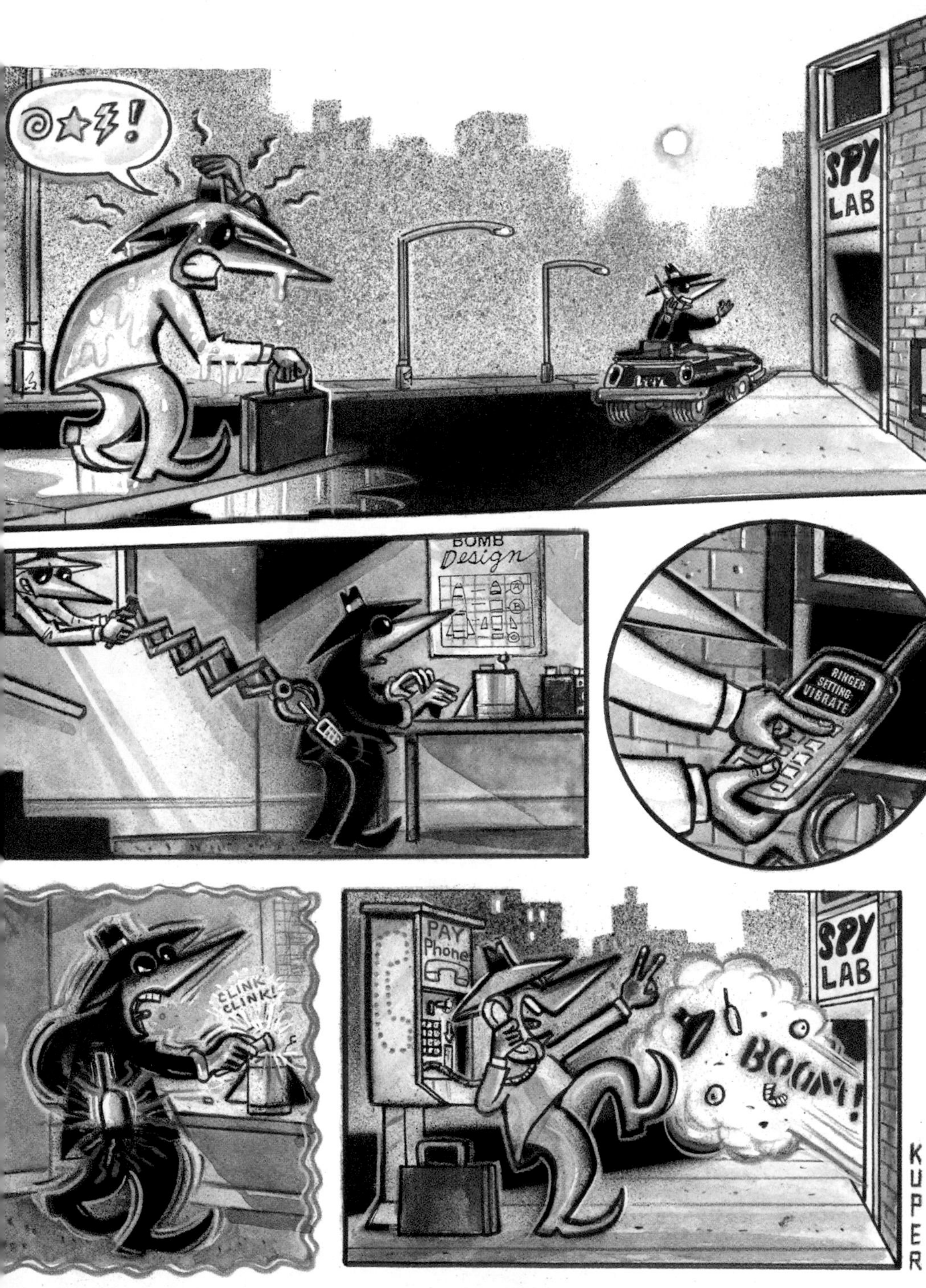
@☆⚡!
SPY LAB
BOMB Design
RINGER SETTING: VIBRATE
CLINK CLINK!
PAY Phone
SPY LAB
BOOM!
KUPER

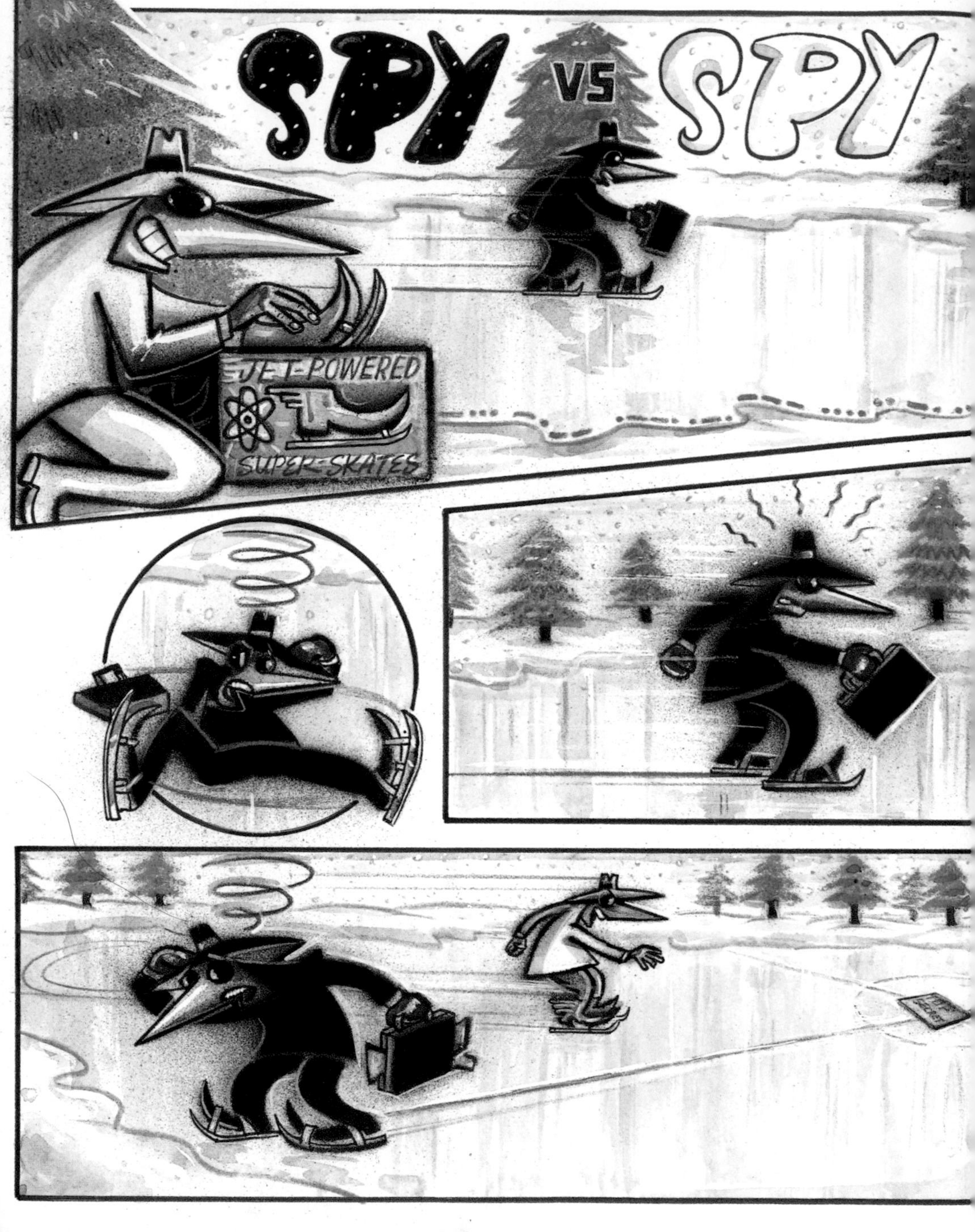
SPY VS SPY
JET-POWERED
SUPER-SKATES

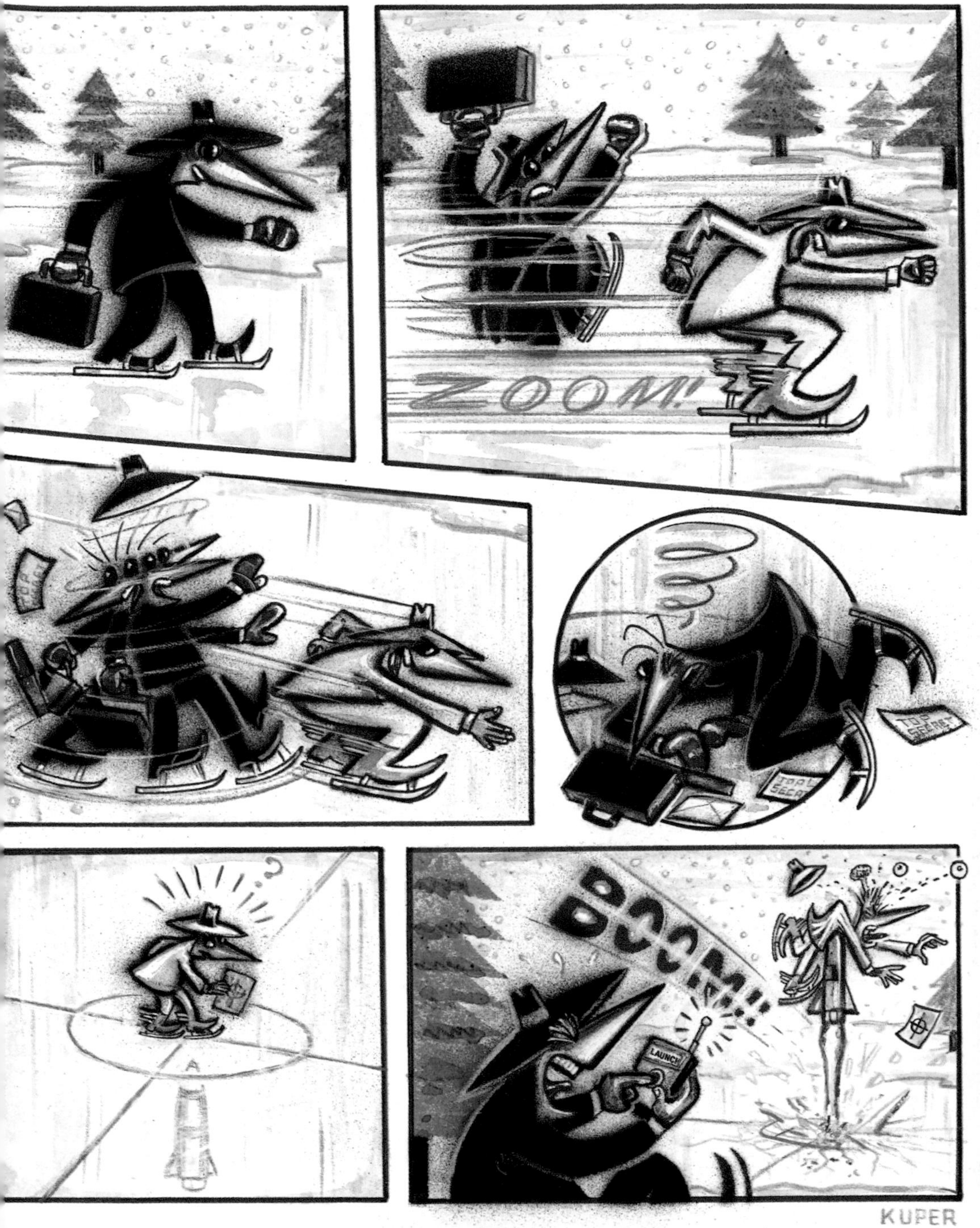
ZOOM!
TOP SECRET
A
BOOM!!
LAUNCH
KUPER

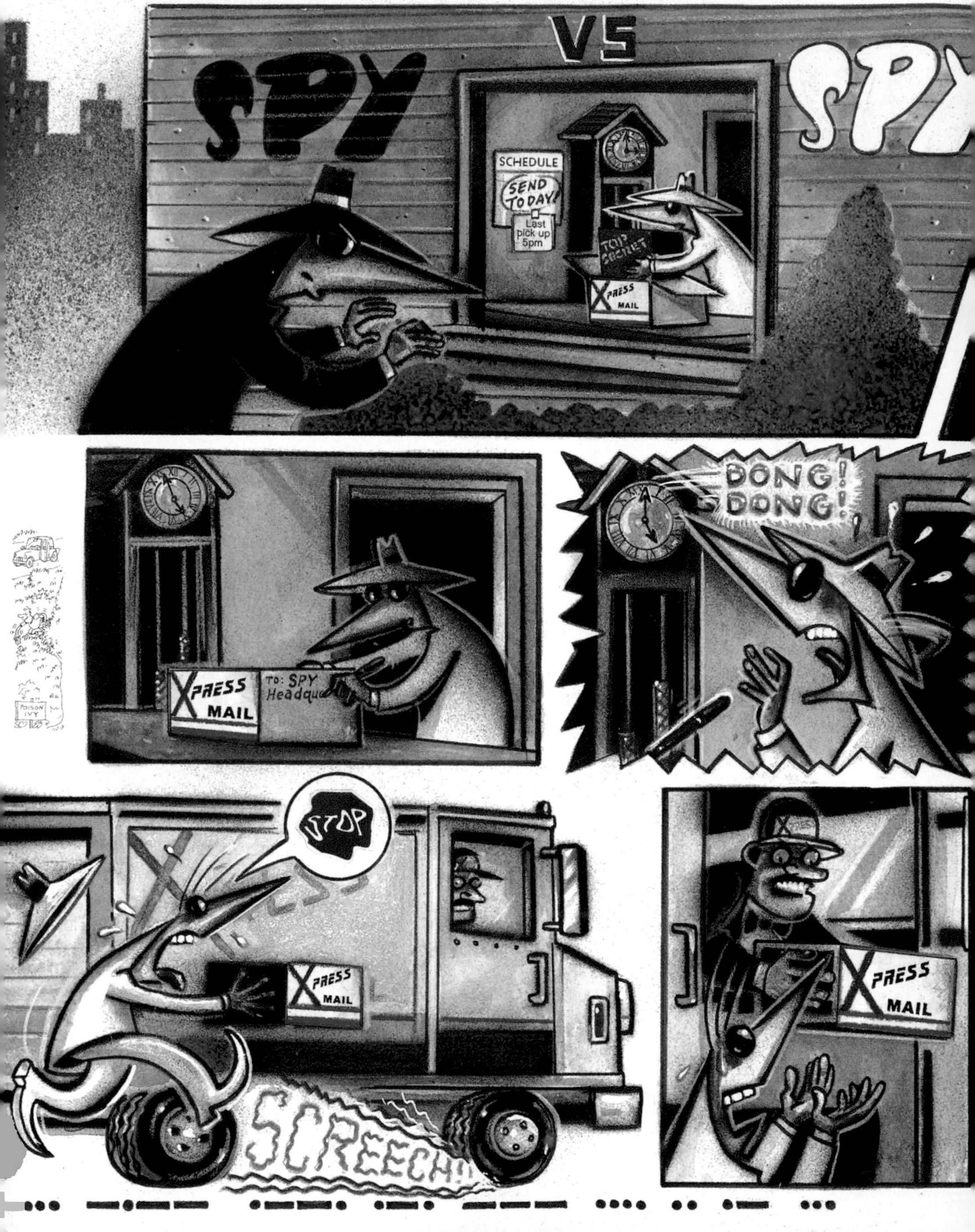
SPY VS SPY
SCHEDULE
SEND TODAY!
Last pick up 5pm
TOP SECRET
XPRESS MAIL
XPRESS MAIL
TO: SPY Headqu
POISON IVY
DONG! DONG!
STOP
XPRESS MAIL
SCREECH!!
XPRESS MAIL

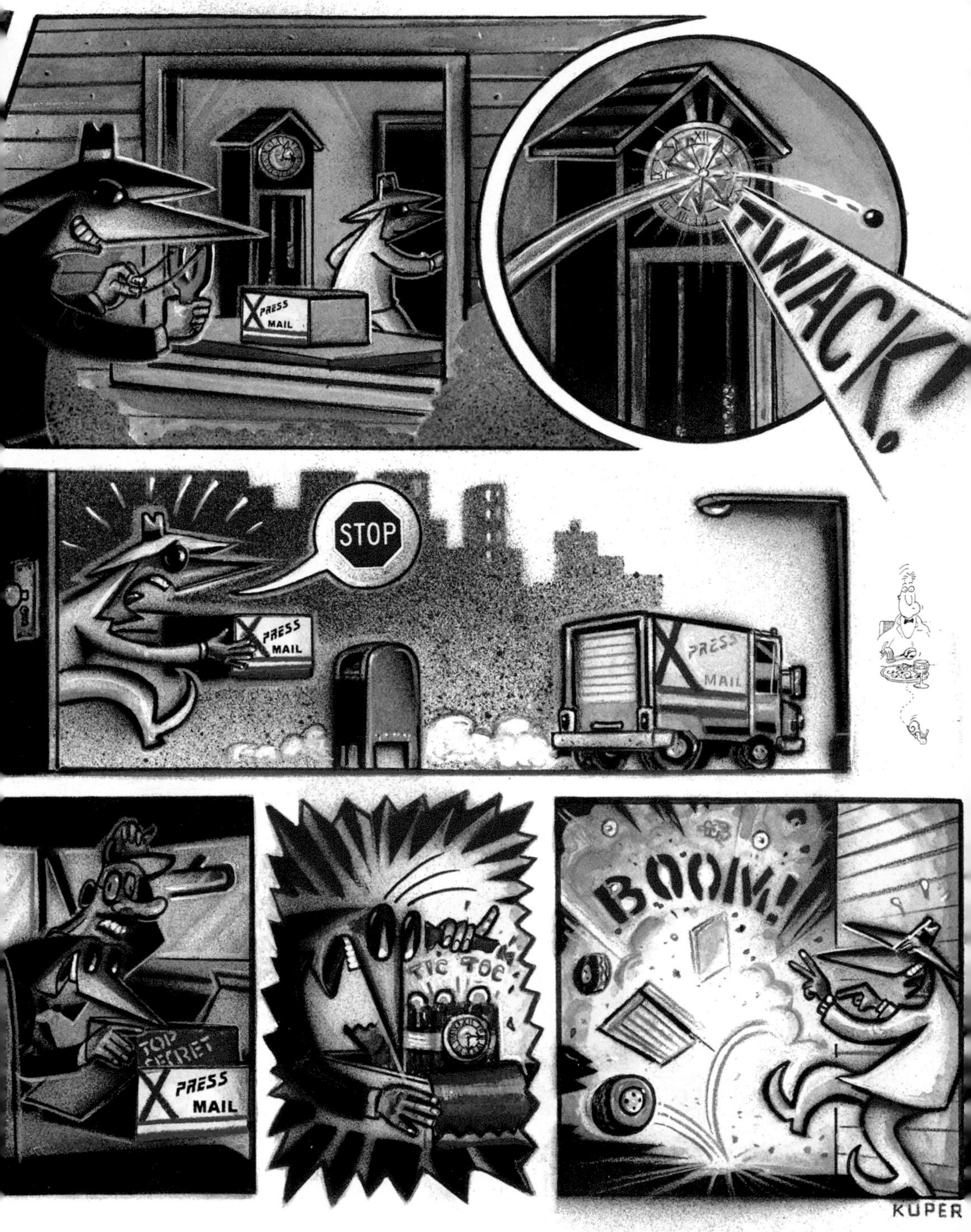
XPRESS MAIL
WACK!
STOP
XPRESS MAIL
XPRESS MAIL
TOP SECRET
XPRESS MAIL
TIC TOC
BOOM!
KUPER

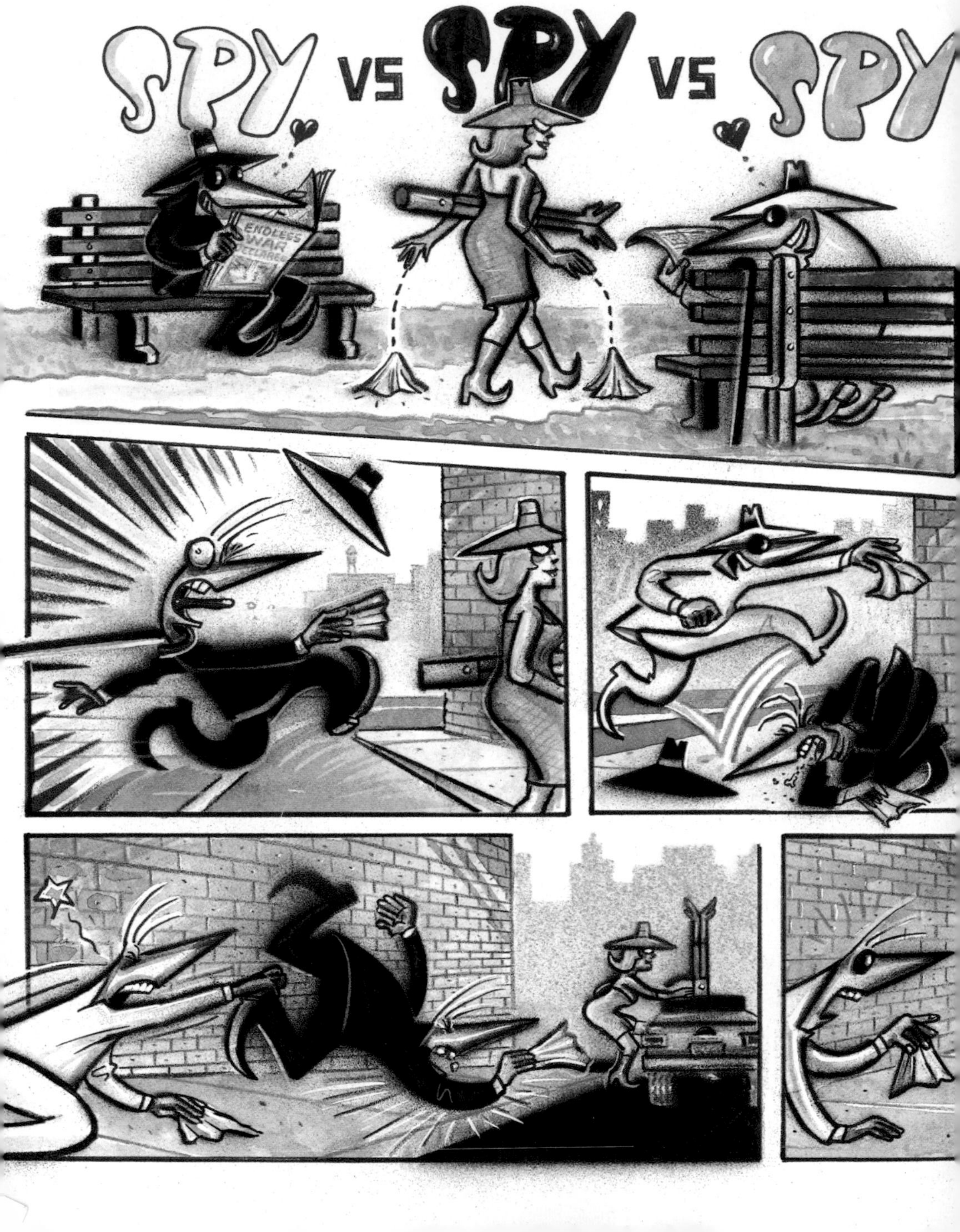
SPY VS SPY VS SPY
ENDLESS WAR DECLARED

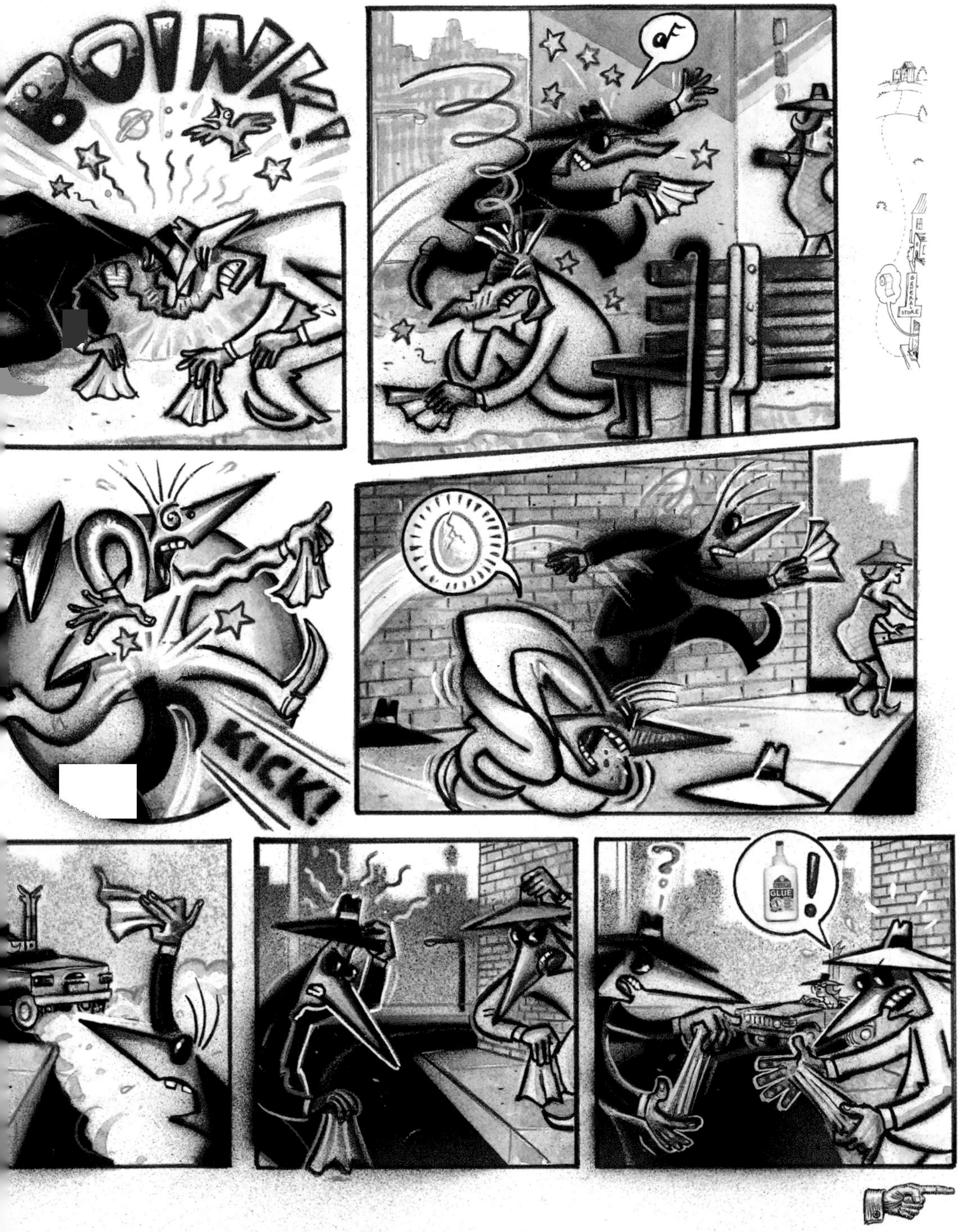
BOINK!
KICK!
GLUE

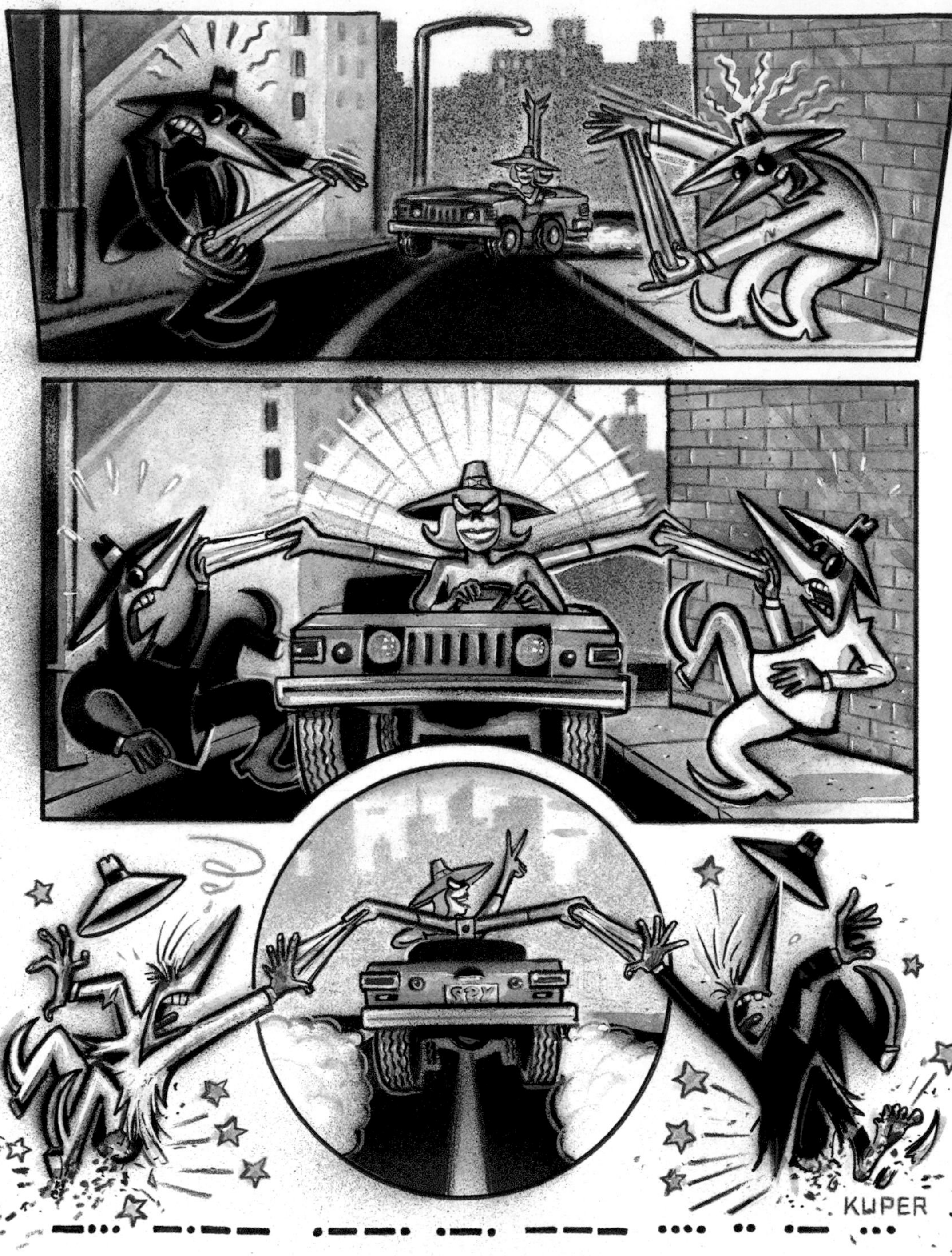
SPY
KUPER

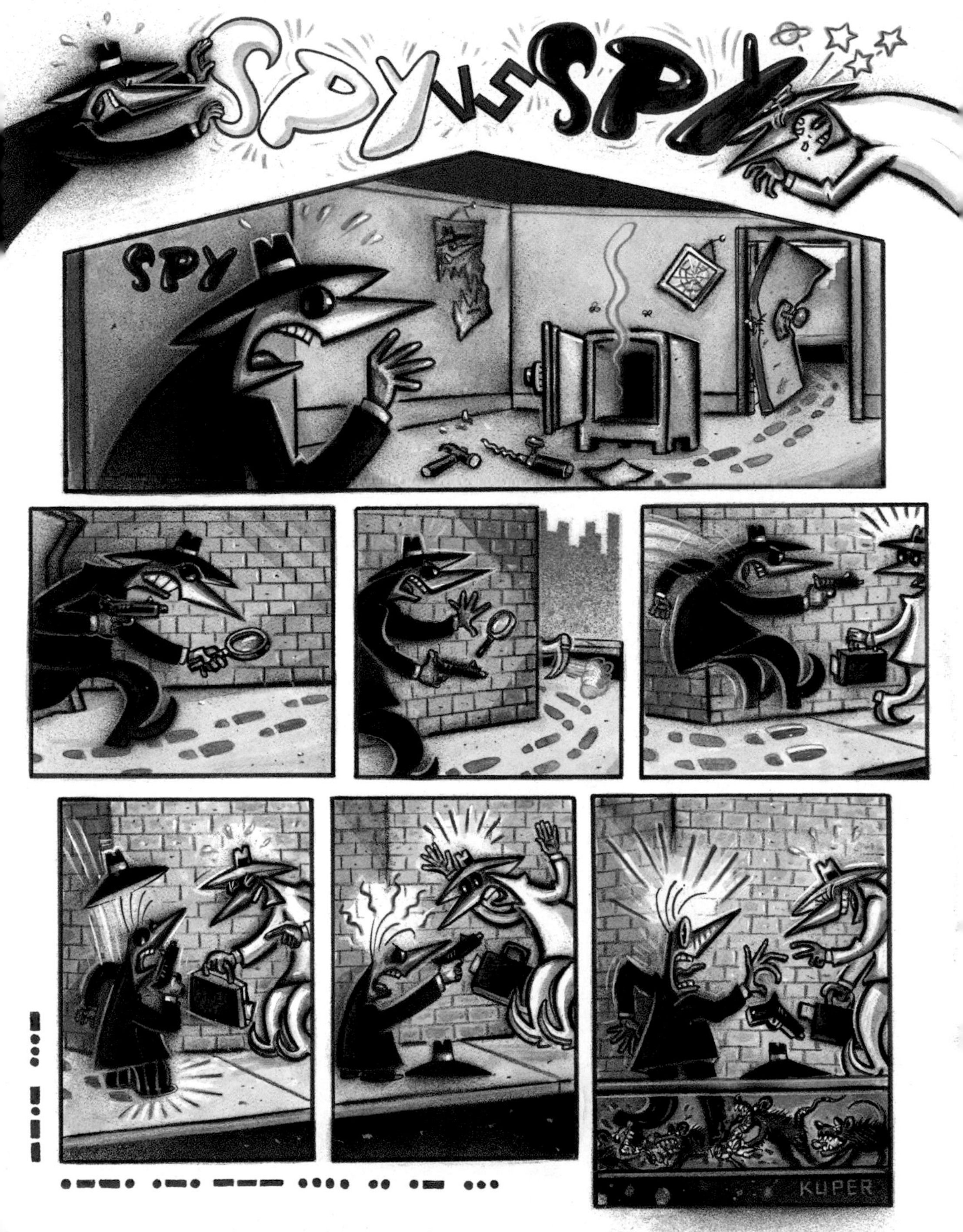
SPY vs SPY
SPY
KUPER

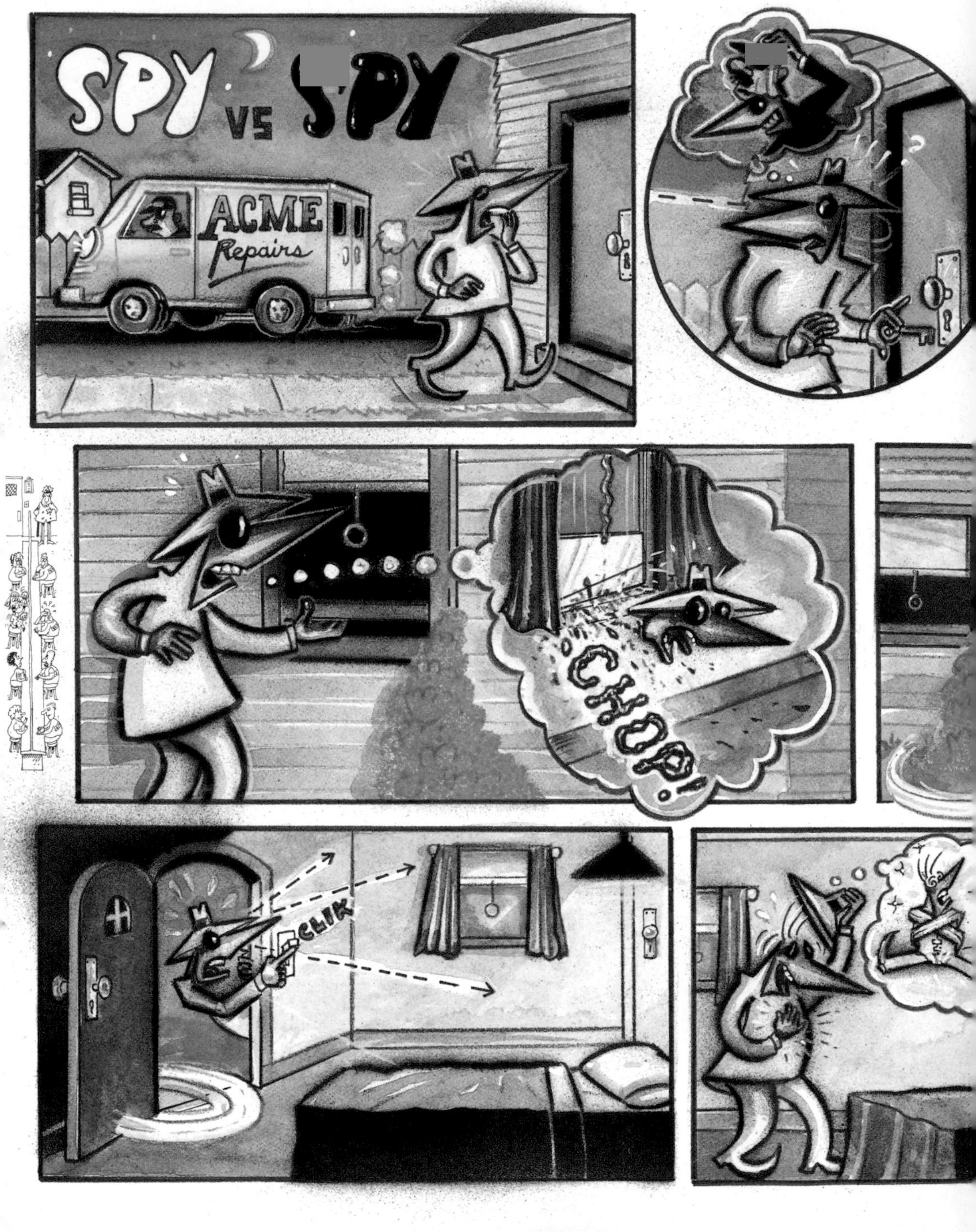
SPY VS SPY
ACME
Repairs
?
CHOP!
CLIK

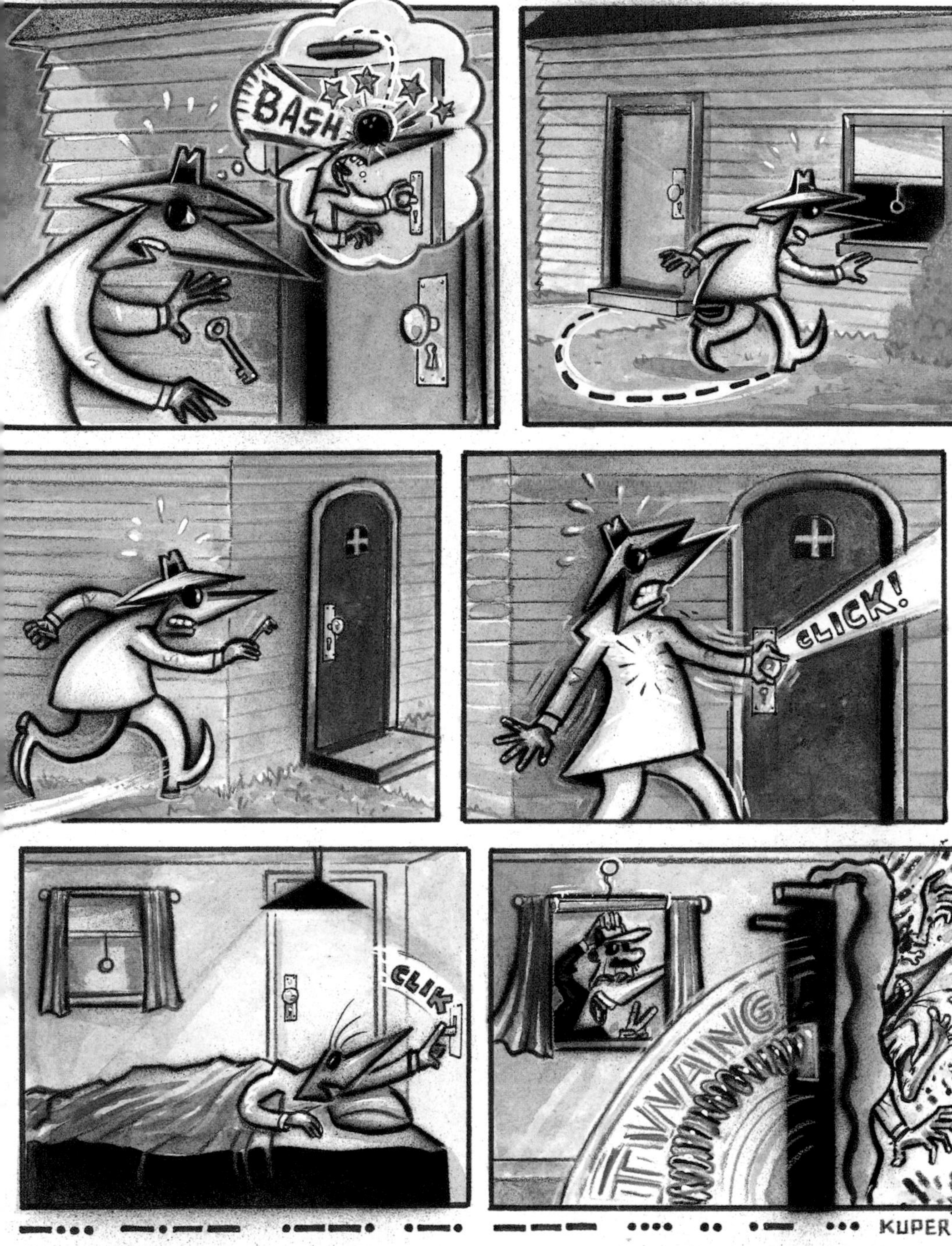
BASH
CLICK!
CLIK
TWANG
KUPER

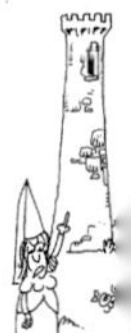

JOKE AND DAGGER DEPT.

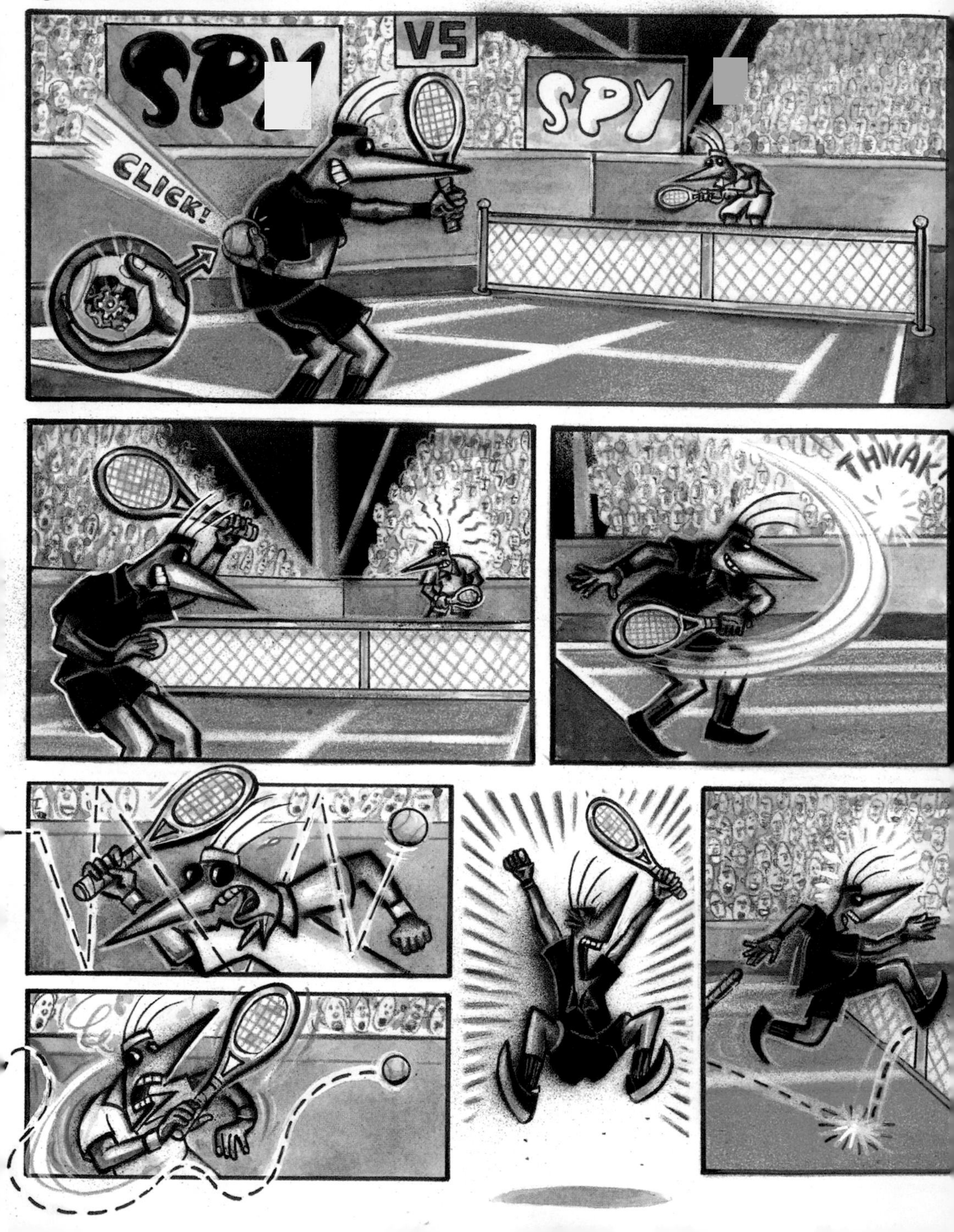
SPY
VS
SPY
CLICK!
THWAK!

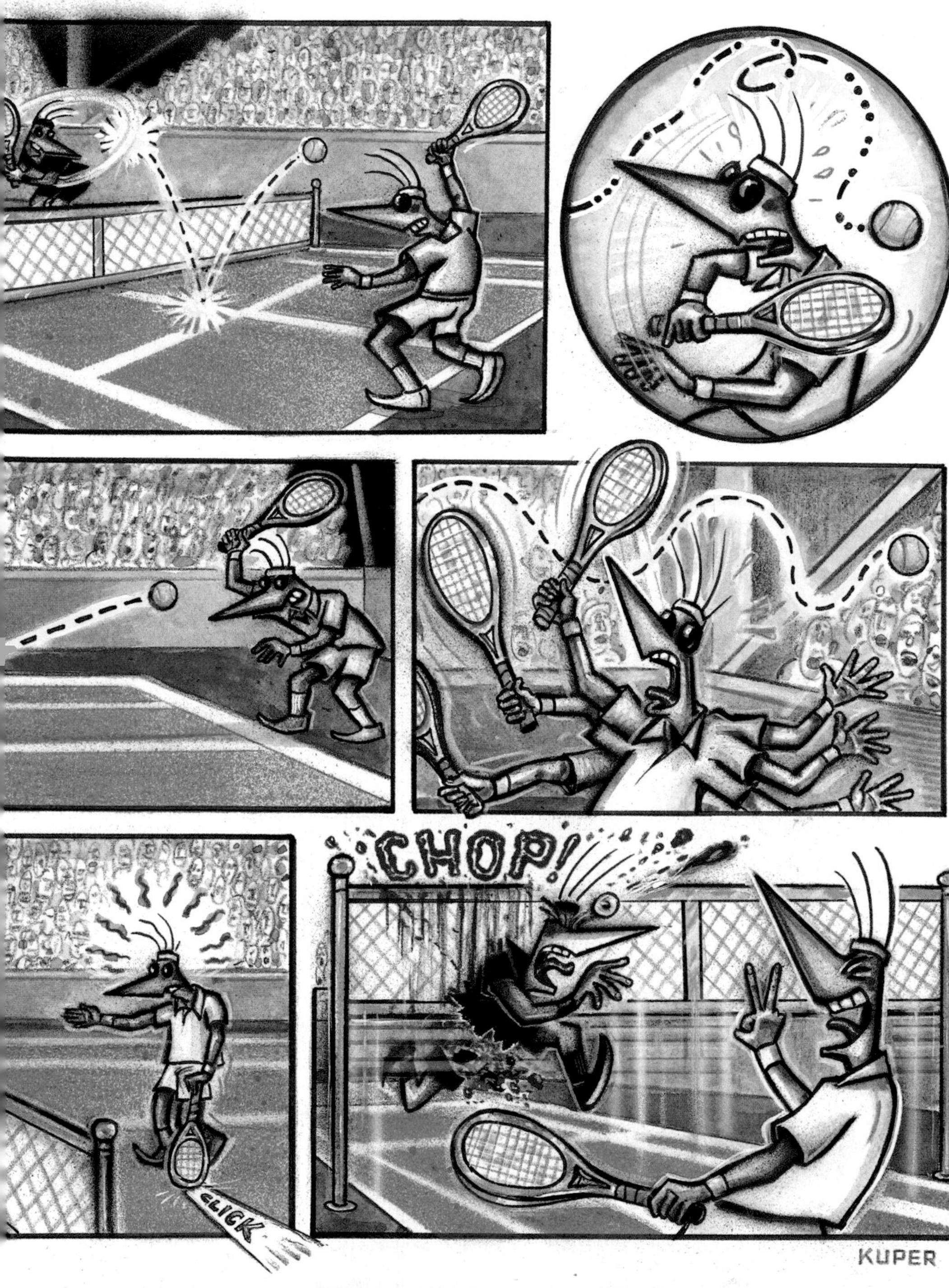
CHOP!
CLICK
KUPER

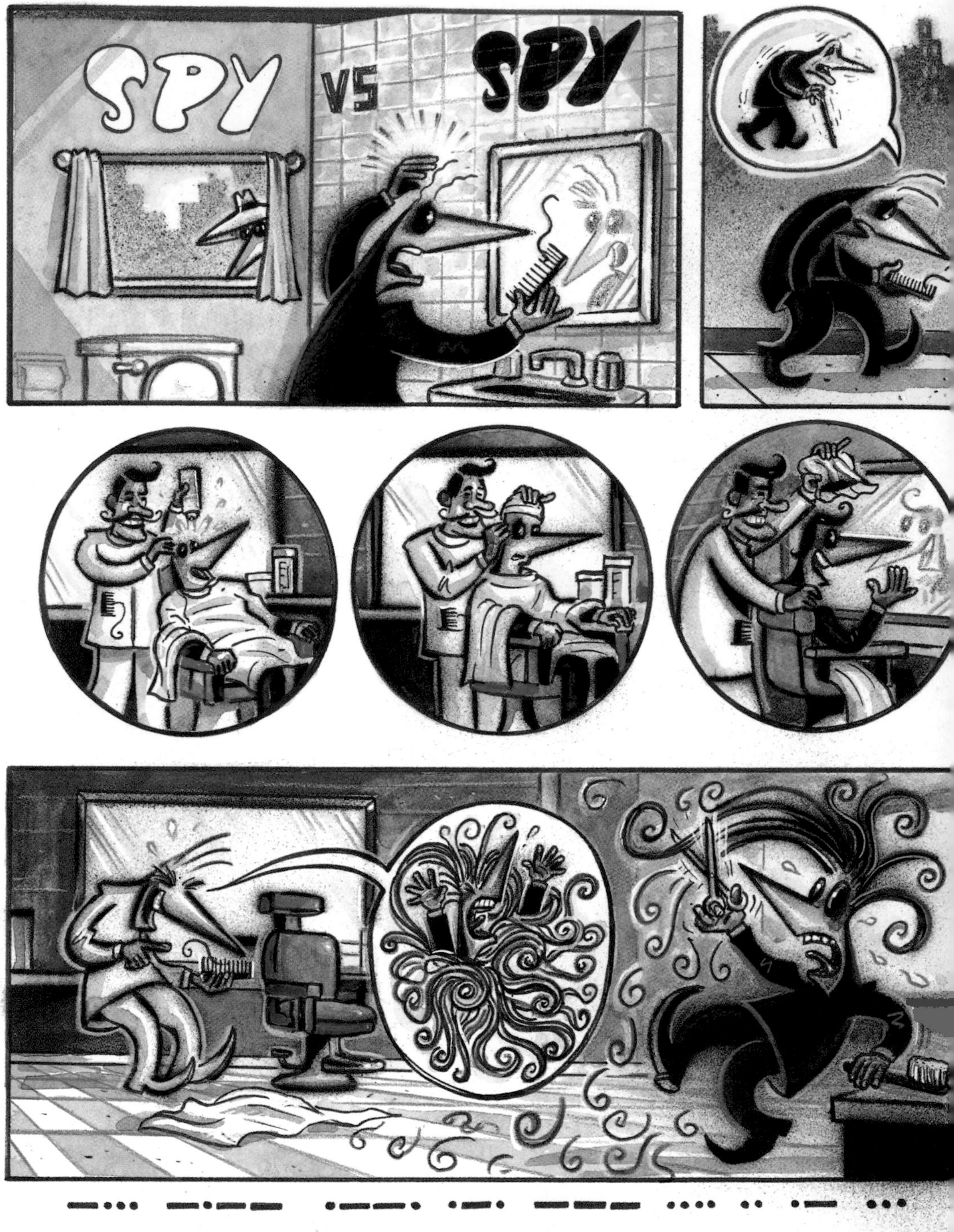
SPY VS SPY

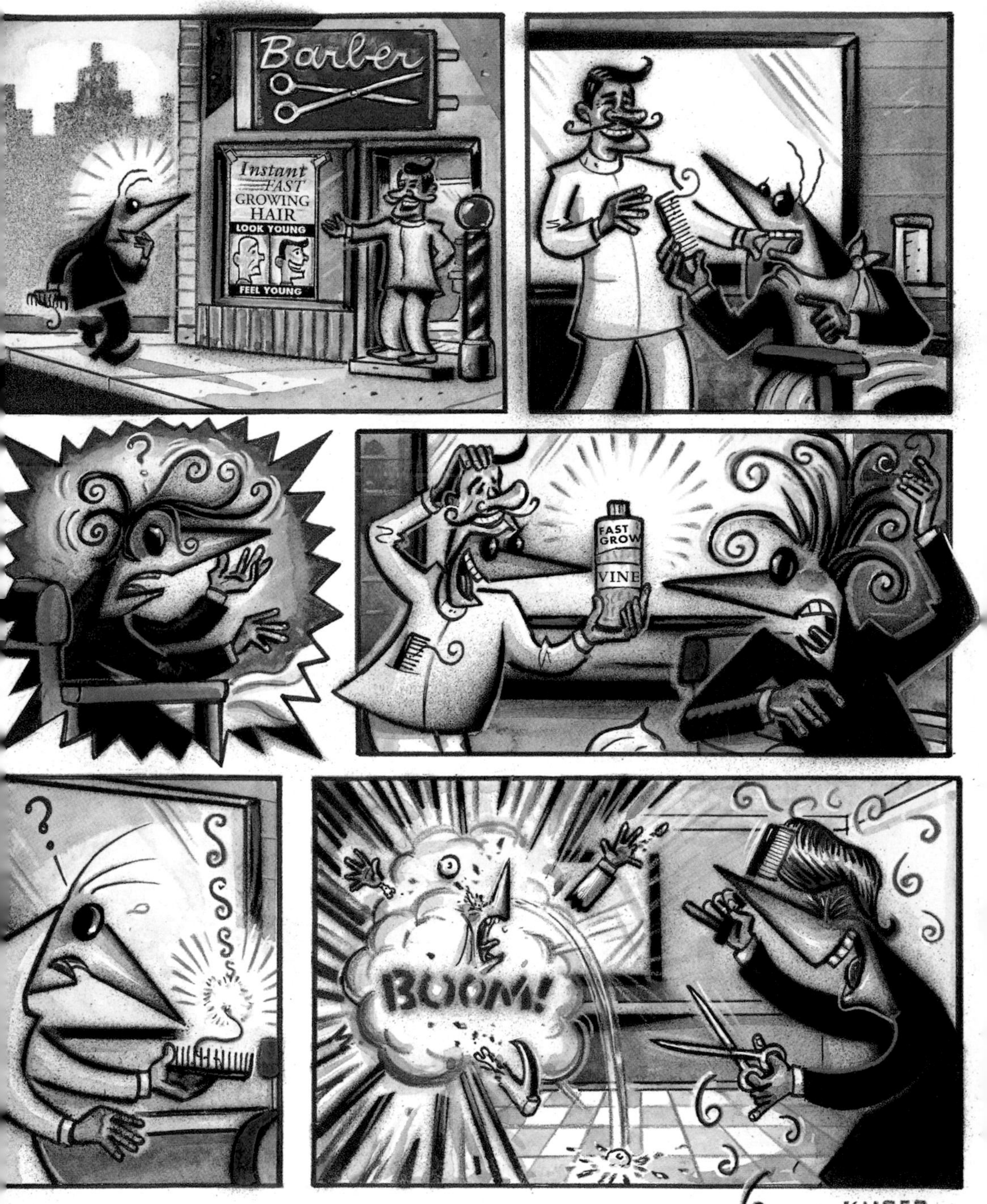

Barber
Instant FAST GROWING HAIR
LOOK YOUNG
FEEL YOUNG
FAST GROW
VINE
BOOM!
KUPER

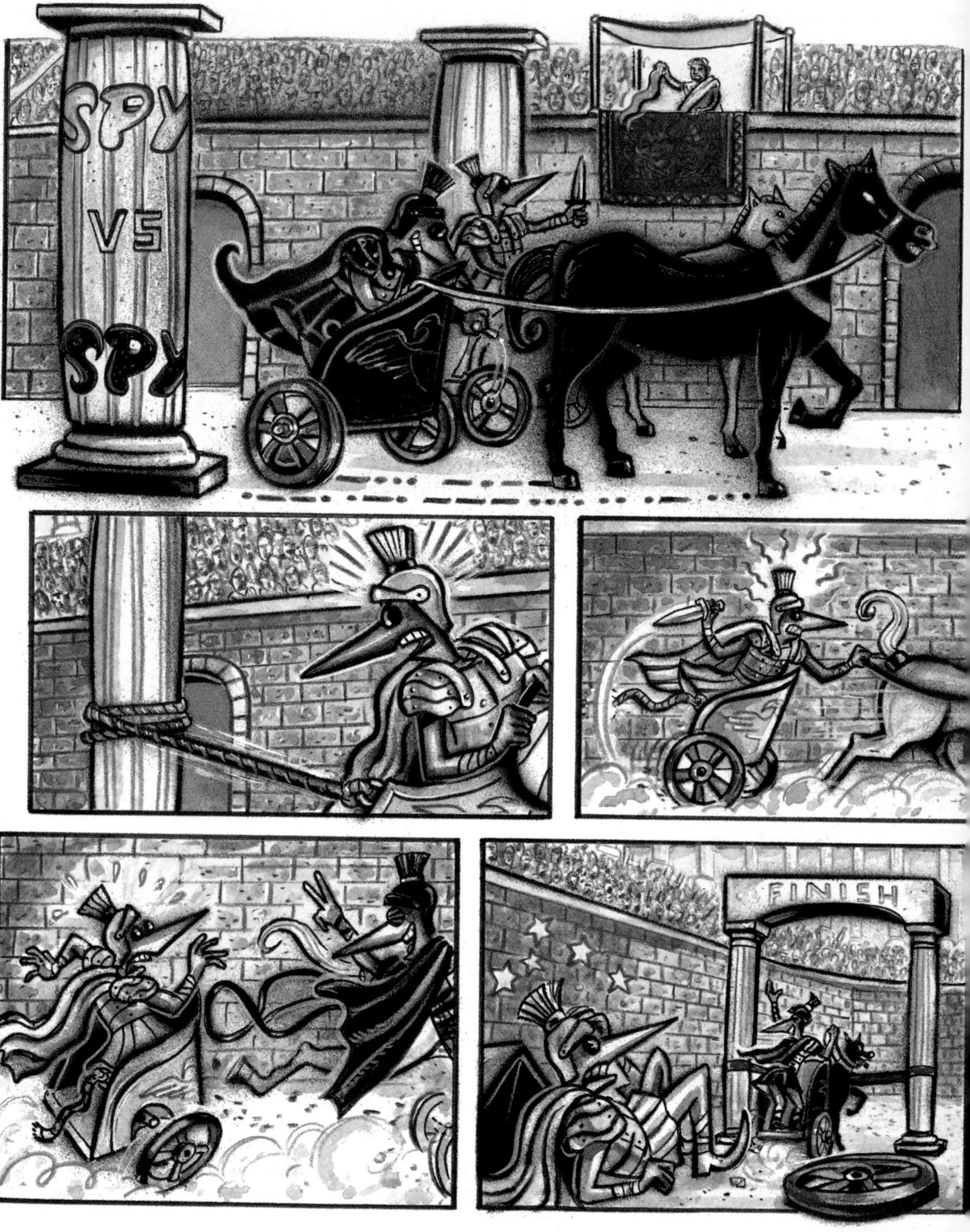
SPY
VS
SPY
FINISH

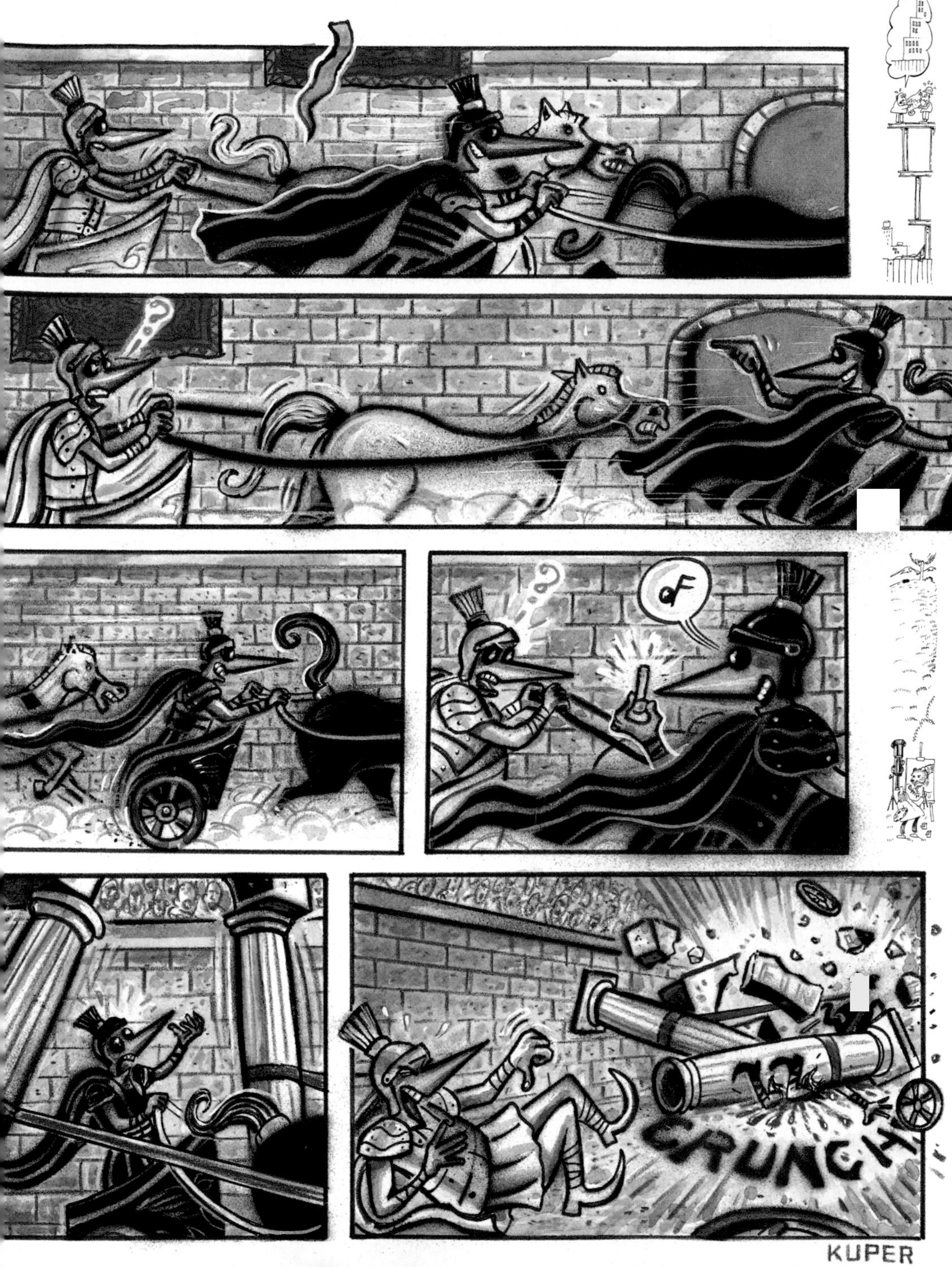

CRUNCH
KUPER

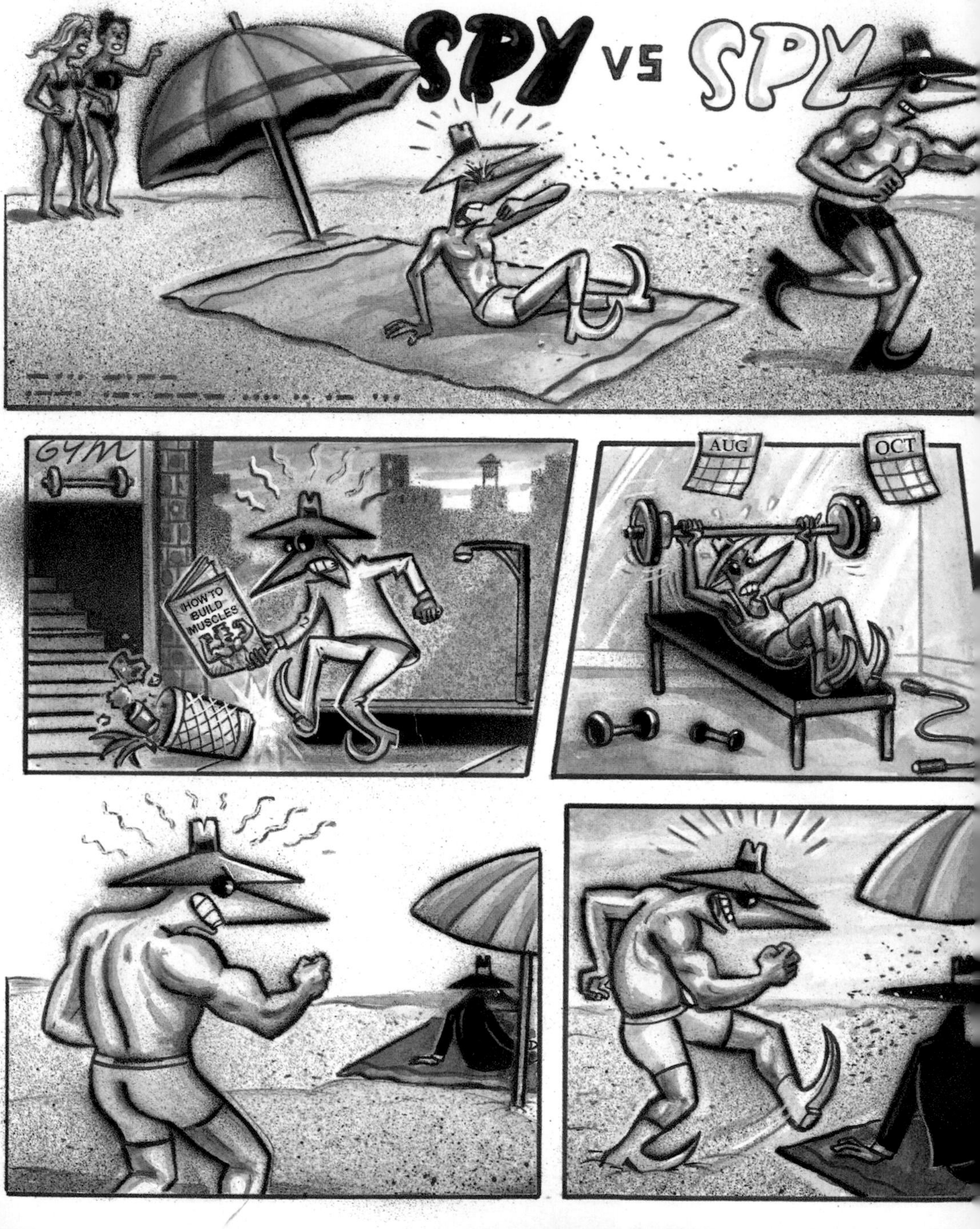
SPY vs SPY
GYM
HOW TO BUILD MUSCLES
AUG
OCT

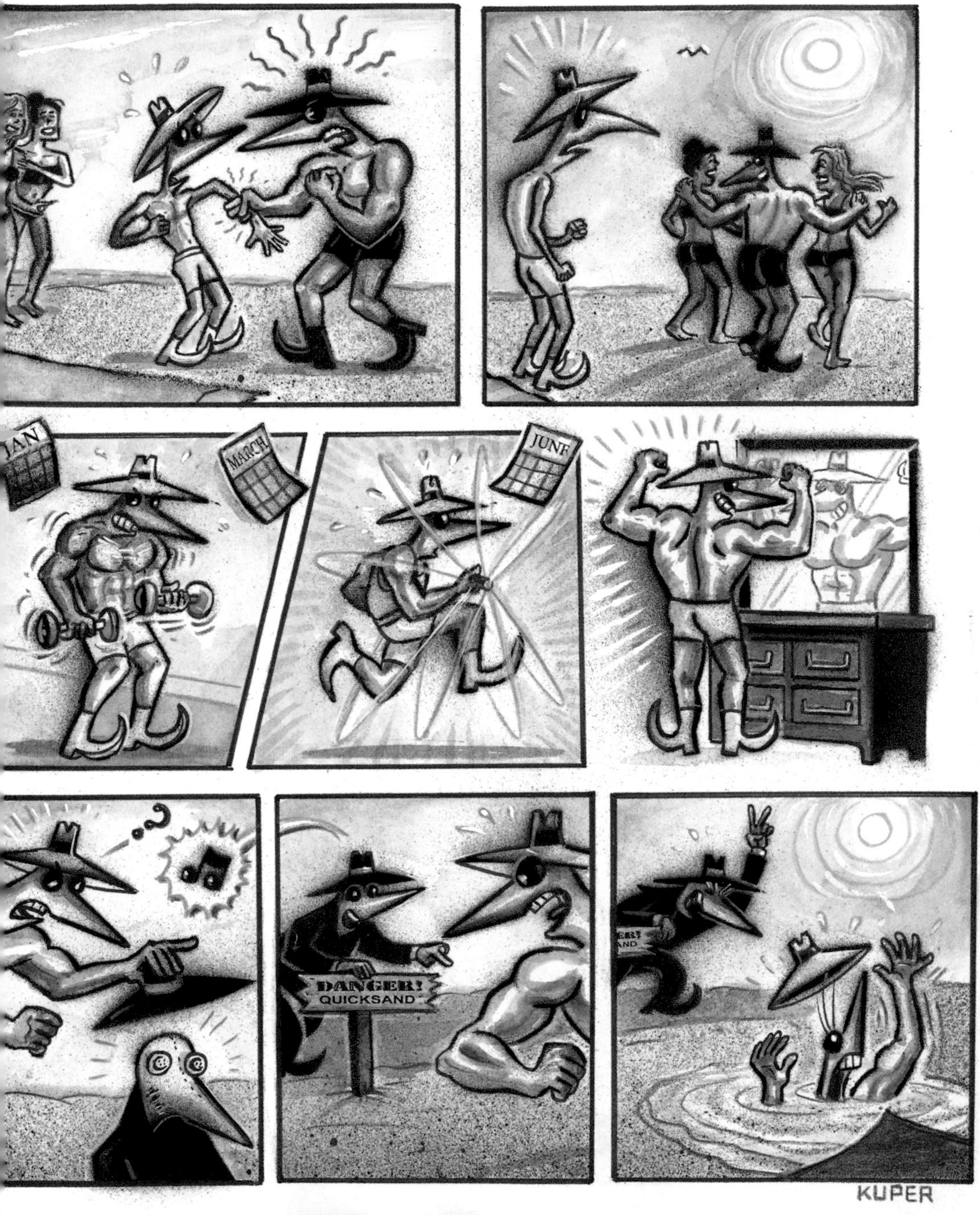
JAN
MARCH
JUNE
DANGER!
QUICKSAND
KUPER

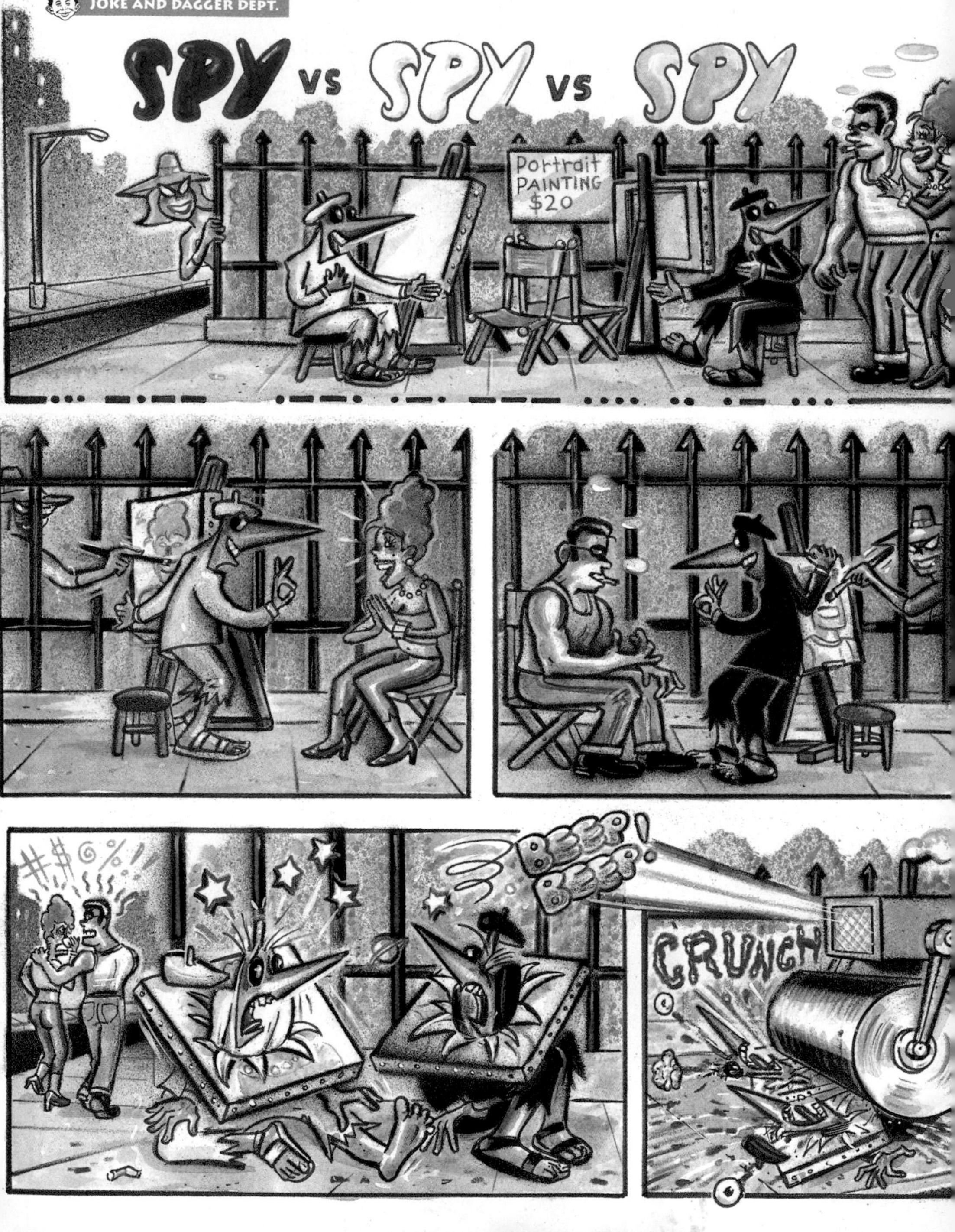
SPY vs SPY vs SPY
Portrait PAINTING $20
#$@%!
BEEP! BEEP!
CRUNCH

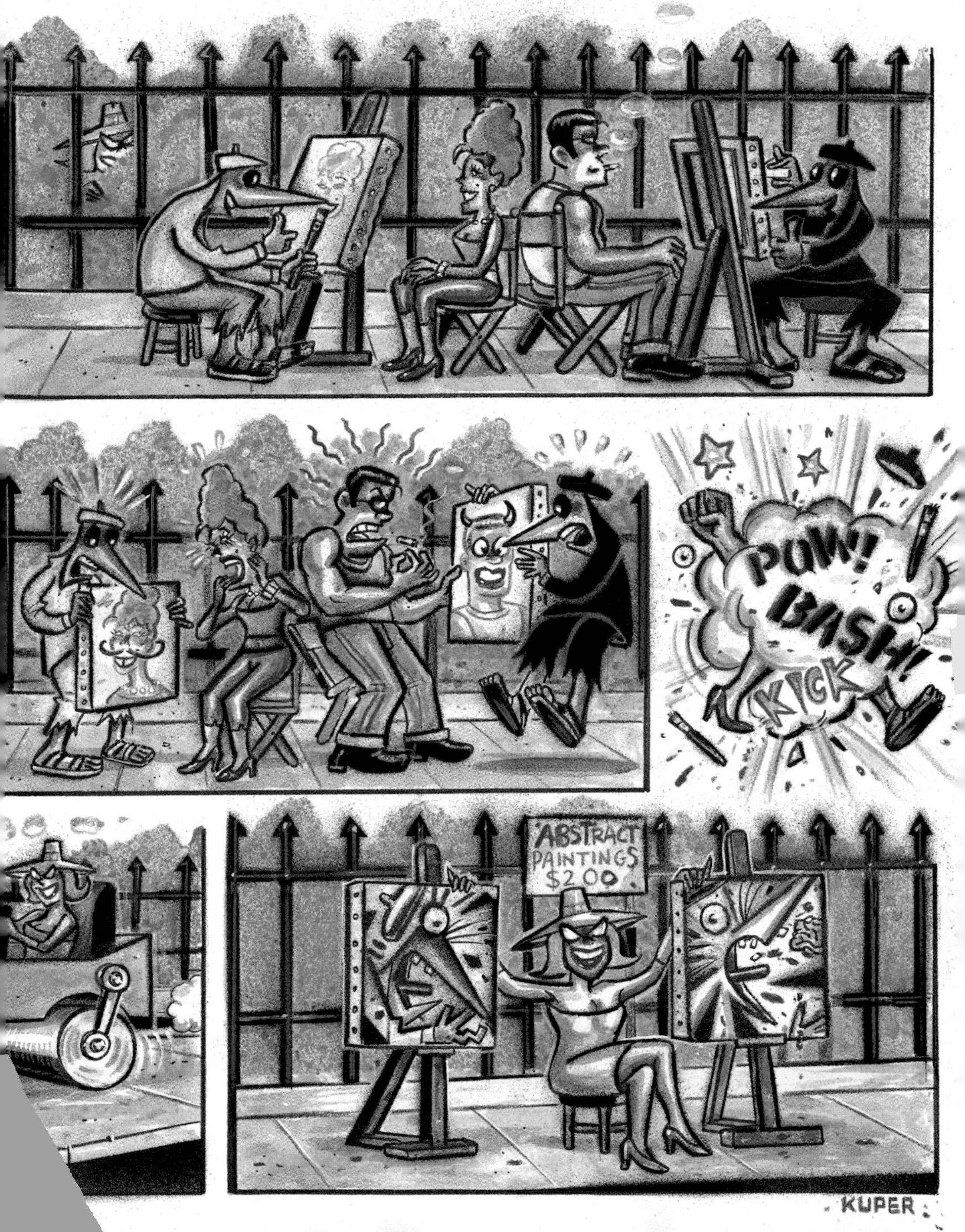
POW!
BASH!
KICK
ABSTRACT
PAINTINGS
$200
KUPER

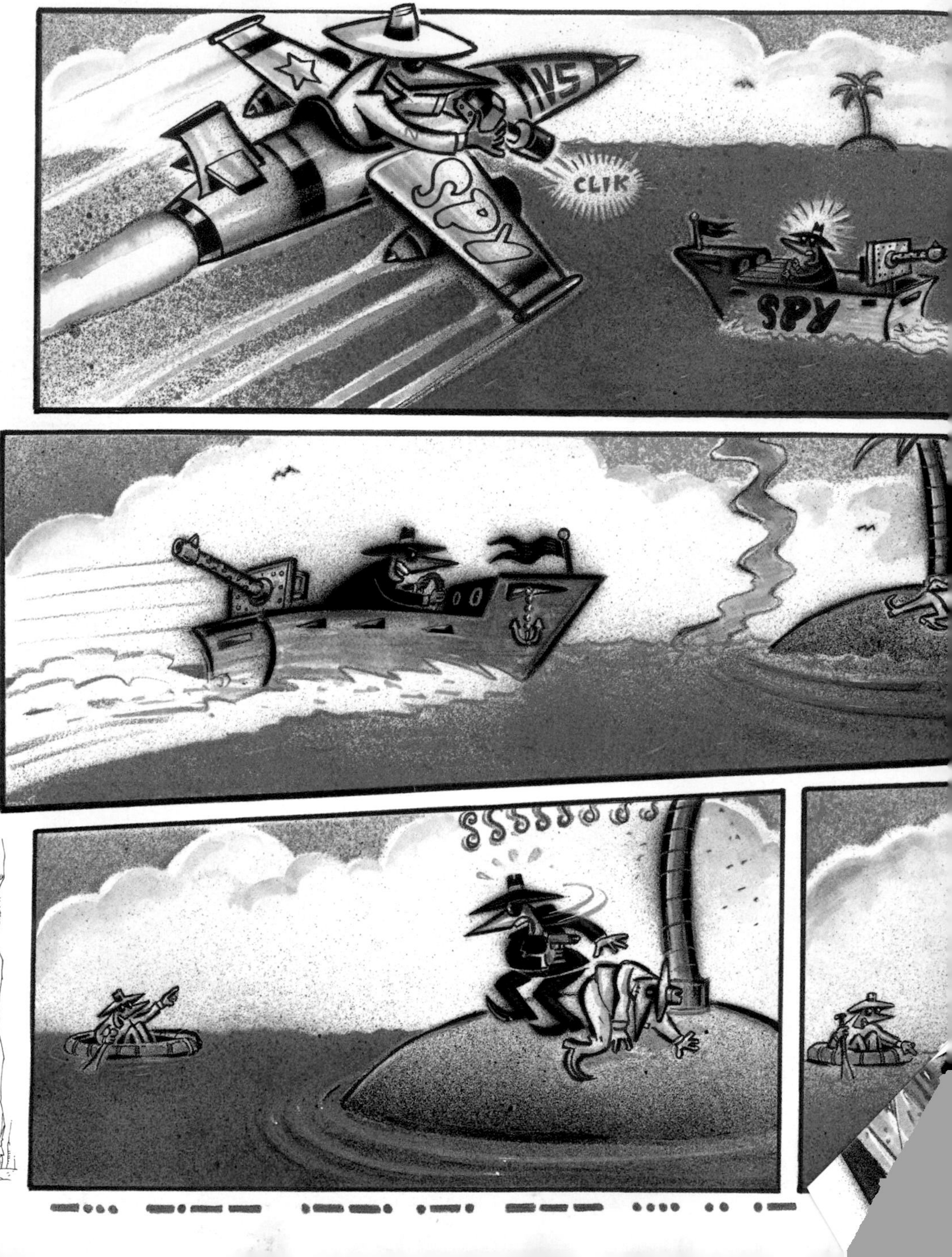
SPY
CLIK
SPY

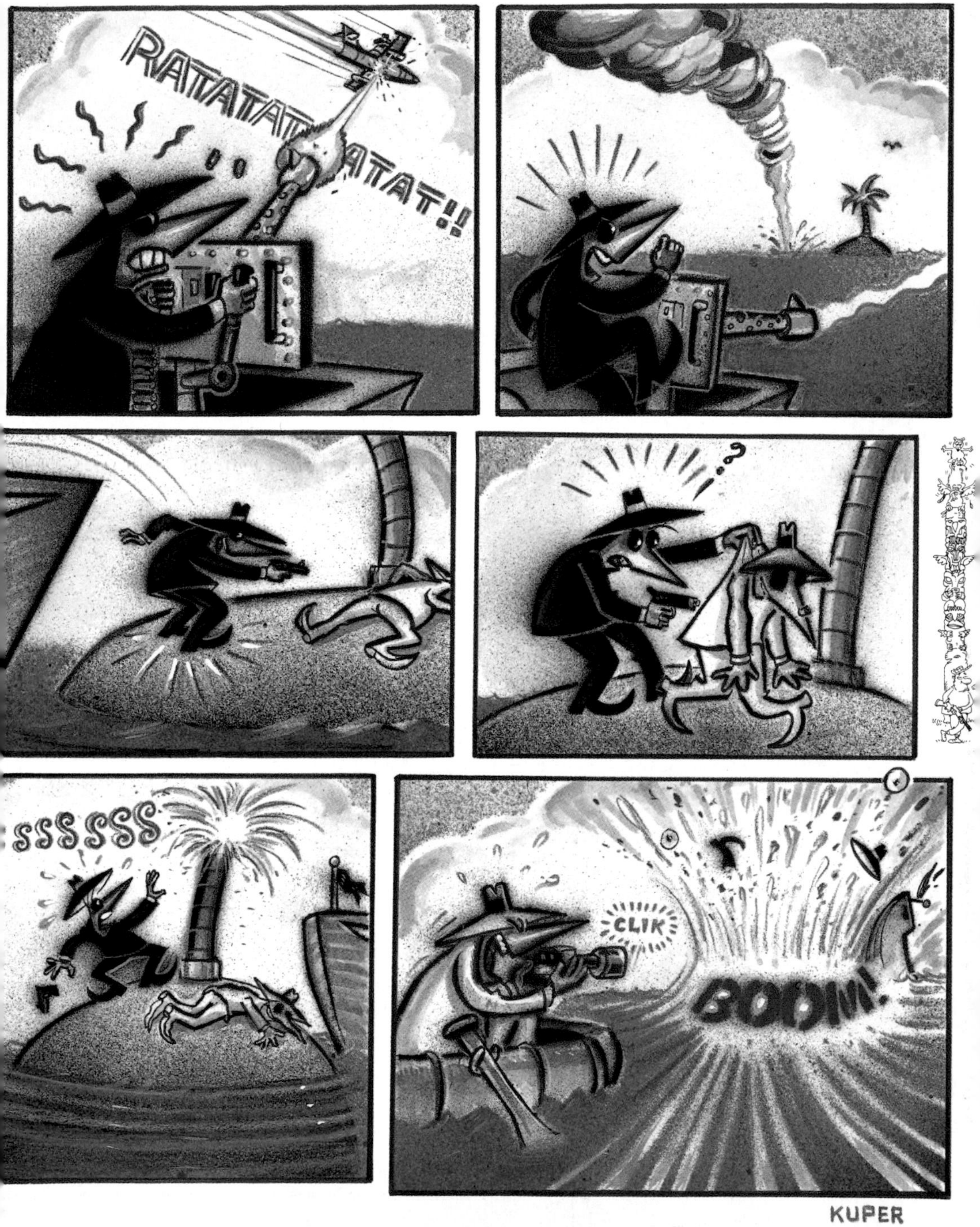
RATATAT ATAT!!
SSSSSS
CLIK
BOOM!

KUPER

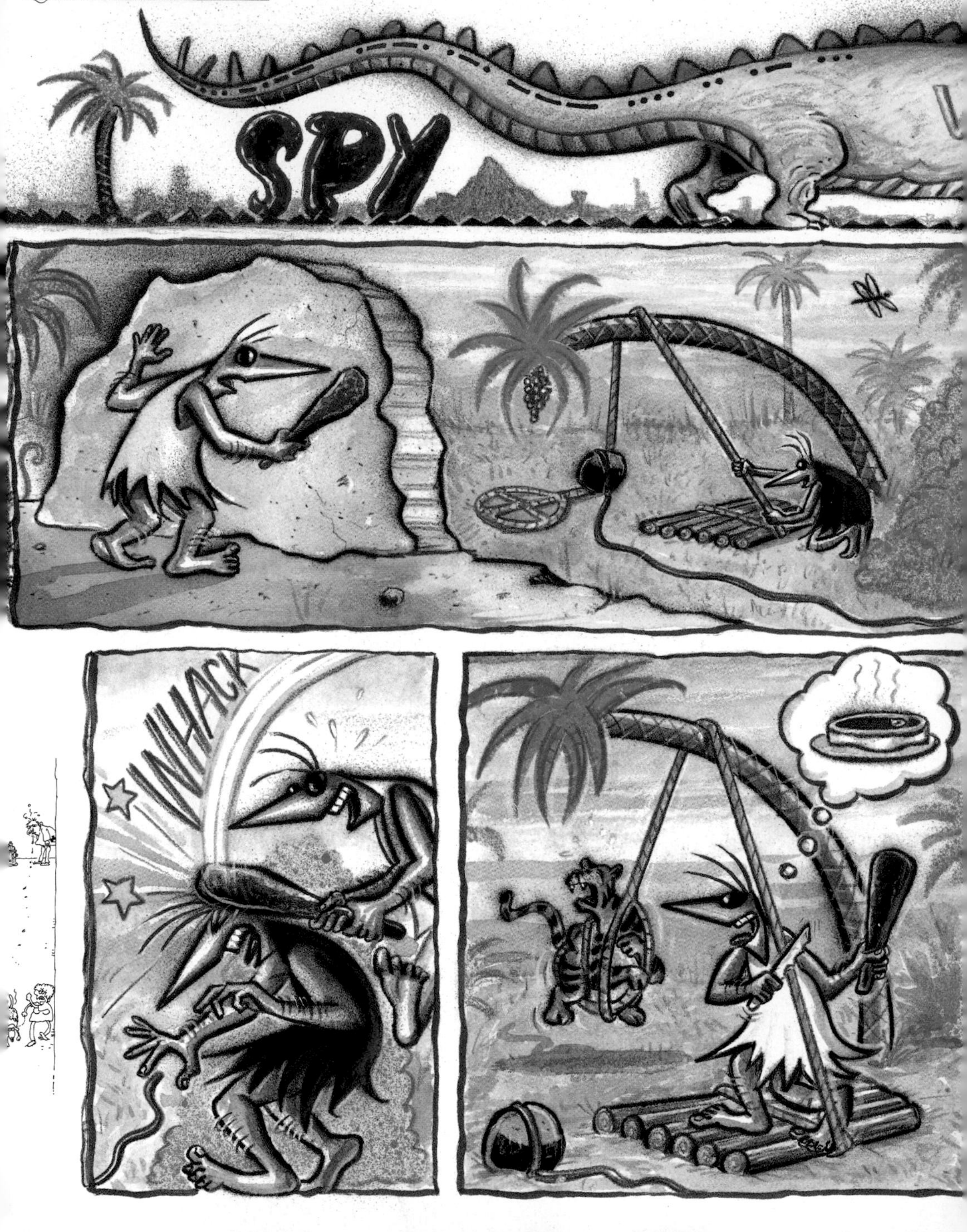
SPY
WHACK

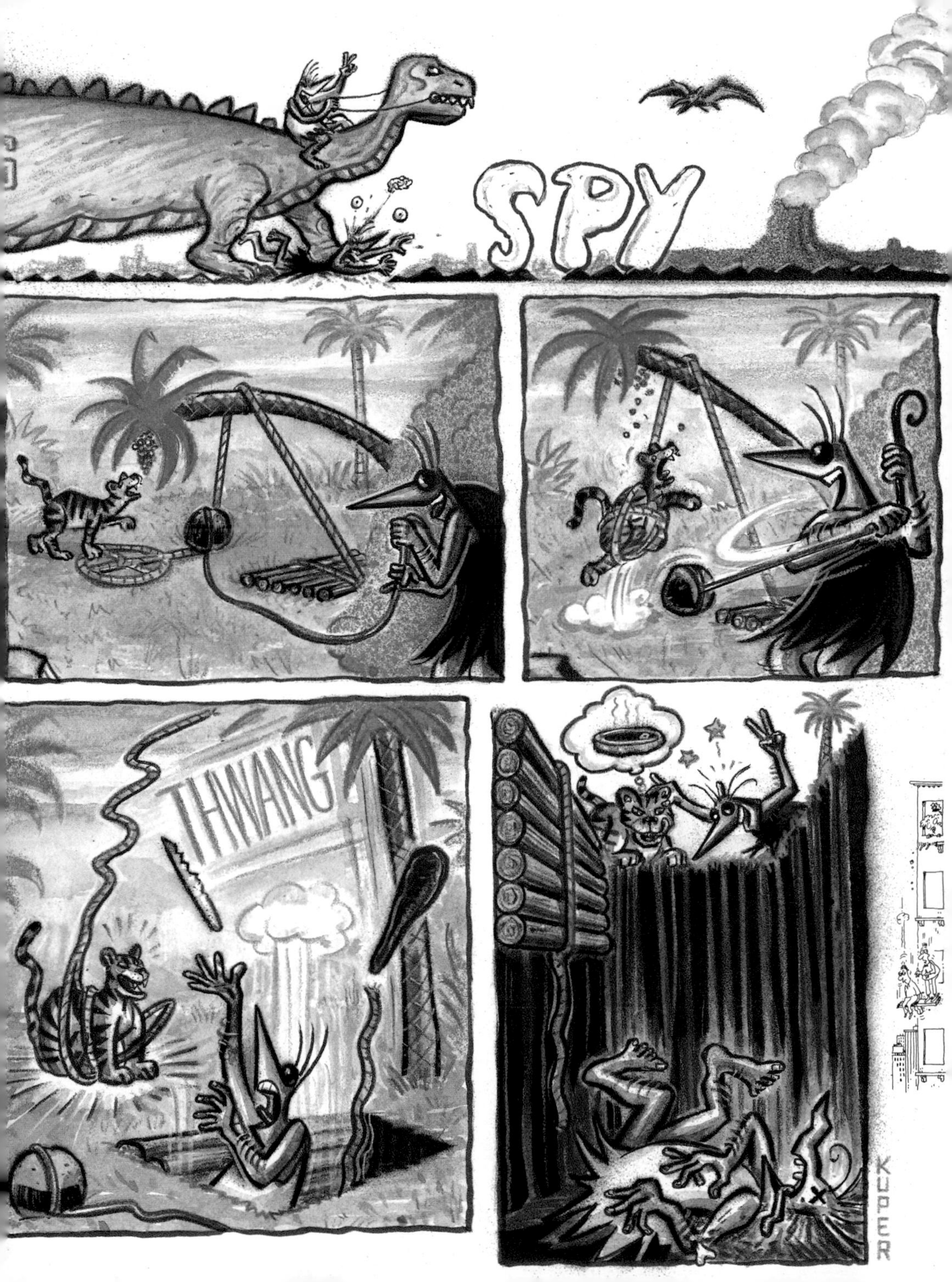
SPY
THWANG
KUPER

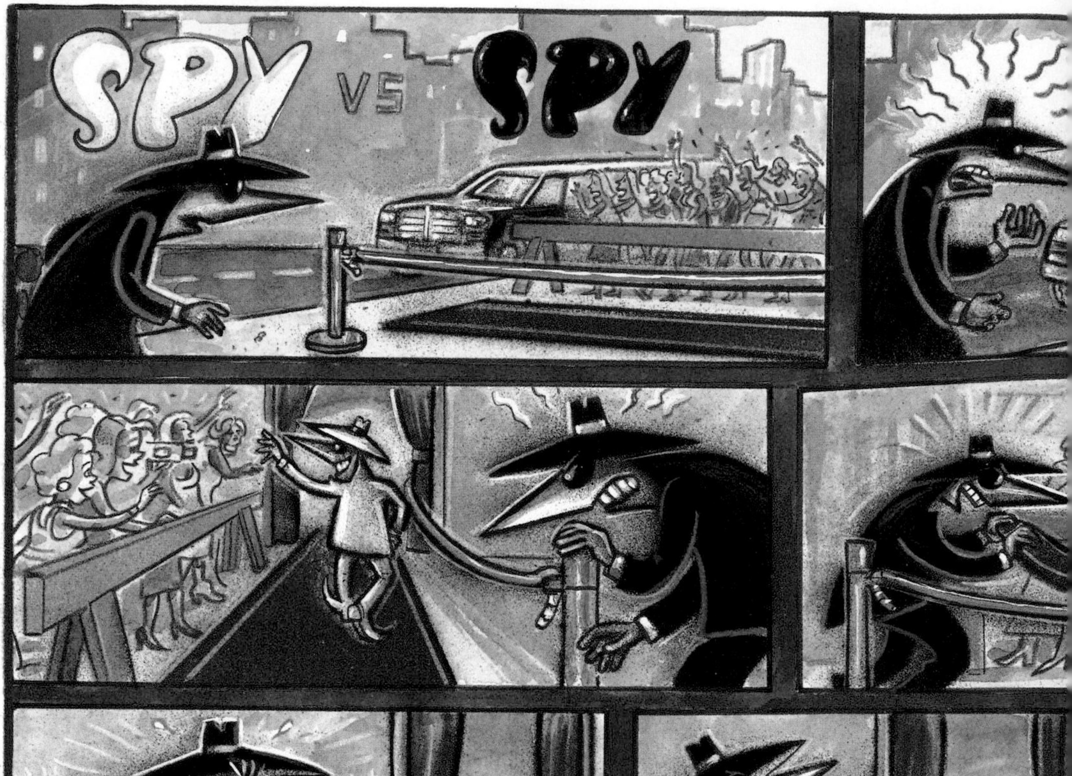
SPY VS SPY

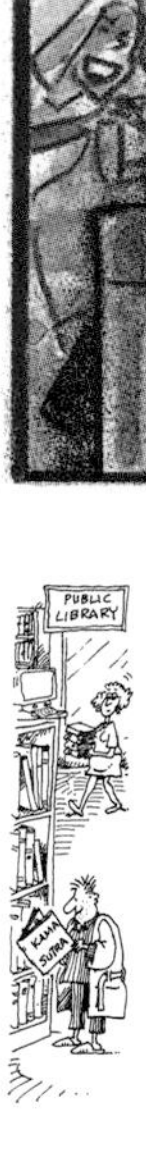
PUBLIC LIBRARY
KAMA SUTRA

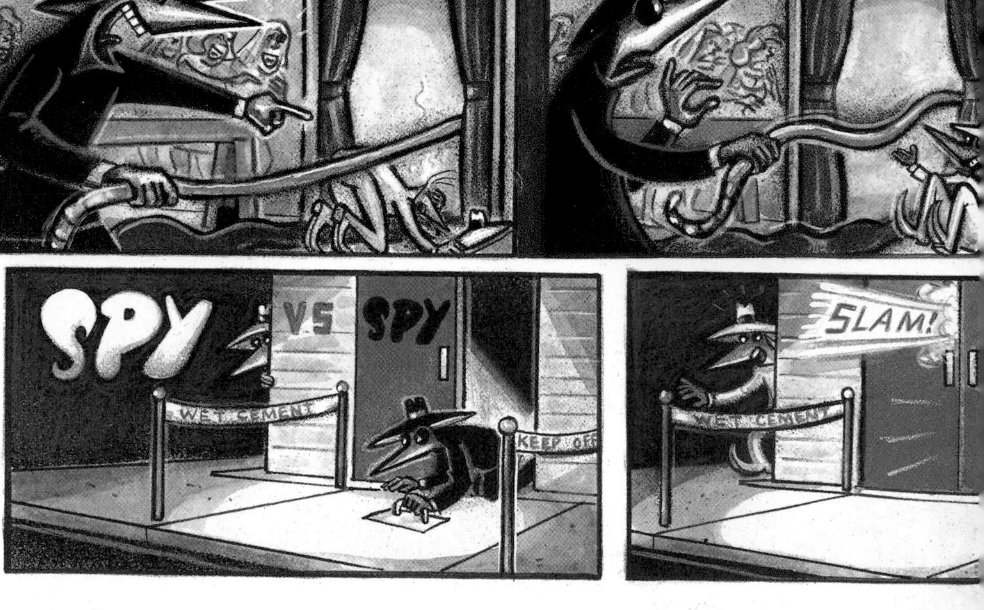
SPY VS SPY
WET CEMENT
KEEP OFF
SLAM!

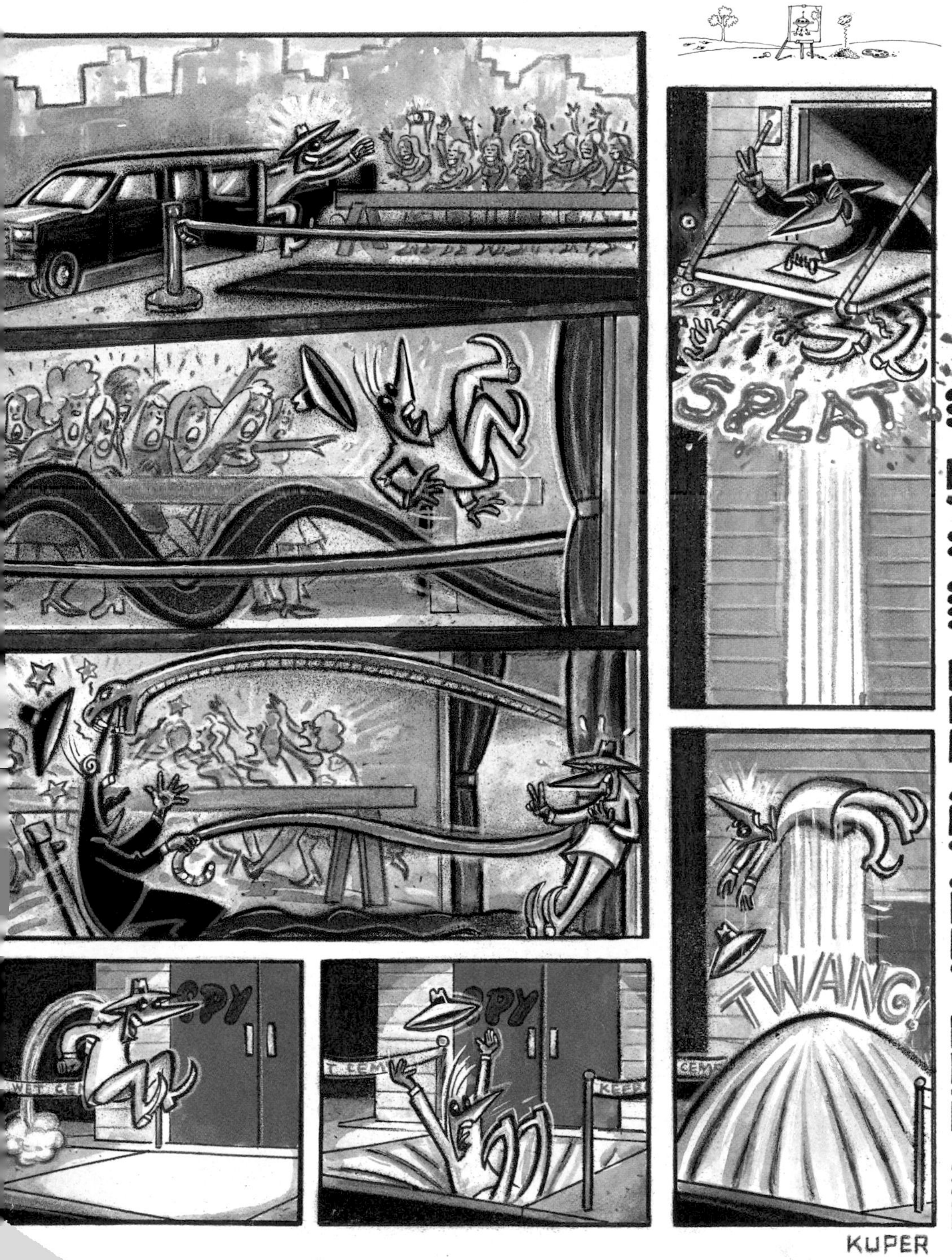
SPLAT
TWANG!
KUPER

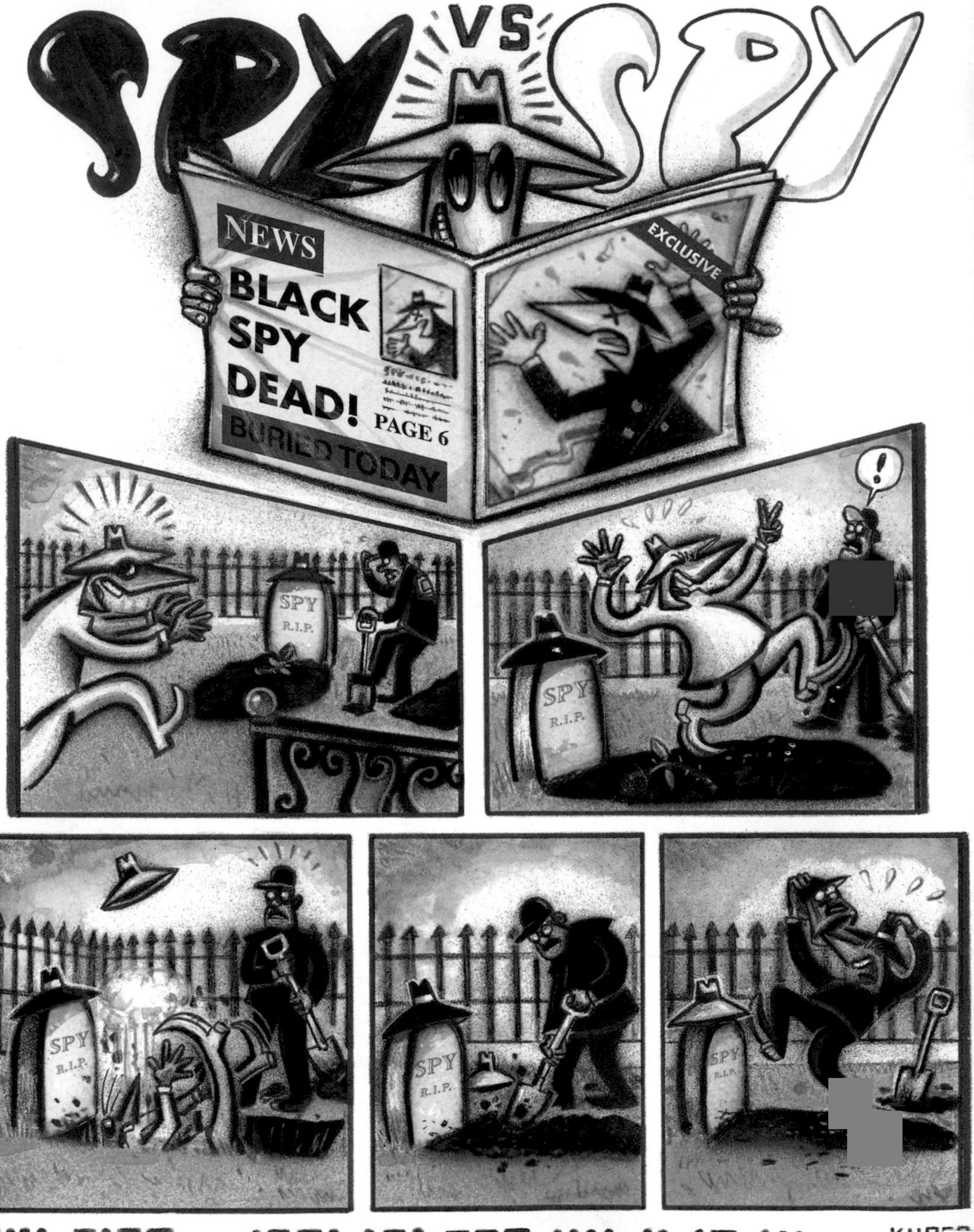
SPY VS SPY
NEWS
BLACK SPY DEAD!
PAGE 6
BURIED TODAY
EXCLUSIVE
SPY R.I.P.
!
SPY R.I.P.
SPY R.I.P.
SPY R.I.P.
SPY R.I.P.

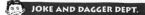

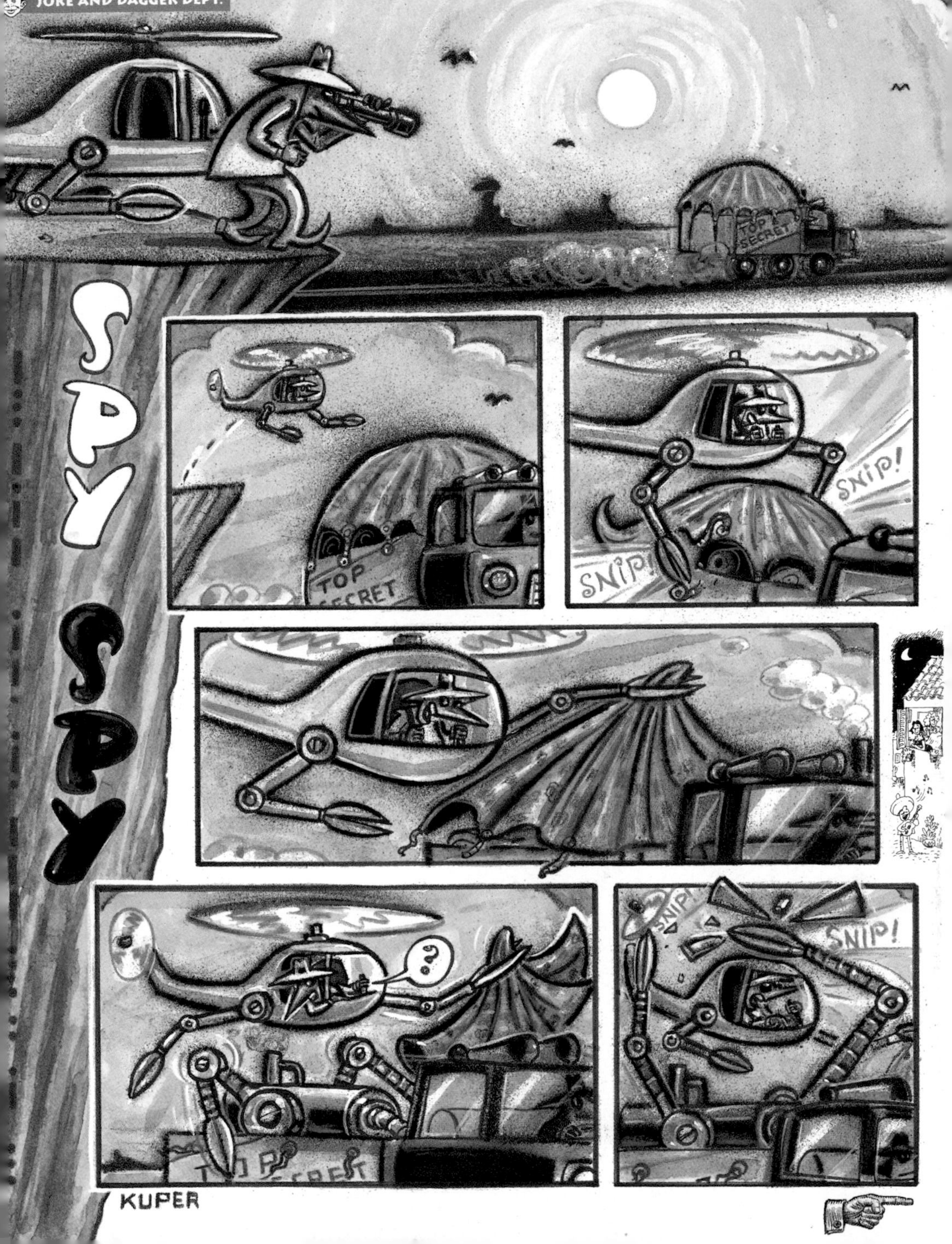
SPY
SPY
TOP SECRET
SNIP!
SNIP!
?
SNIP!
SNIP!
KUPER

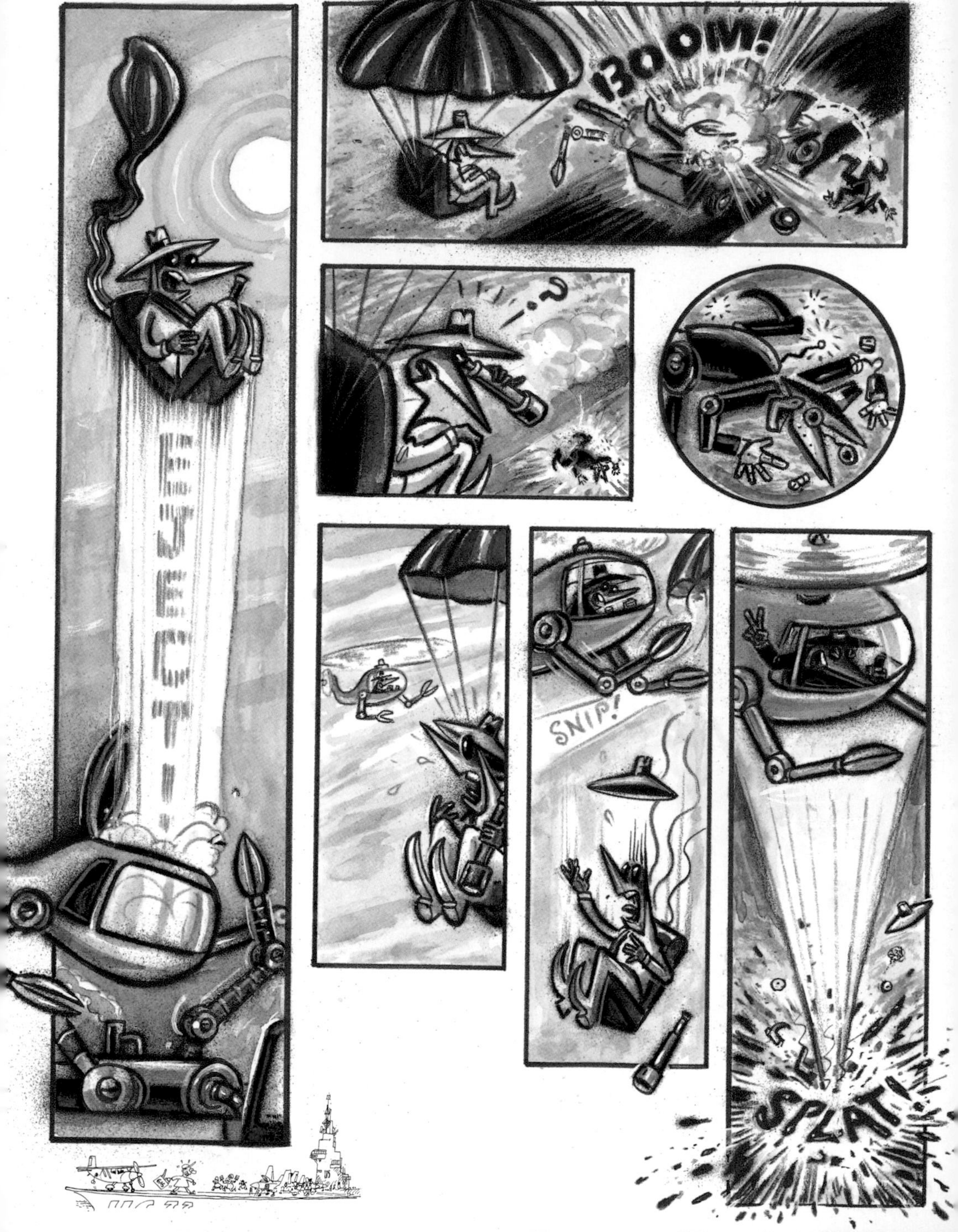
EJECT!
BOOM!
...?
SNIP!
SPLAT!

JOKE AND DAGGER DEPT.

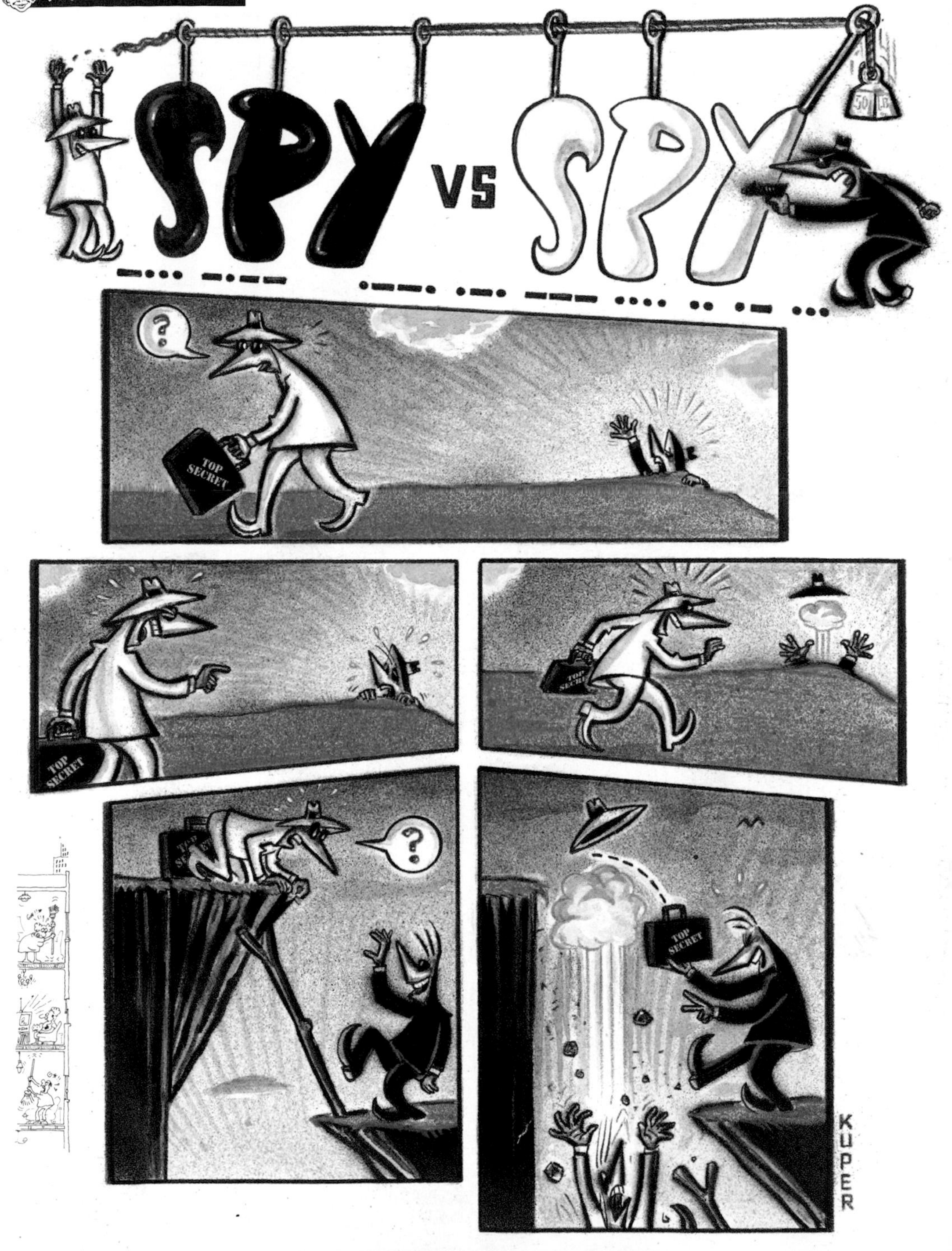
SPY VS SPY
50 LB
?
TOP SECRET
TOP SECRET
TOP SECRET
TOP SECRET
?
TOP SECRET
KUPER

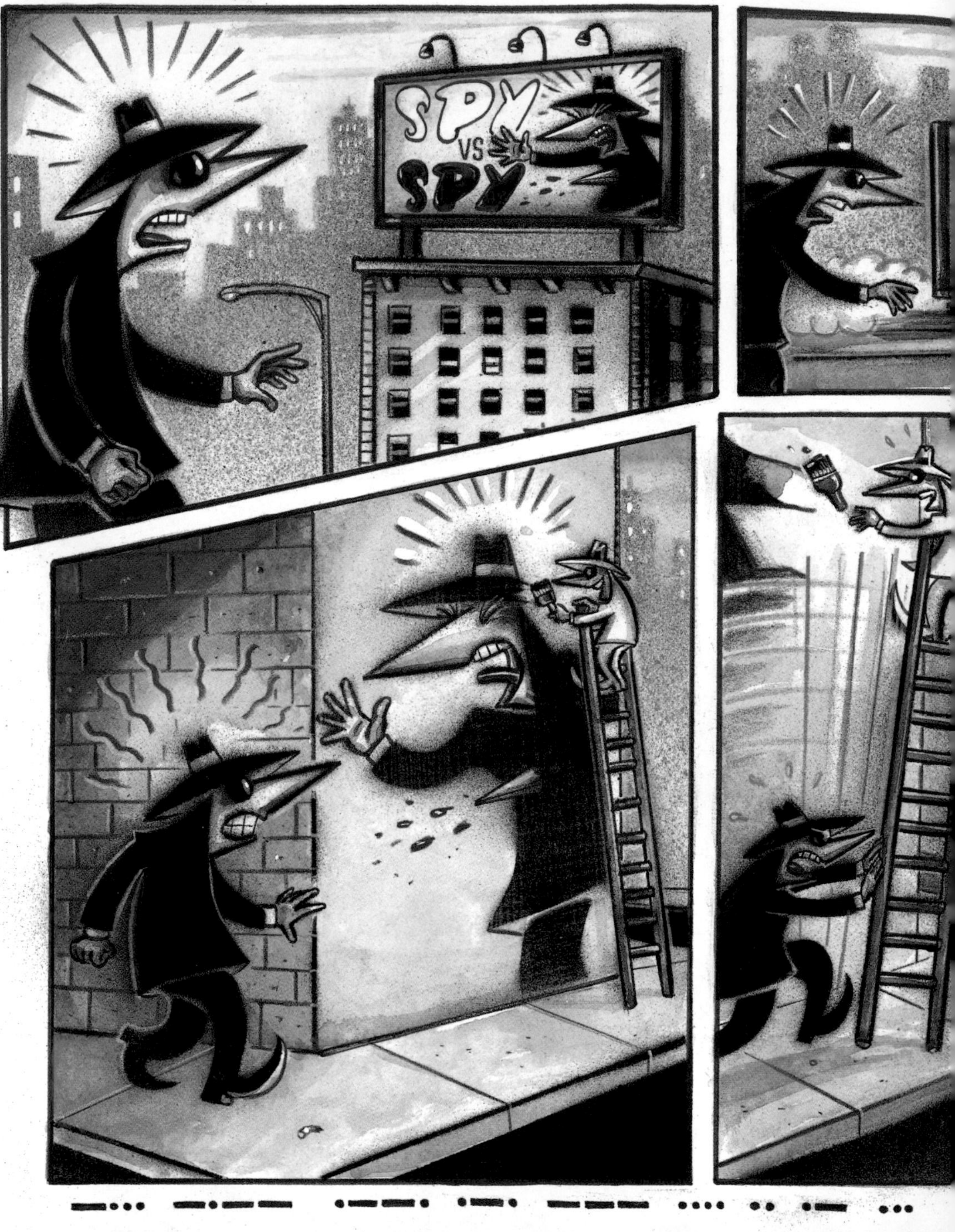
SPY
VS
SPY

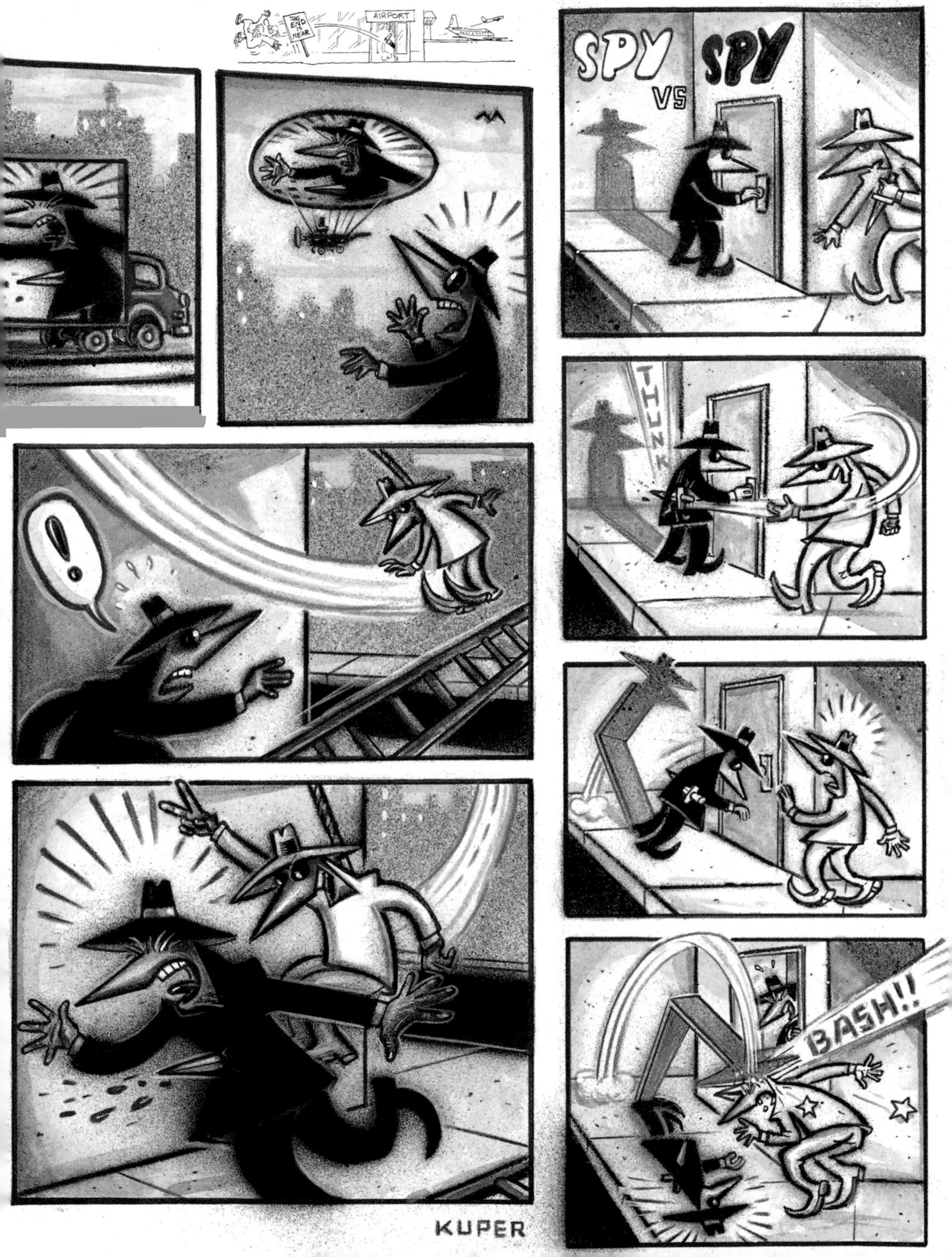
THE END IS NEAR
AIRPORT
SPY VS SPY
!
THUNK
BASH!!
KUPER

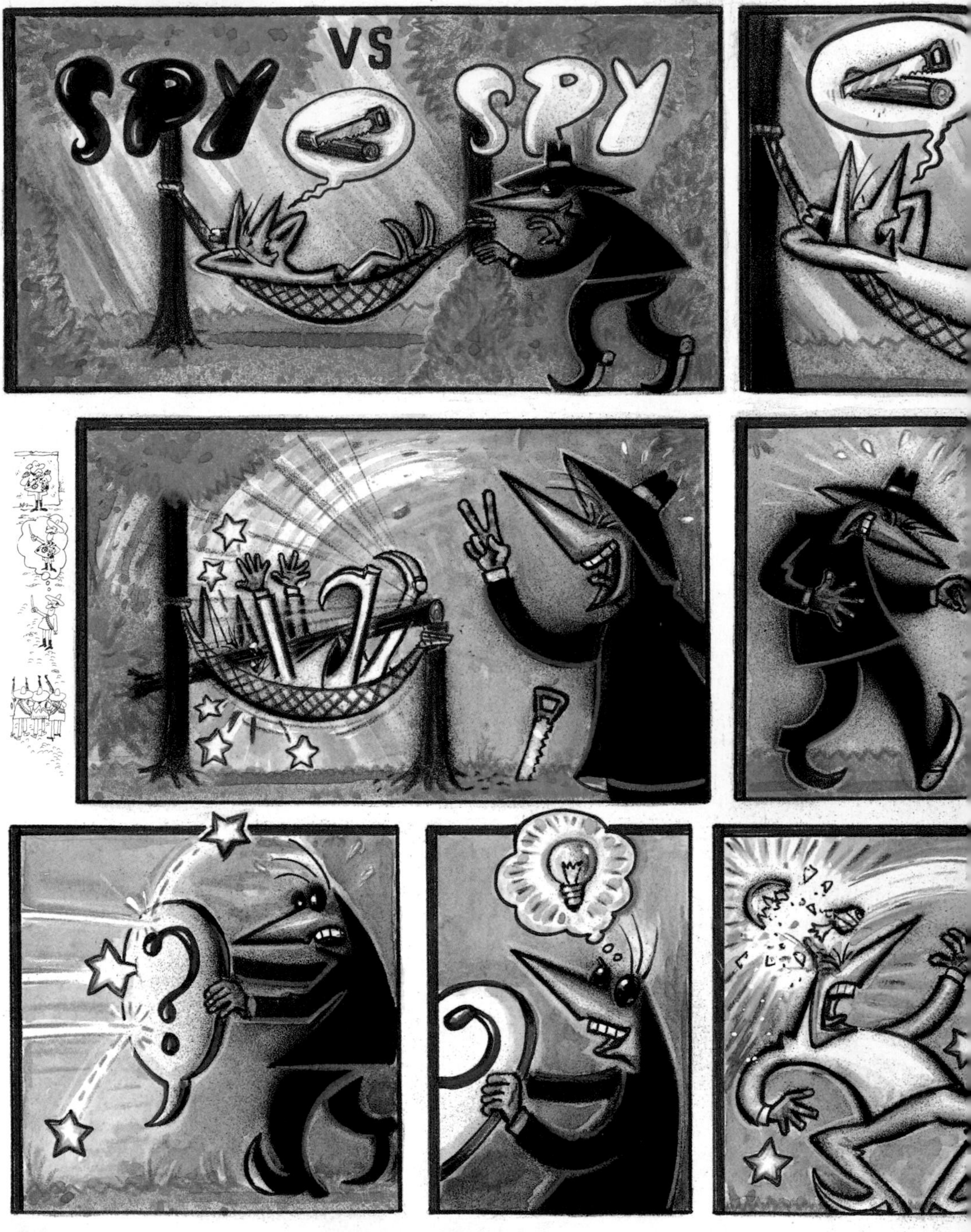
SPY VS SPY

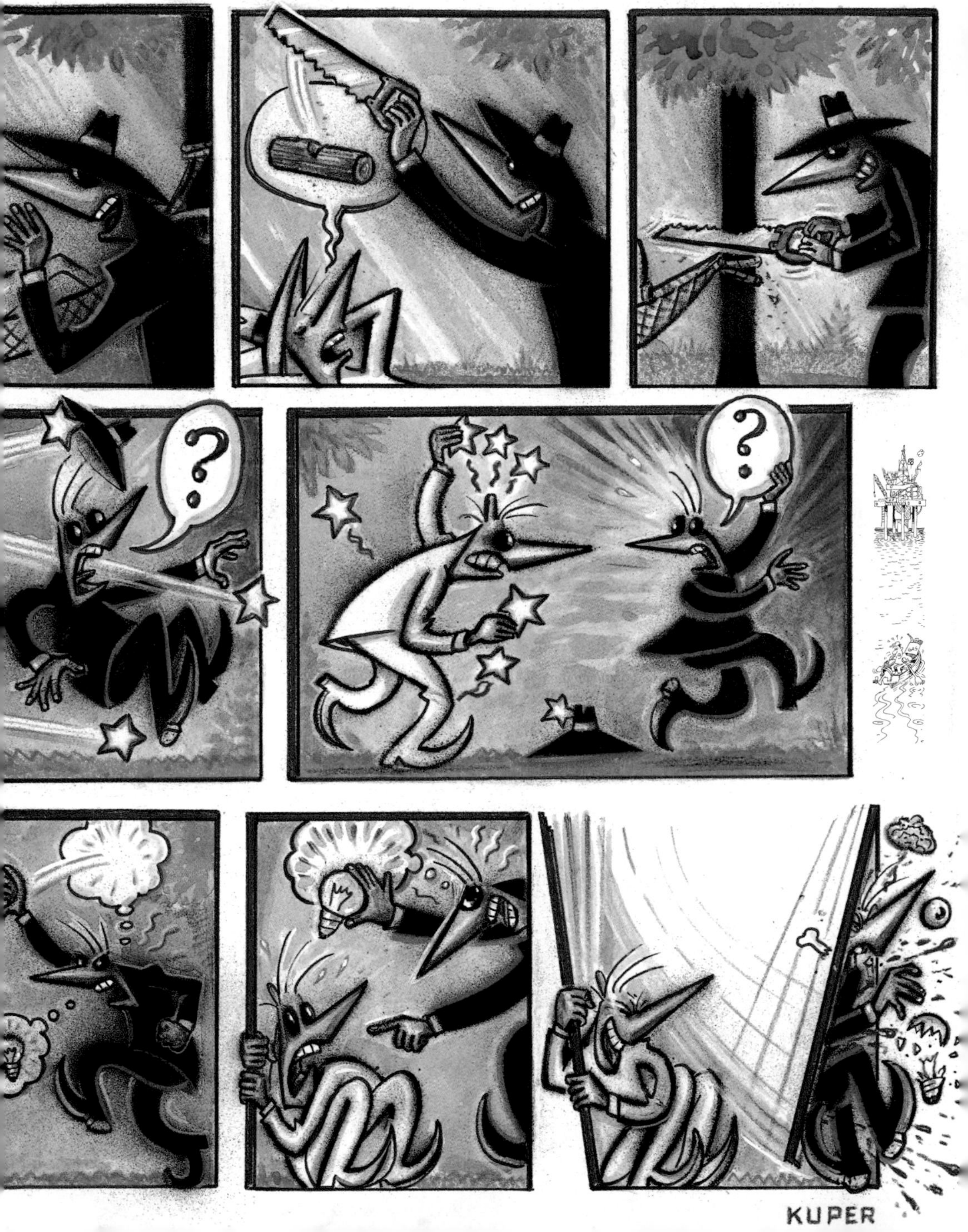
?
?
KUPER

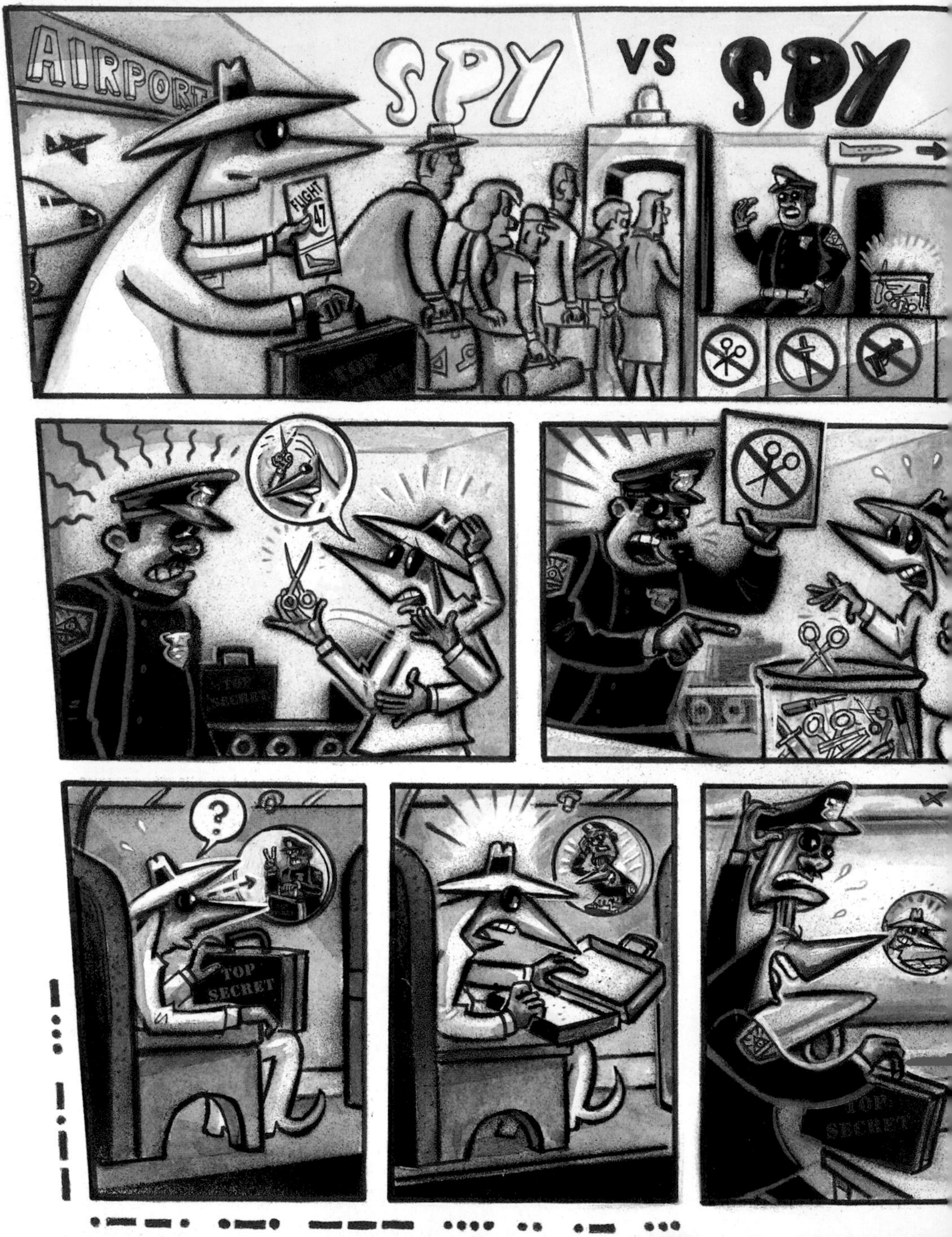
AIRPORT
SPY VS SPY
FLIGHT 47
TOP SECRET
TOP SECRET
?
TOP SECRET
TOP SECRET

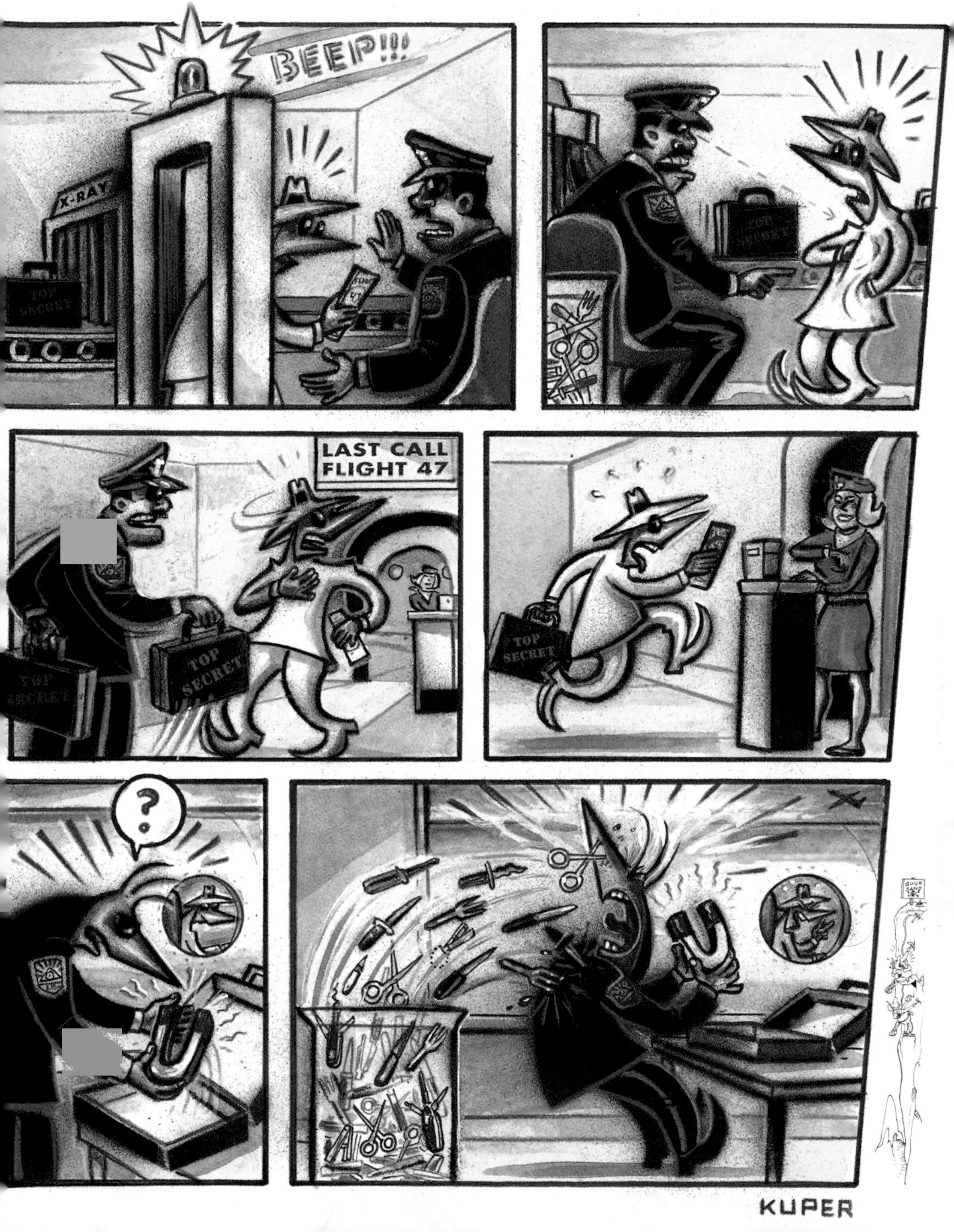
BEEP!!!
X-RAY
TOP SECRET
LAST CALL
FLIGHT 47
TOP SECRET
TOP SECRET
?

KUPER

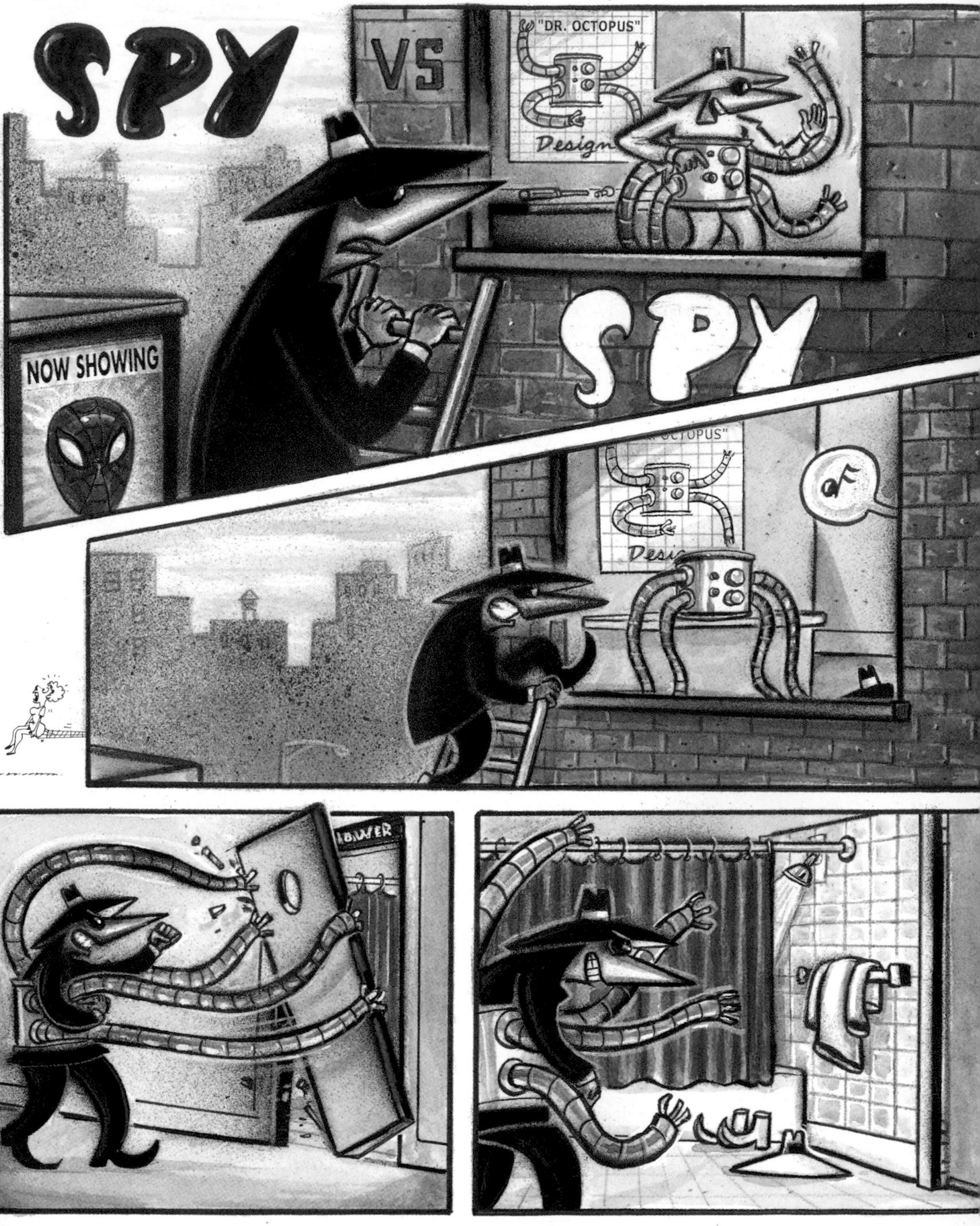
SPY
VS
SPY
"DR. OCTOPUS"
Design
NOW SHOWING

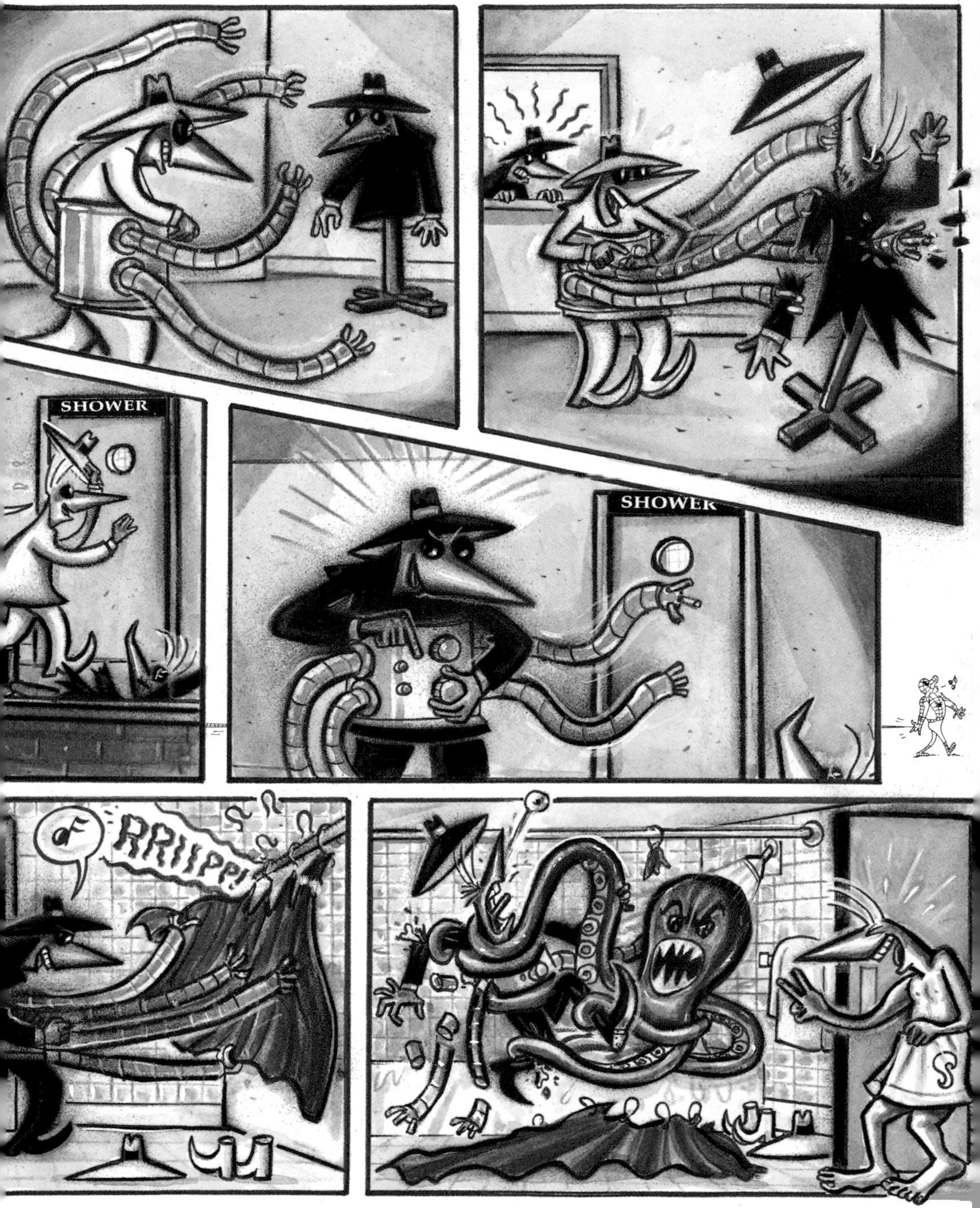

SHOWER
SHOWER
RRIIPP!
KUPER

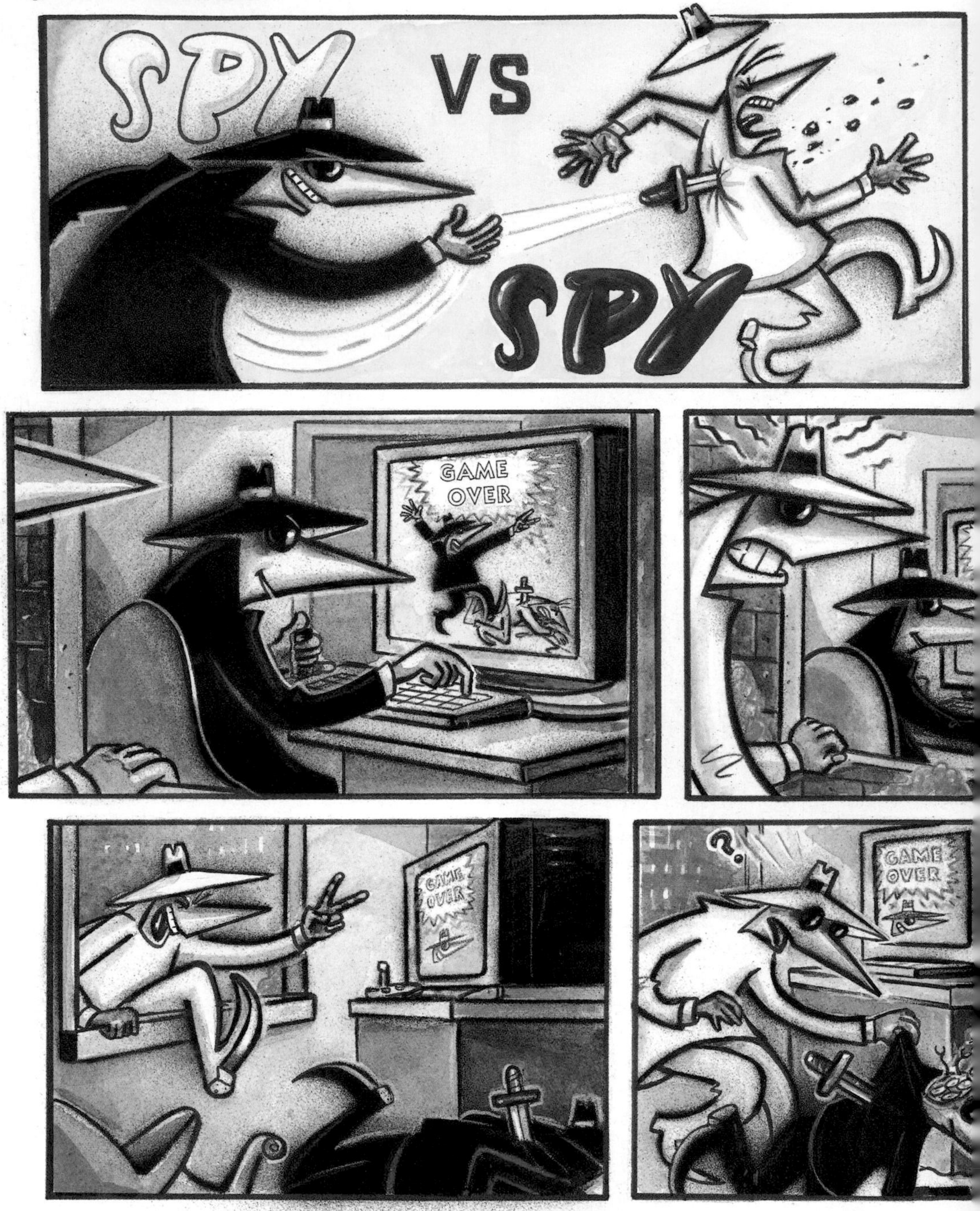
SPY
VS
SPY
GAME OVER
GAME OVER
?
GAME OVER

SPY vs SPY

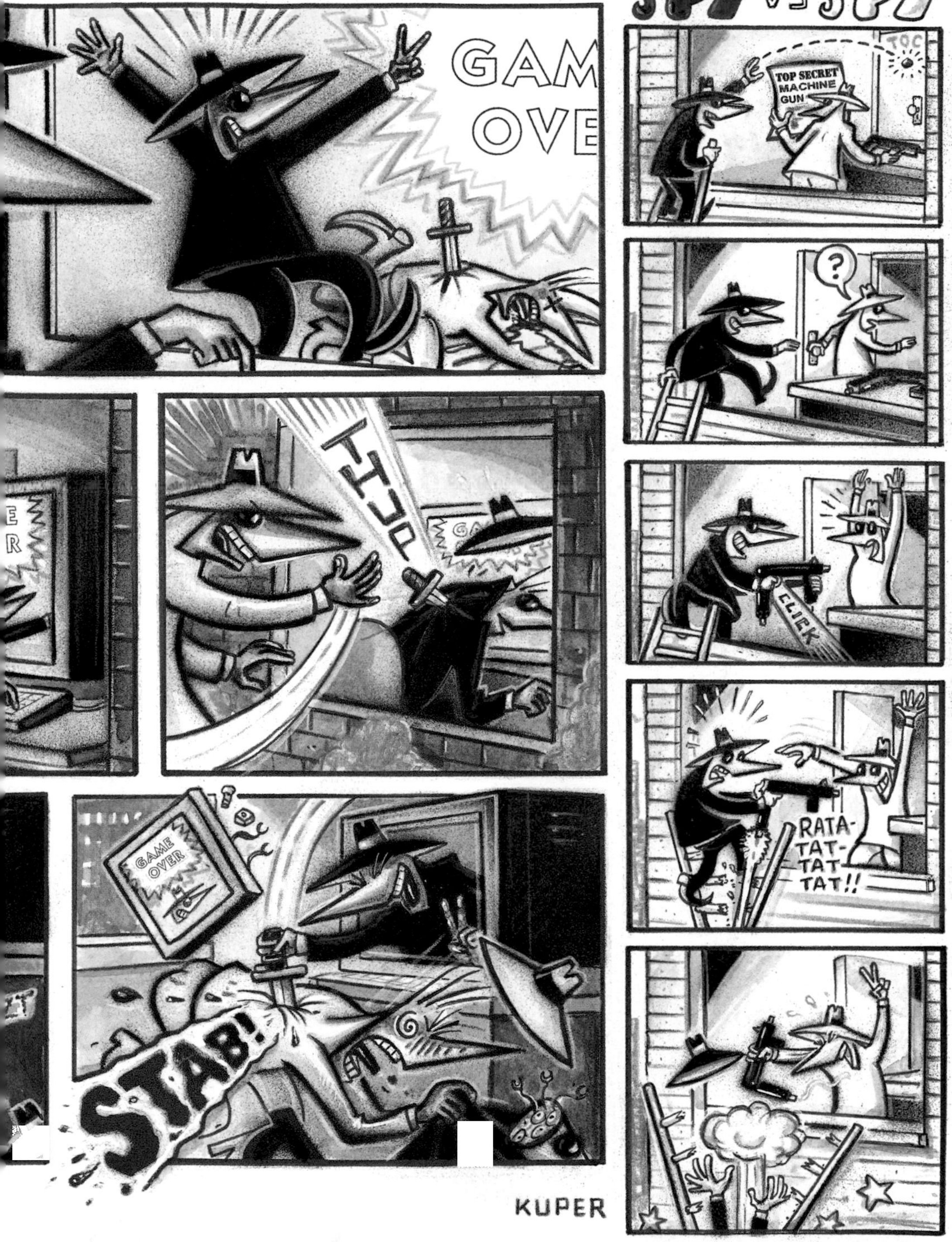

GAME OVER
THUD
GAME OVER
STAB!
KUPER
TOC
TOP SECRET MACHINE GUN
?
CLICK
RATA-TAT-TAT-TAT!!

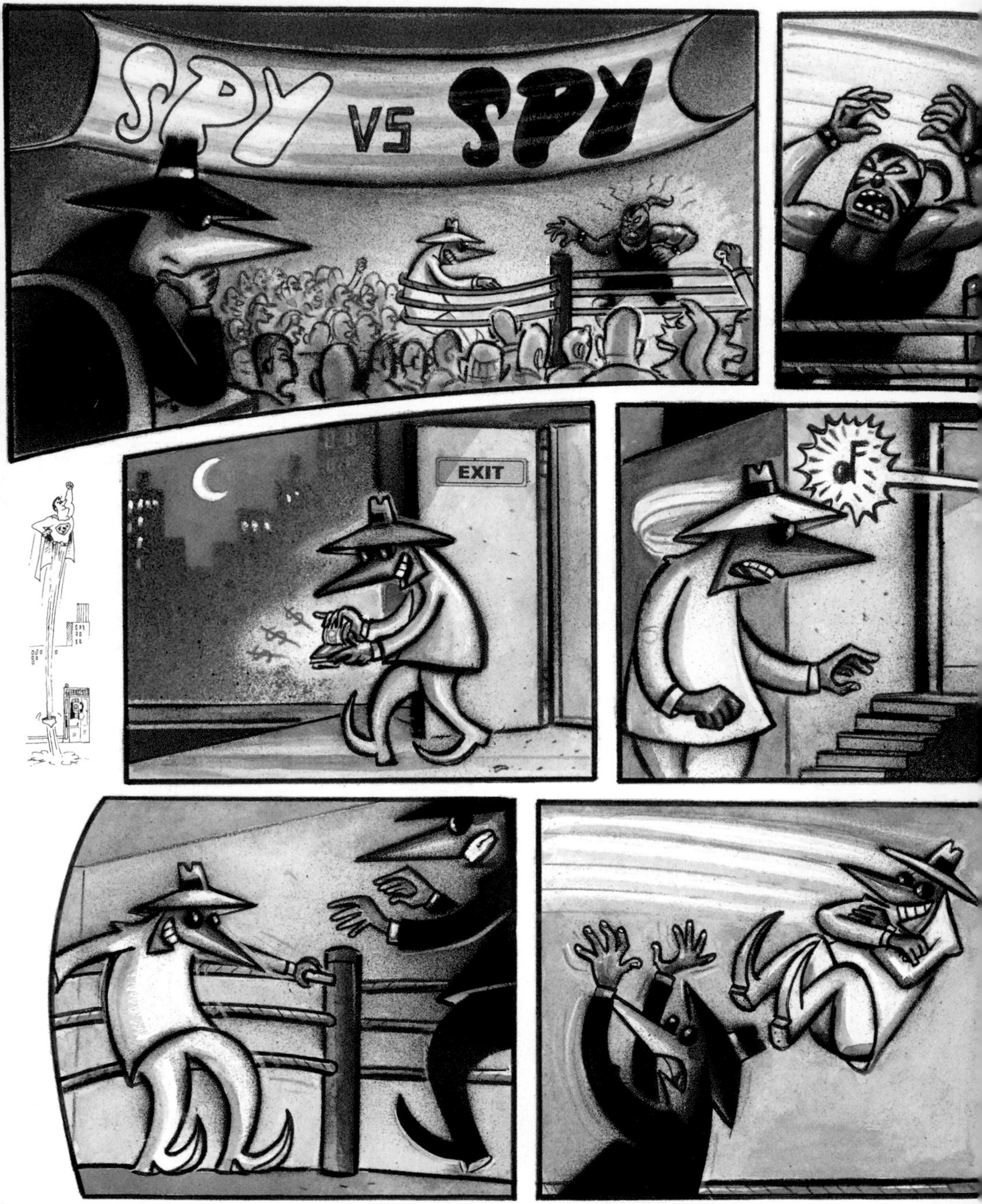
SPY VS SPY
EXIT

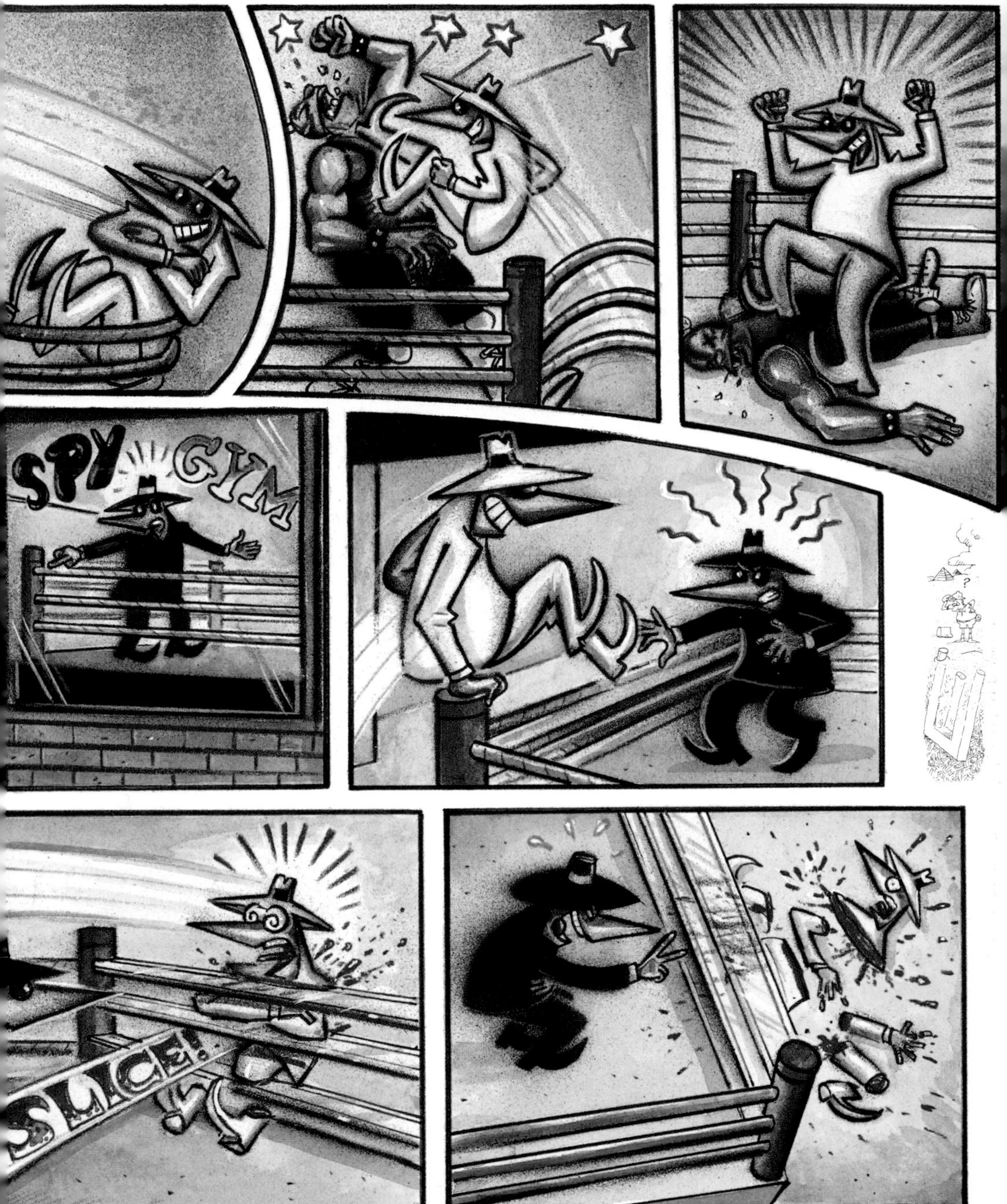
SPY GYM
SLICE!
KUPER

JOKE AND DAGGER DEPT.

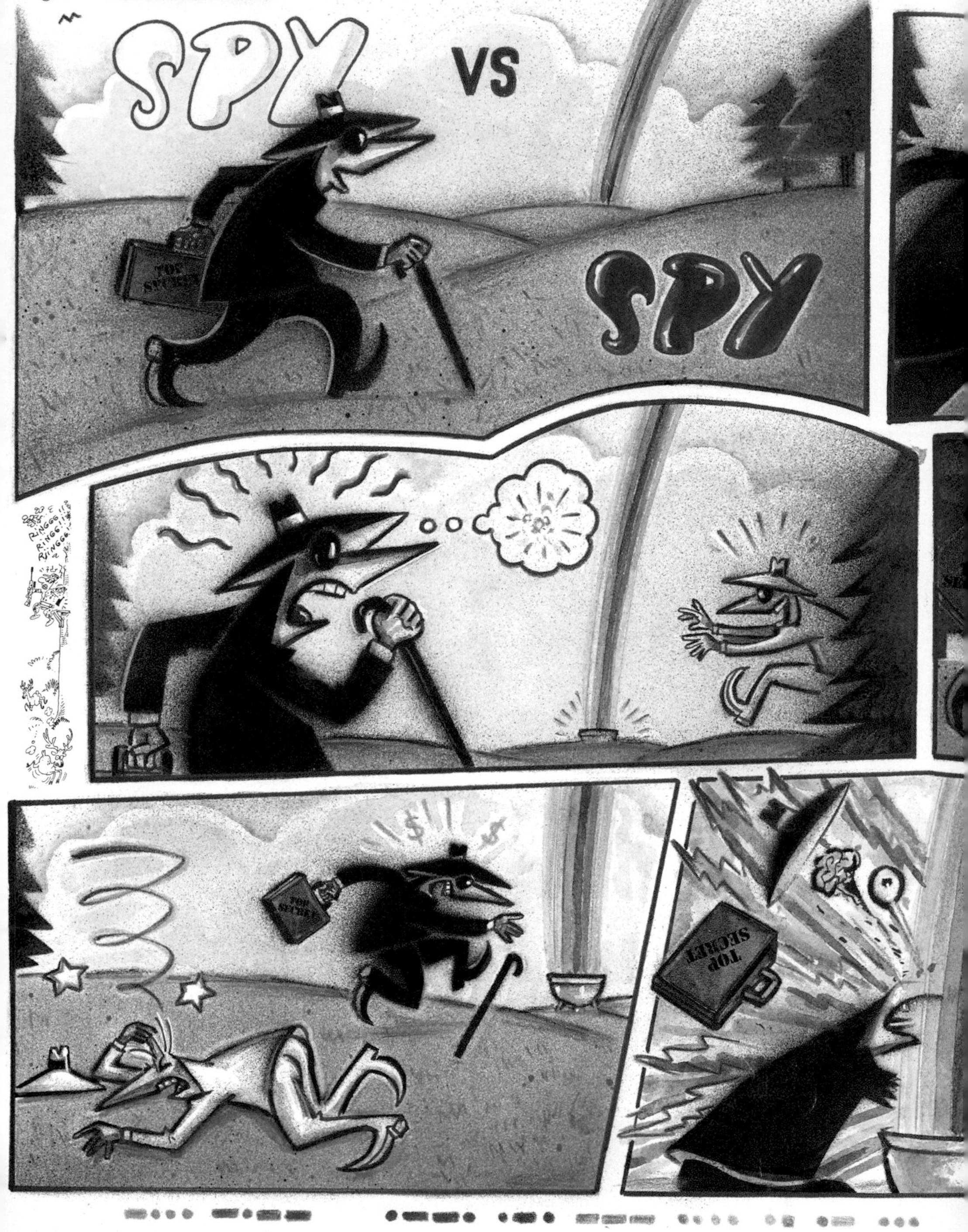
SPY
VS
SPY
TOP SECRET
TOP SECRET
TOP SECRET

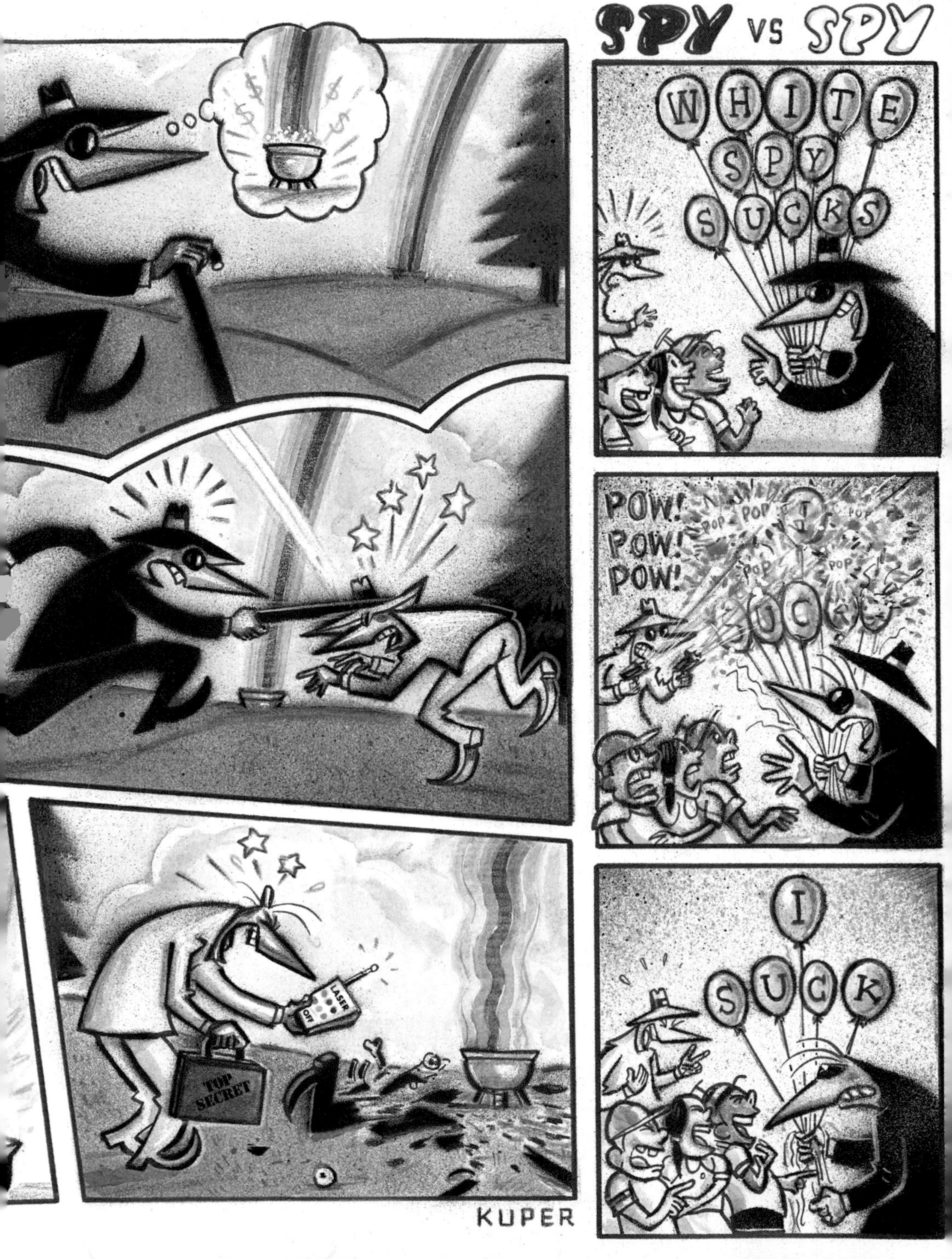

SPY VS SPY
$
LASER
OFF
TOP SECRET
KUPER
WHITE SPY SUCKS
POW! POW! POW!
POP POP POP POP POP
I SUCK

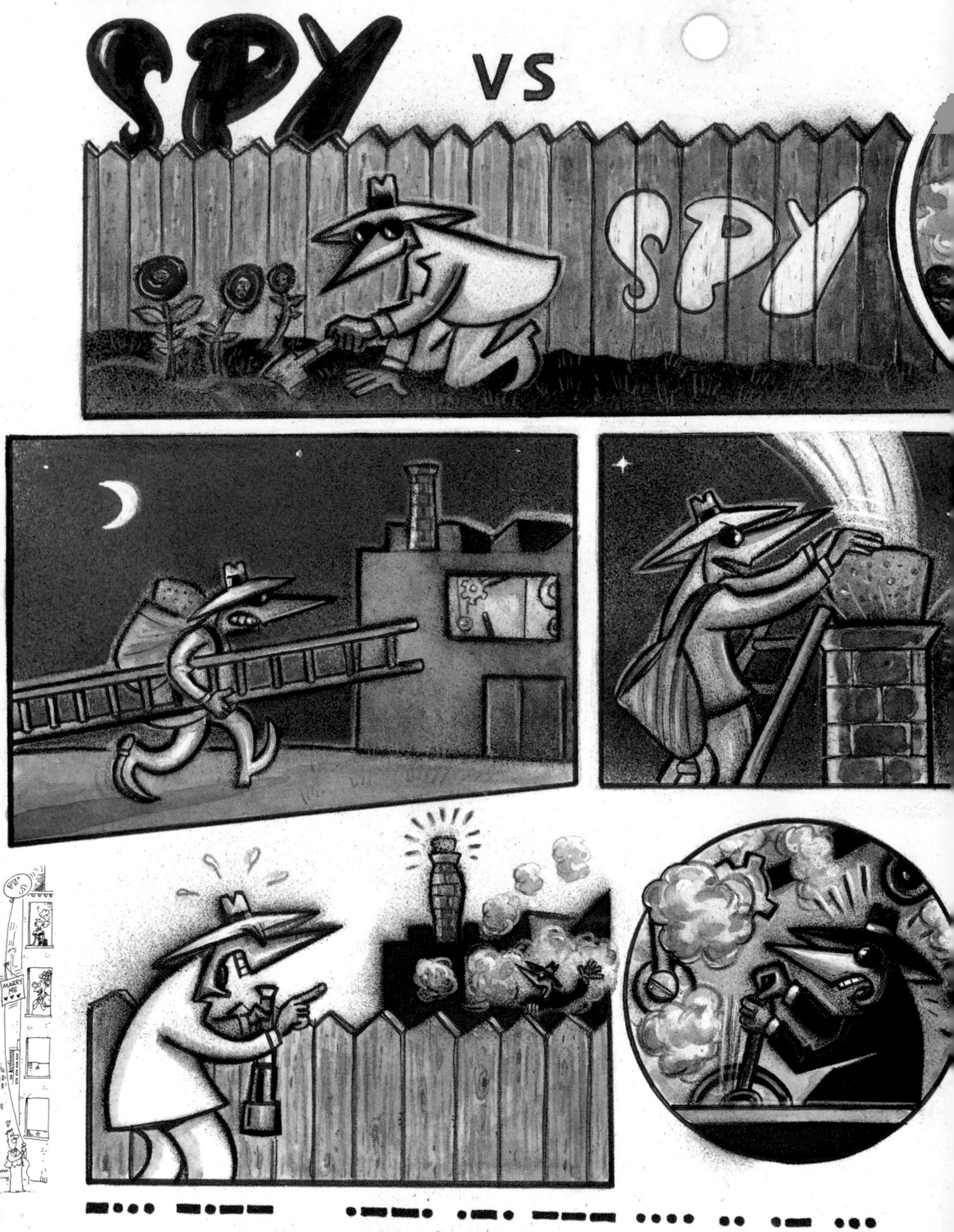
SPY VS SPY
MARRY ME

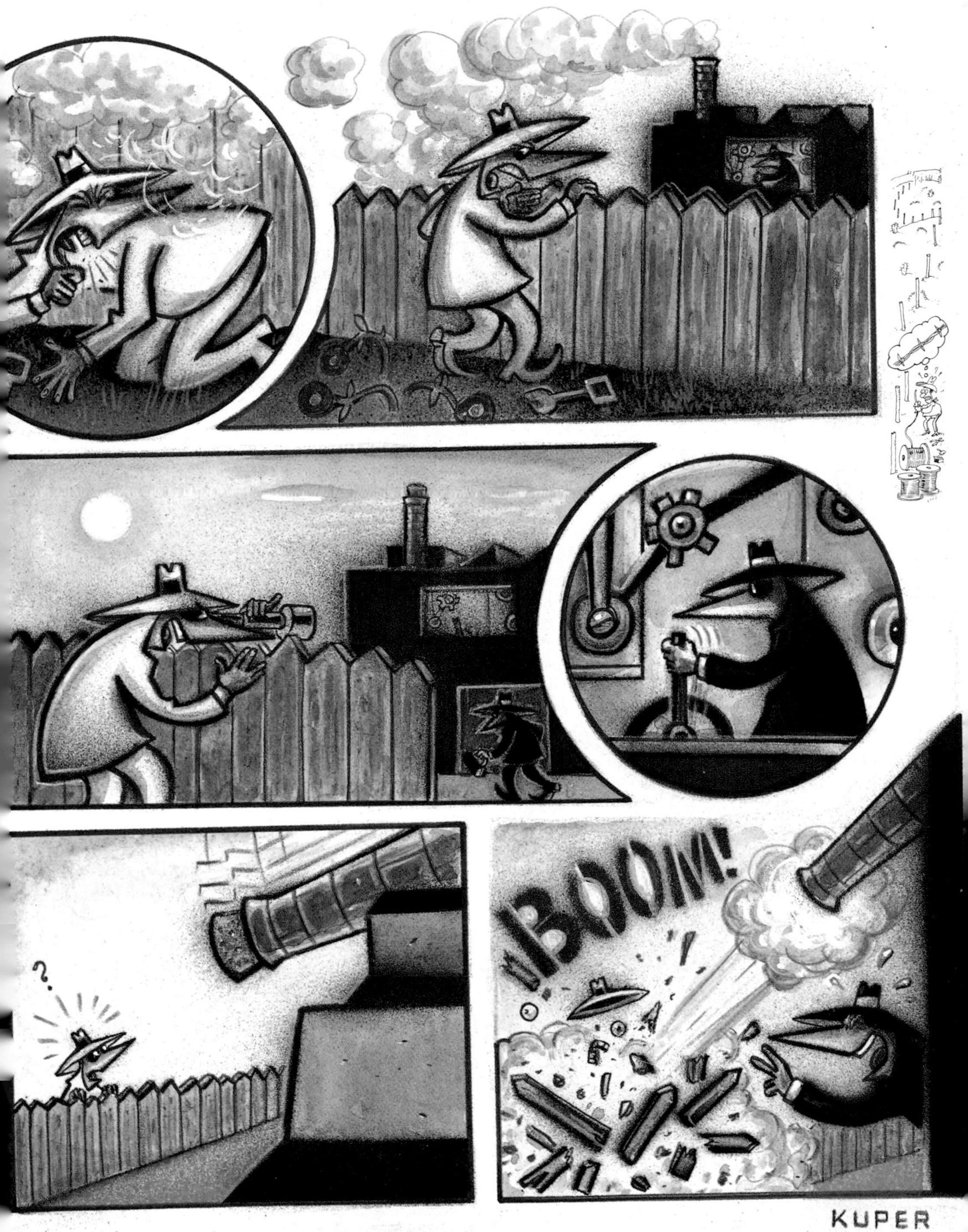
?
BOOM!
KUPER

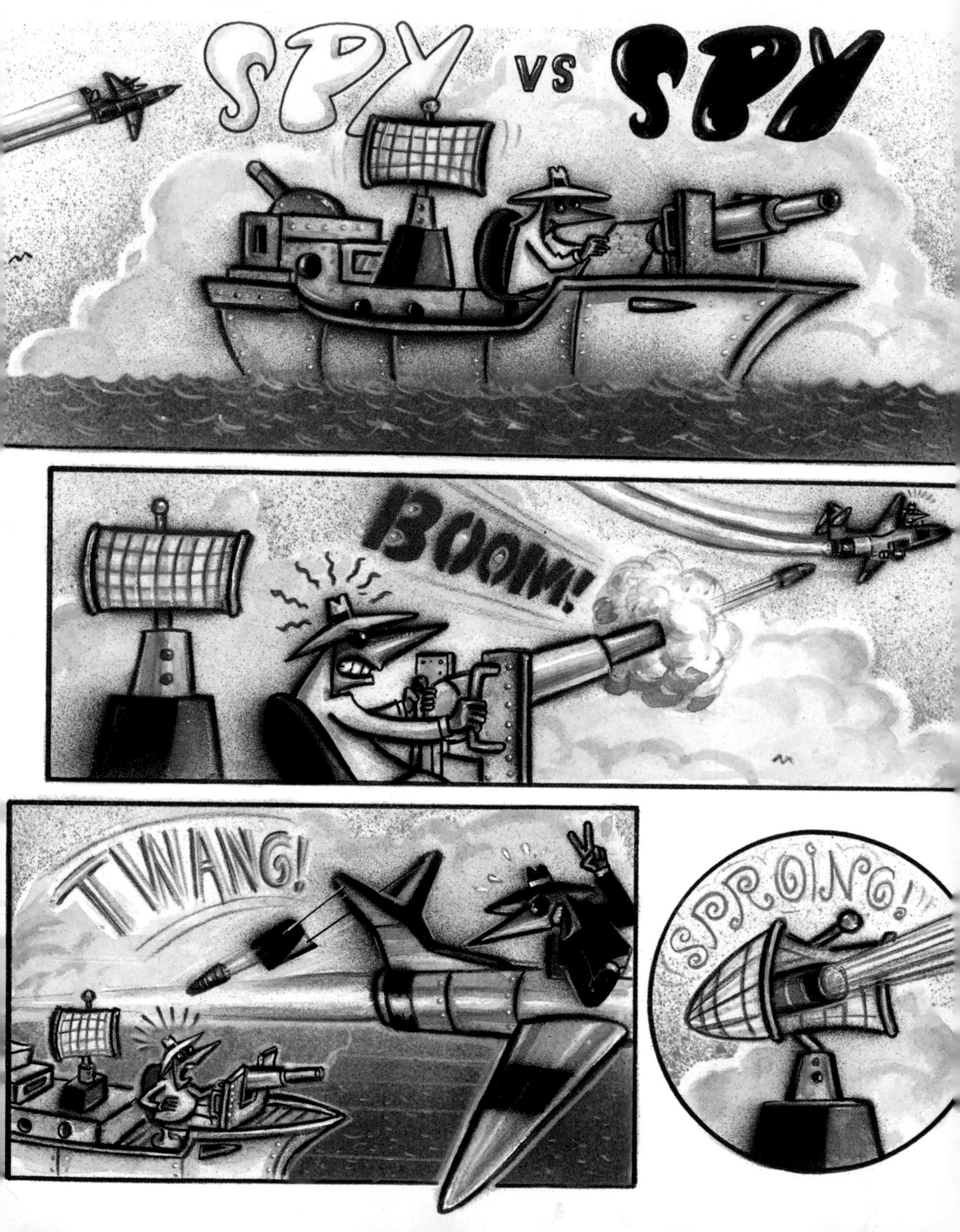
SPY VS SPY
BOOM!
TWANG!
SPROING!

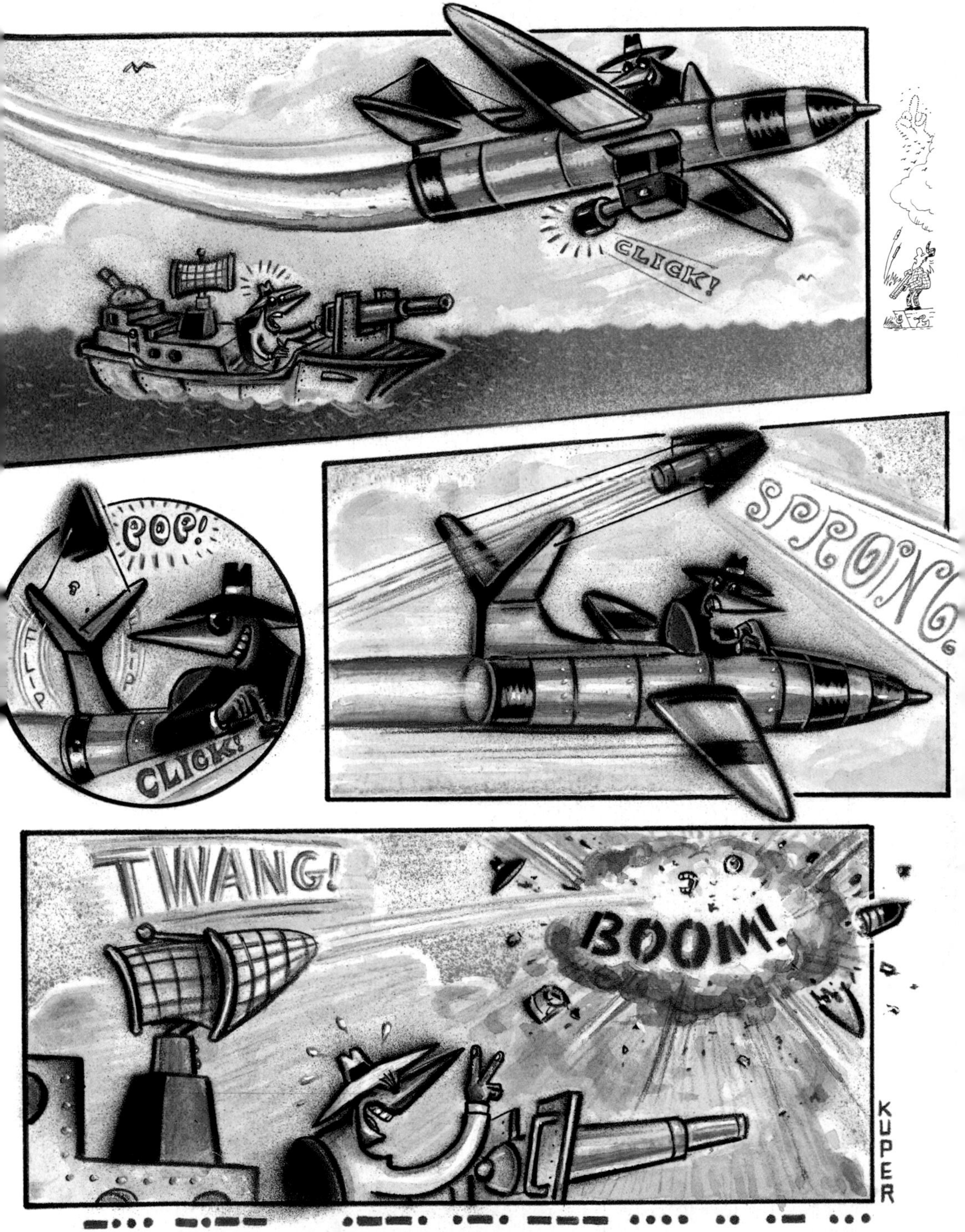
CLICK!
POP!
FLIP
FLIP
CLICK!
SPRONG
TWANG!
BOOM!
KUPER

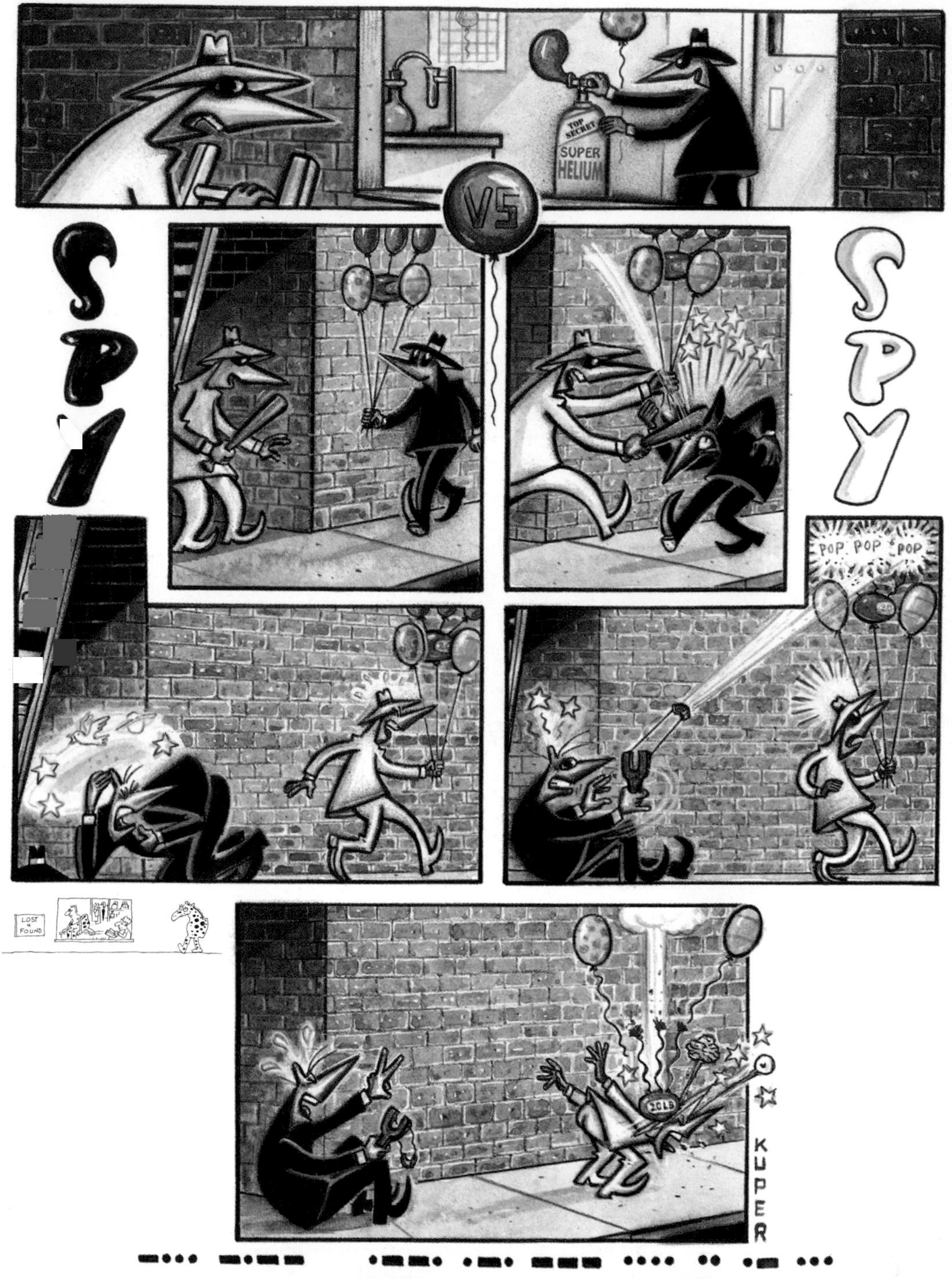
TOP SECRET
SUPER HELIUM
VS
SPY
SPY
POP POP POP
LOST & FOUND
KUPER

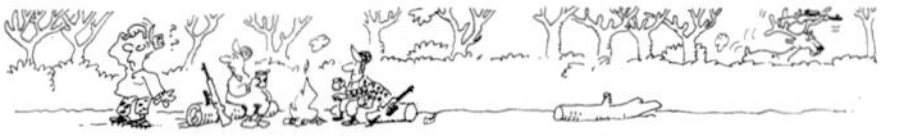

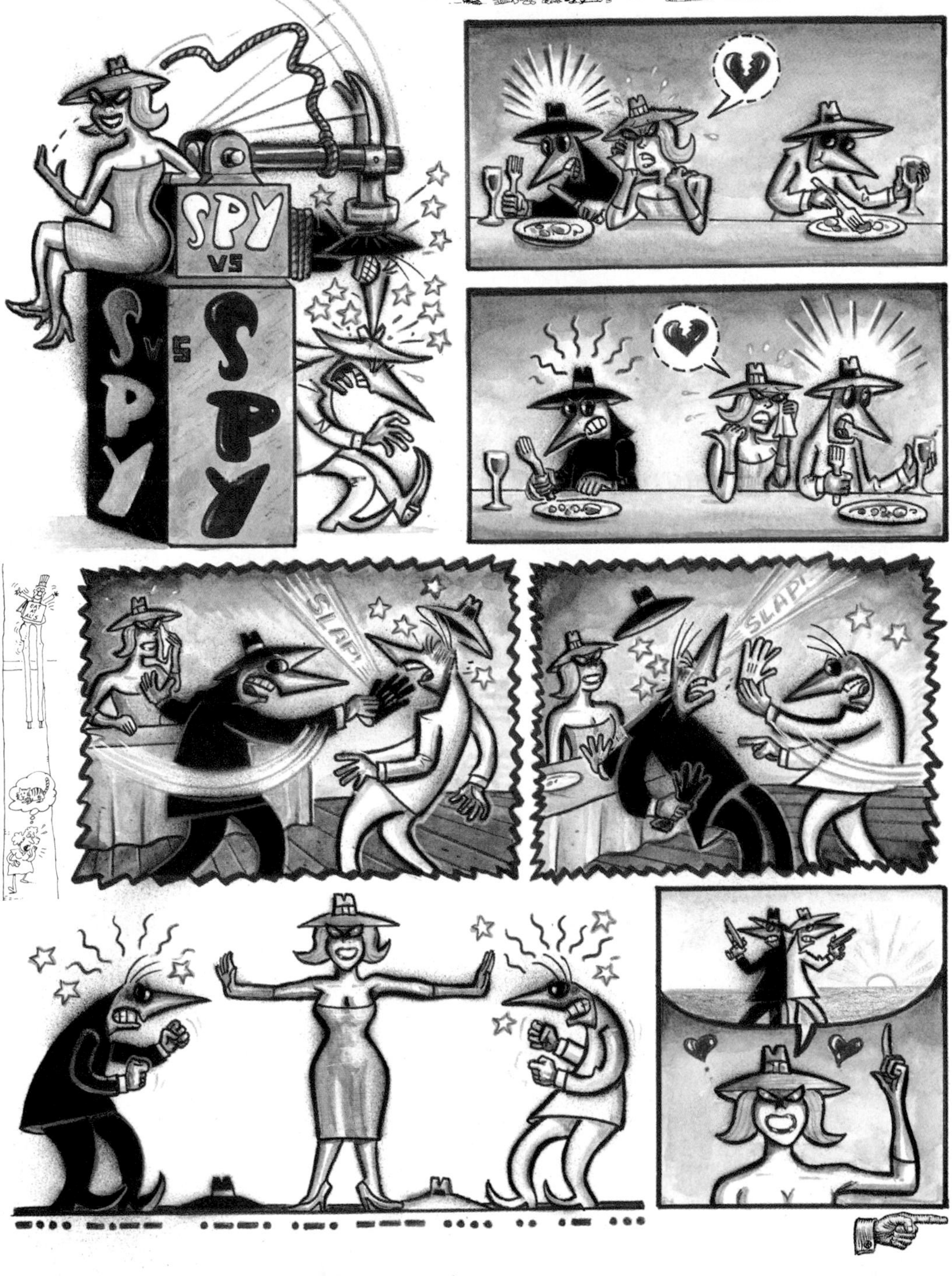
SPY VS SPY
SPY VS SPY
SLAP!
SLAP!

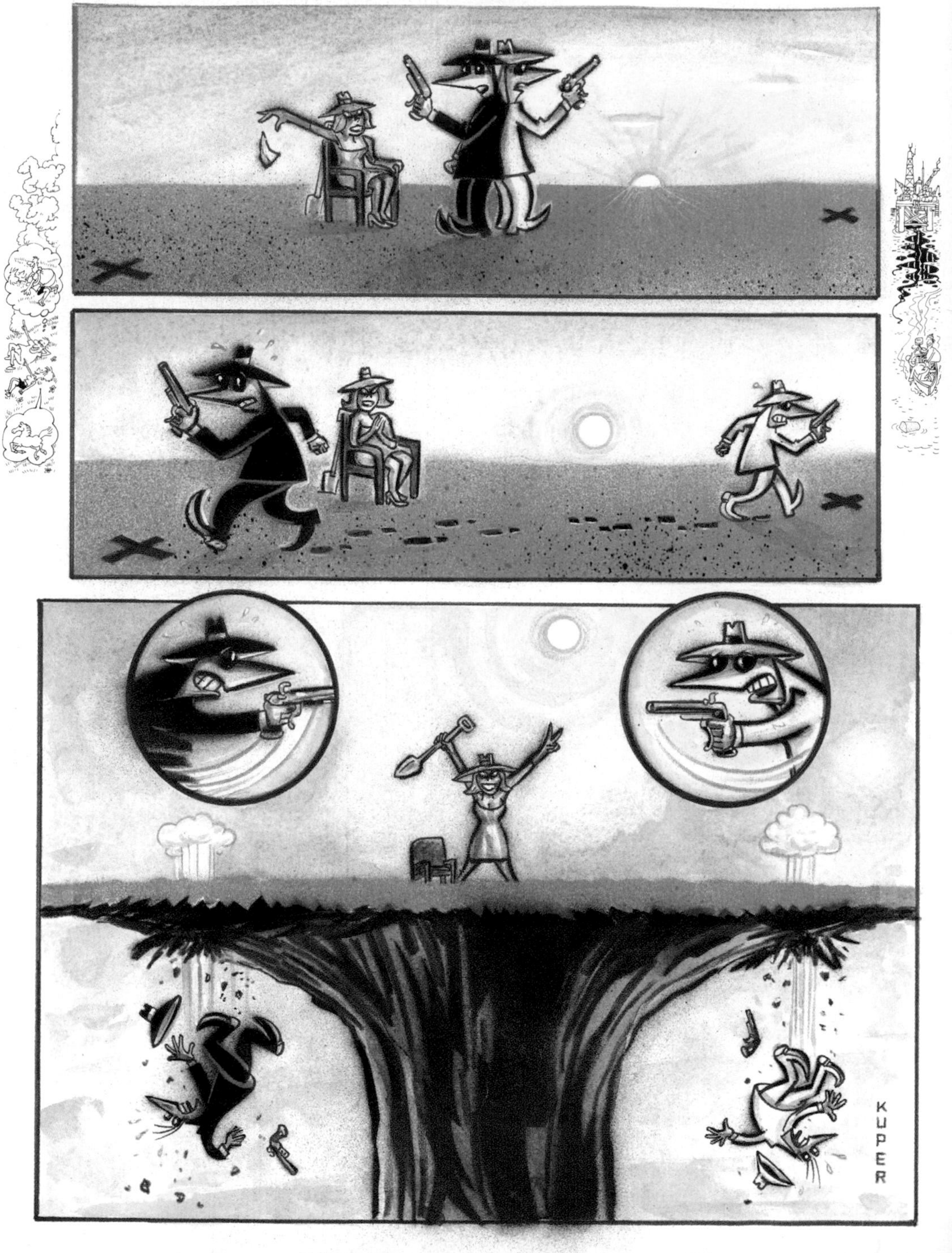
KUPER

JOKE AND DAGGER DEPT.

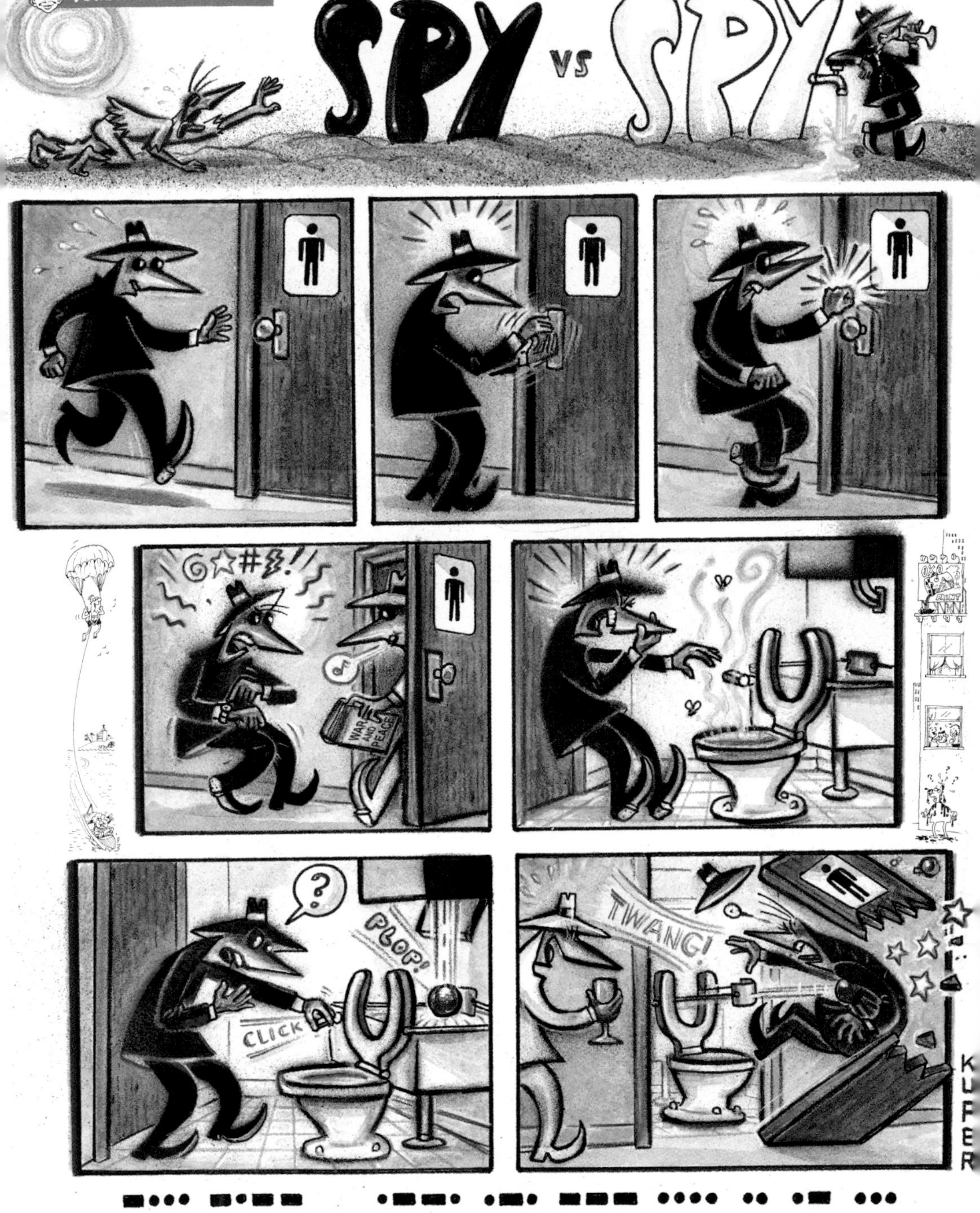
SPY vs SPY
WAR AND PEACE
?
PLOP!
CLICK
TWANG!
KUPER

JOKE AND DAGGER DEPT.

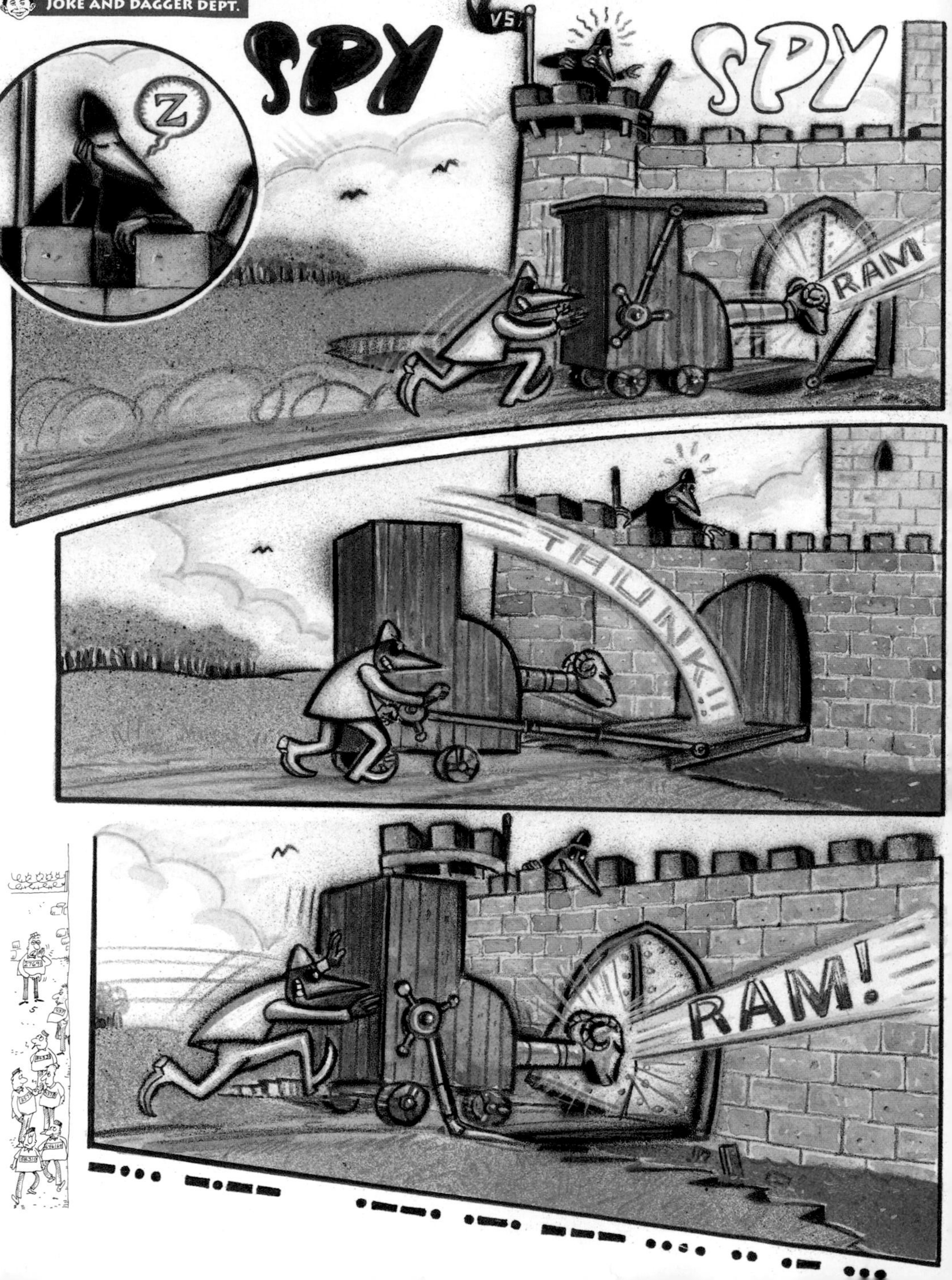
SPY VS SPY
Z
RAM
THUNK!!
RAM!

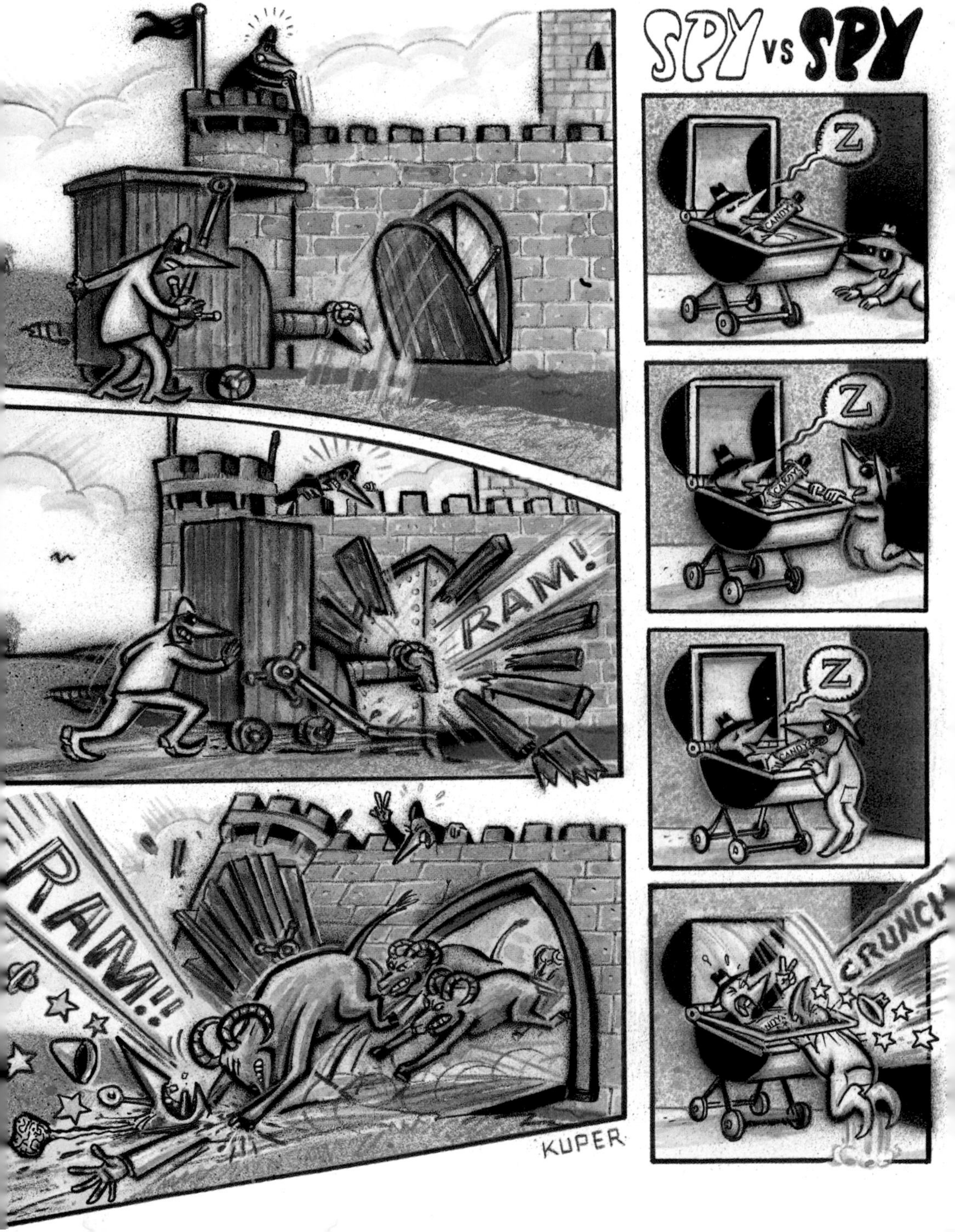
SPY vs SPY
Z
CANDY
Z
CANDY
Z
CANDY
CRUNCH
RAM!
RAM!!!
KUPER

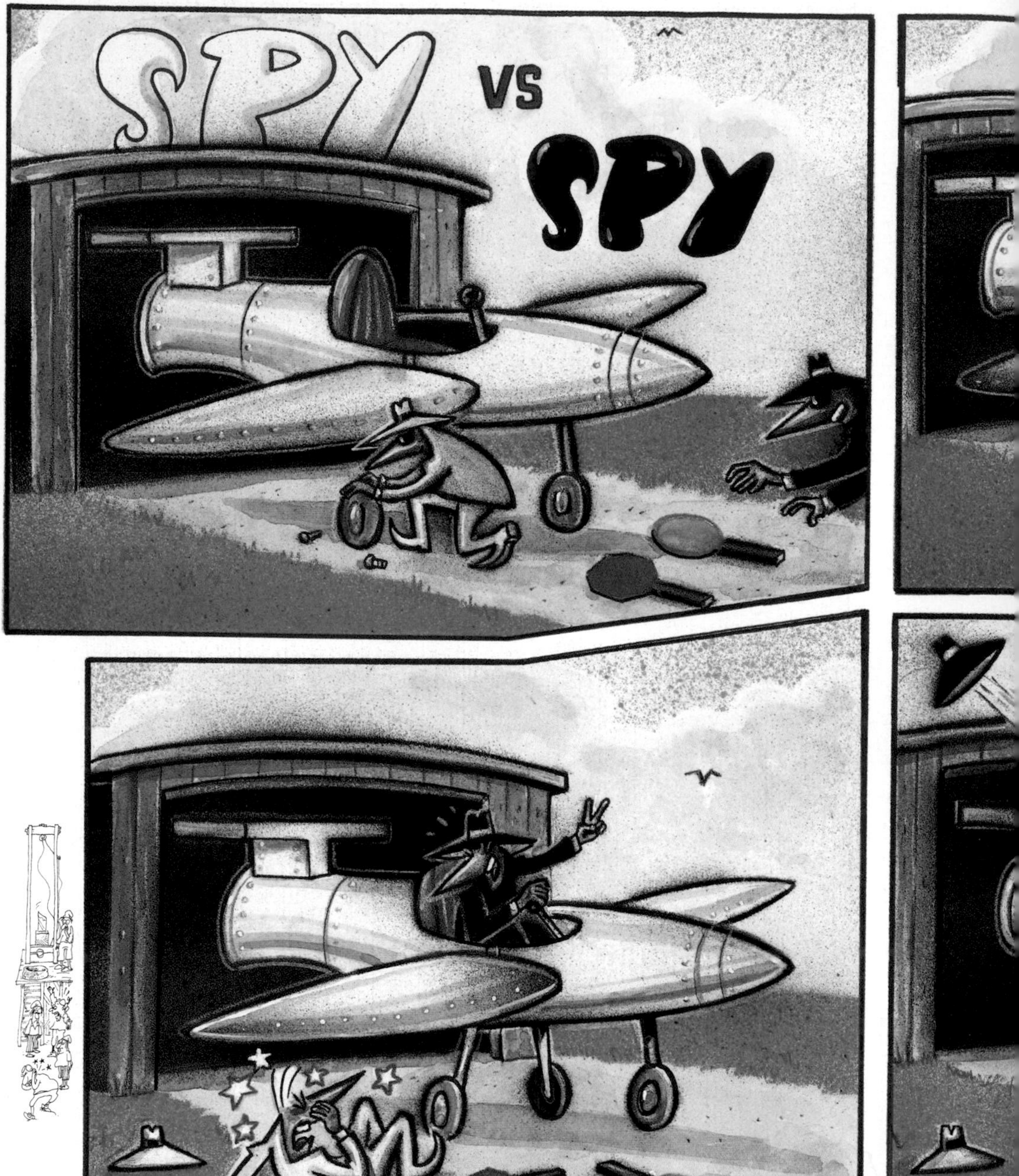
SPY
VS
SPY

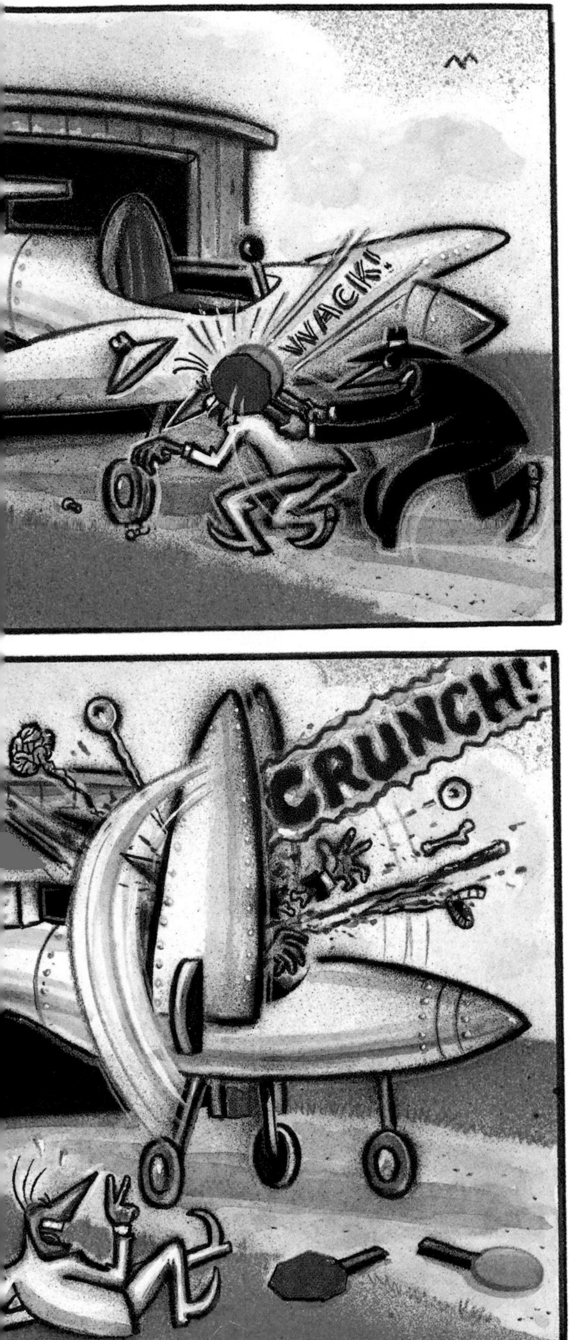
WACK!
CRUNCH!

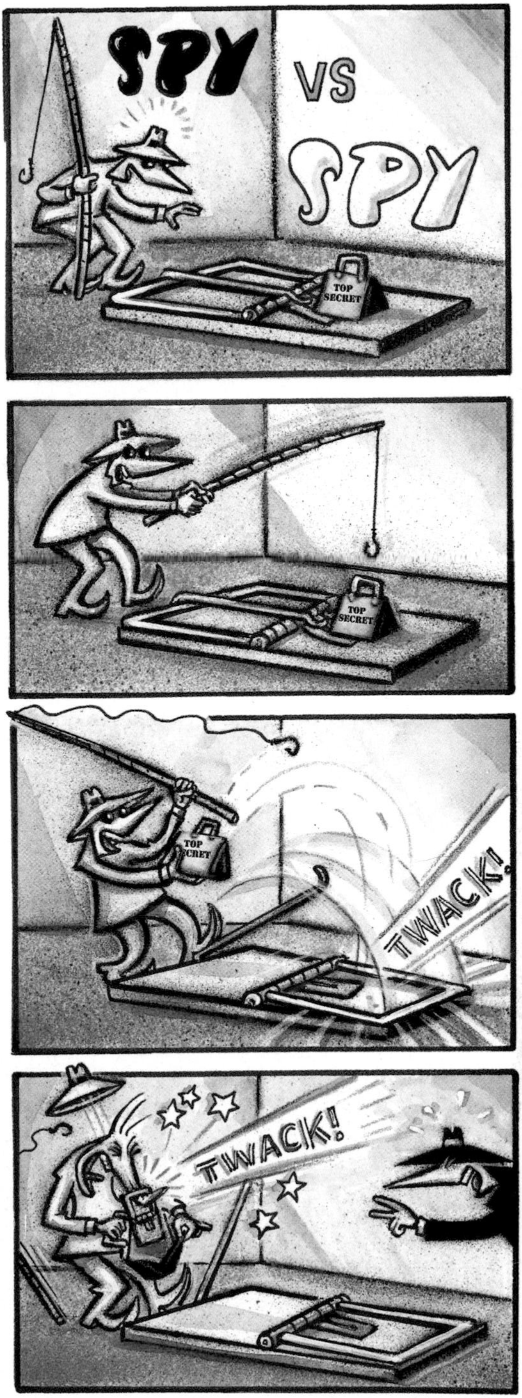
SPY VS SPY
TOP SECRET
TOP SECRET
TOP SECRET
TWACK!
TWACK!

KUPER

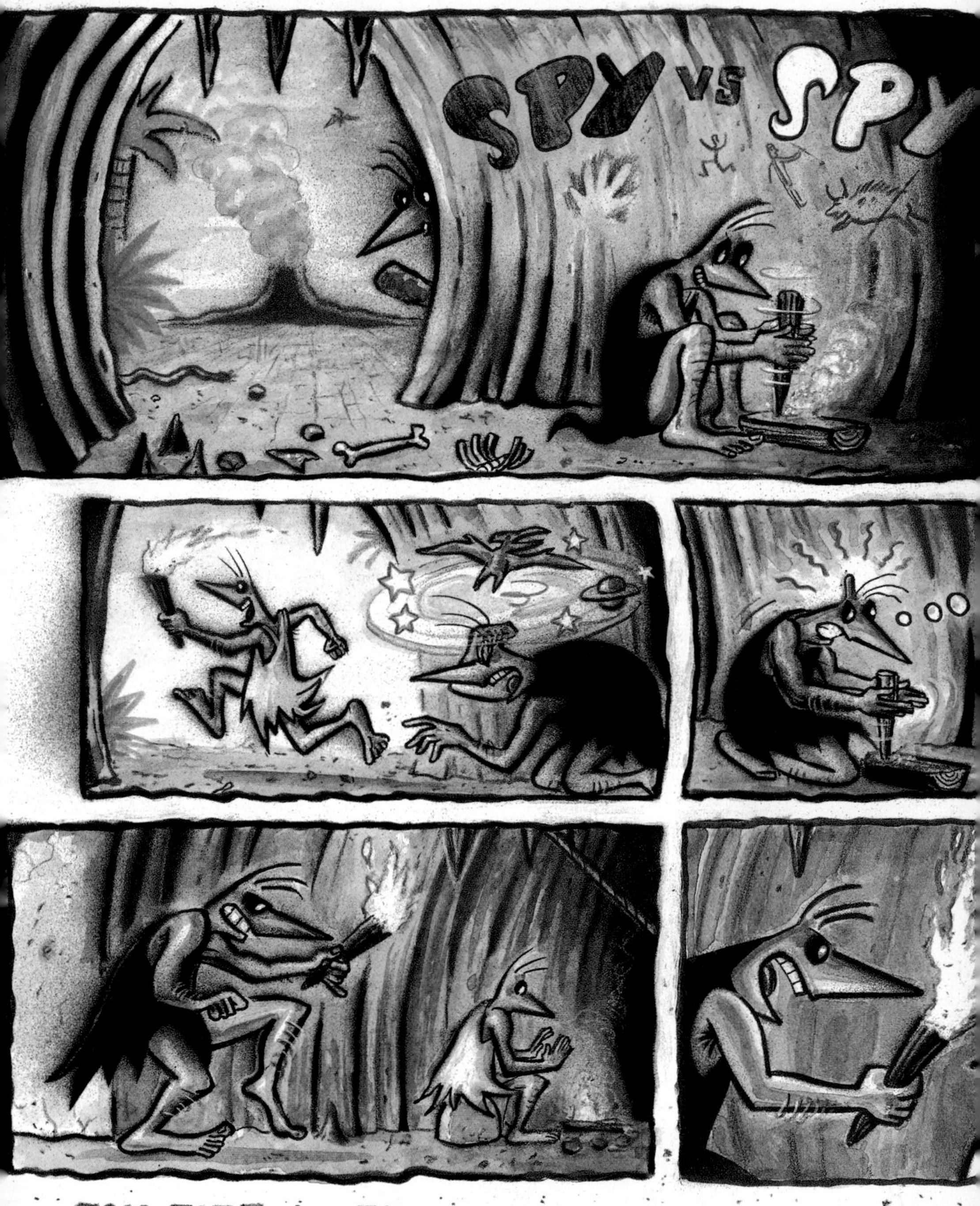
SPY vs SPY

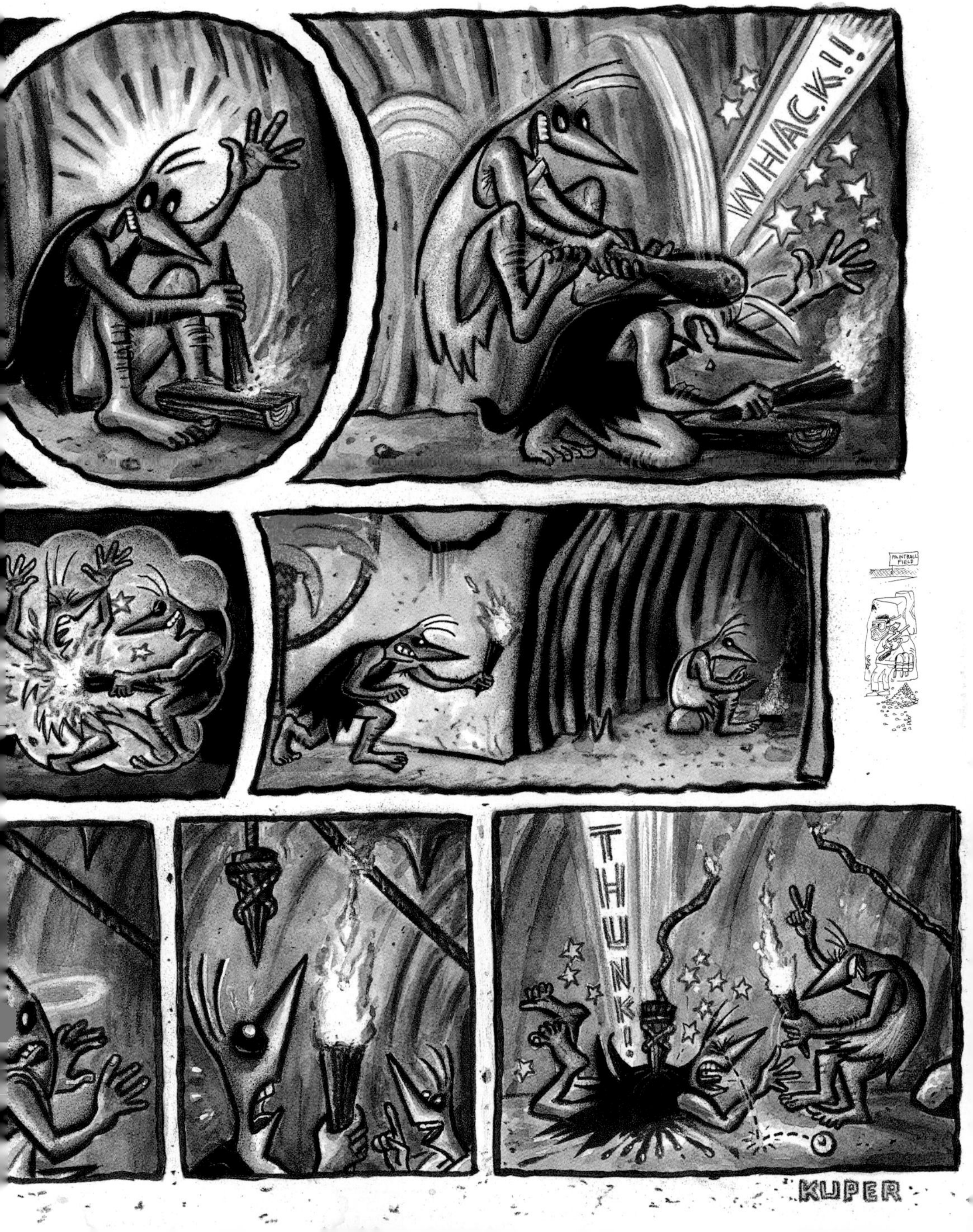
WHACK!!
THUNK!
PAINTBALL FIELD
KUPER

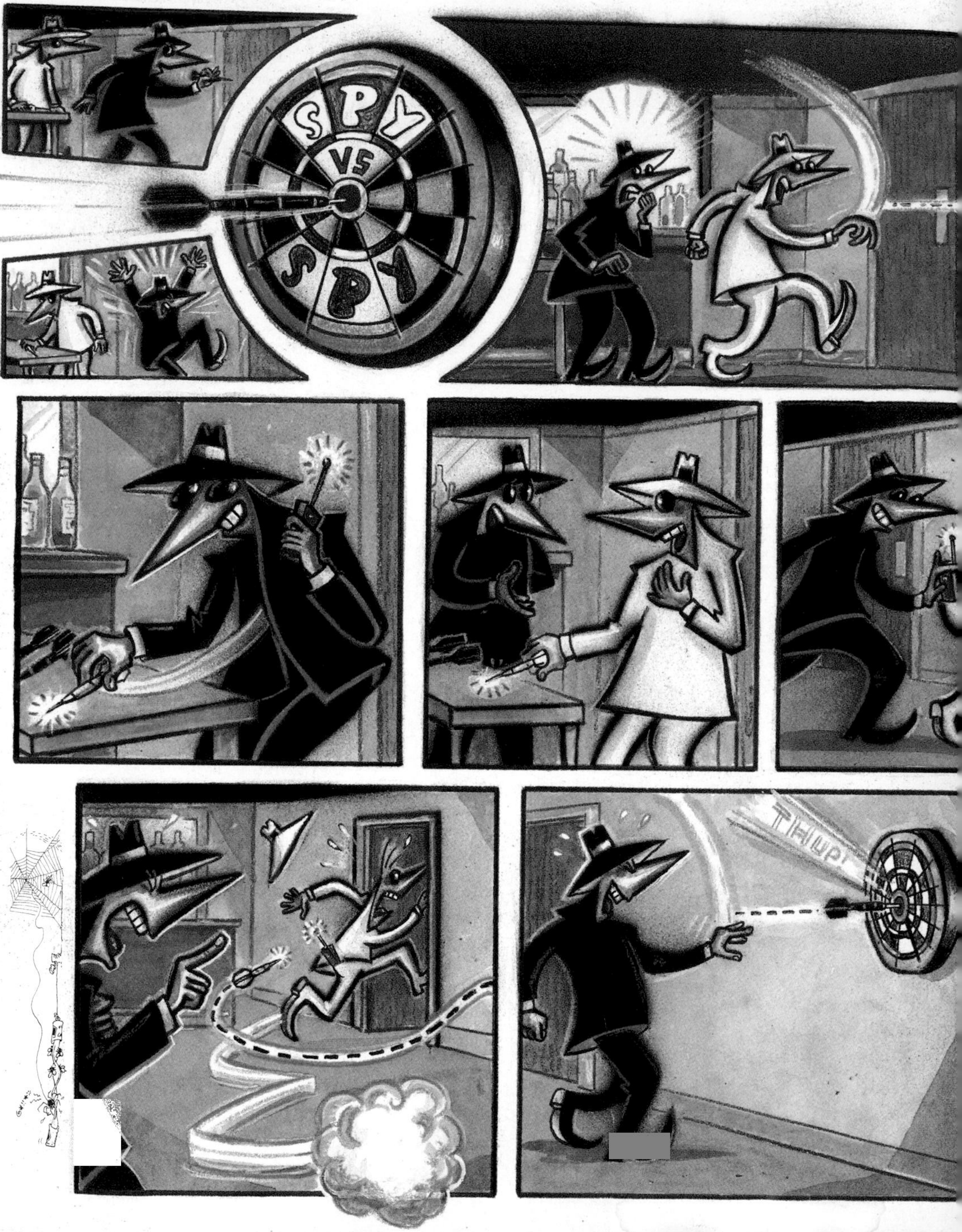
SPY
VS
SPY
THUP!

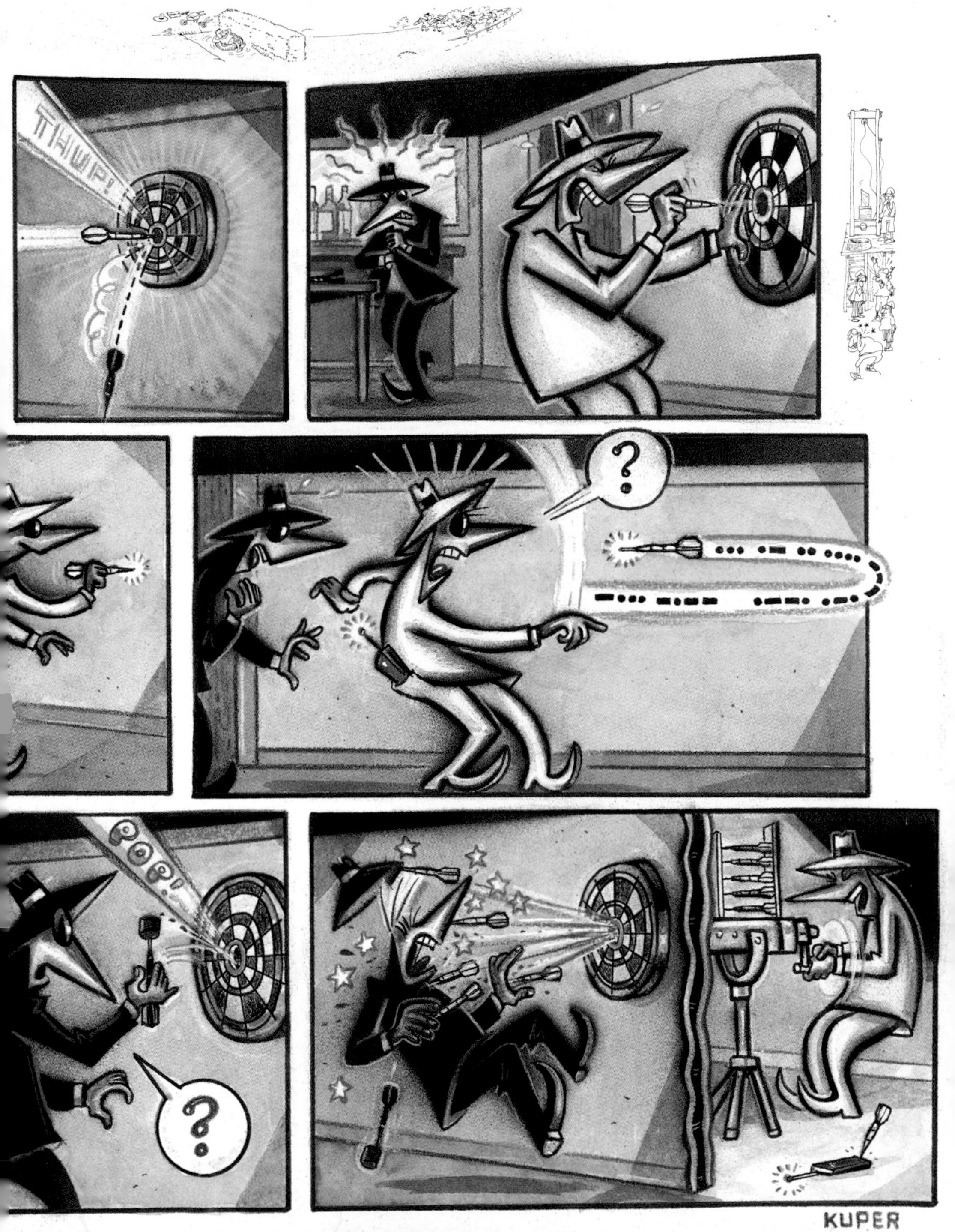
THWP!
?
POP!
?
KUPER

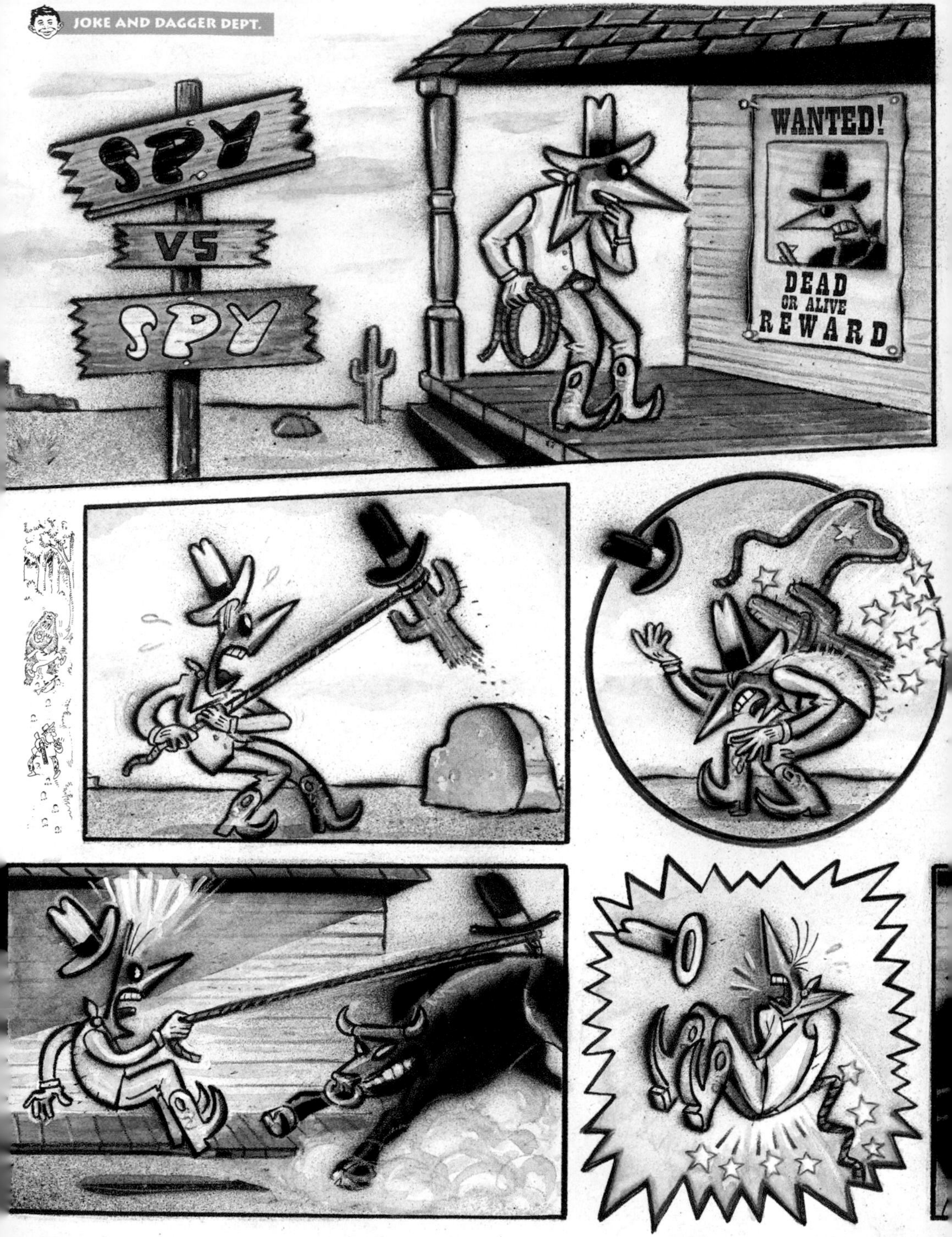
SPY
VS
SPY
WANTED!
DEAD
OR ALIVE
REWARD

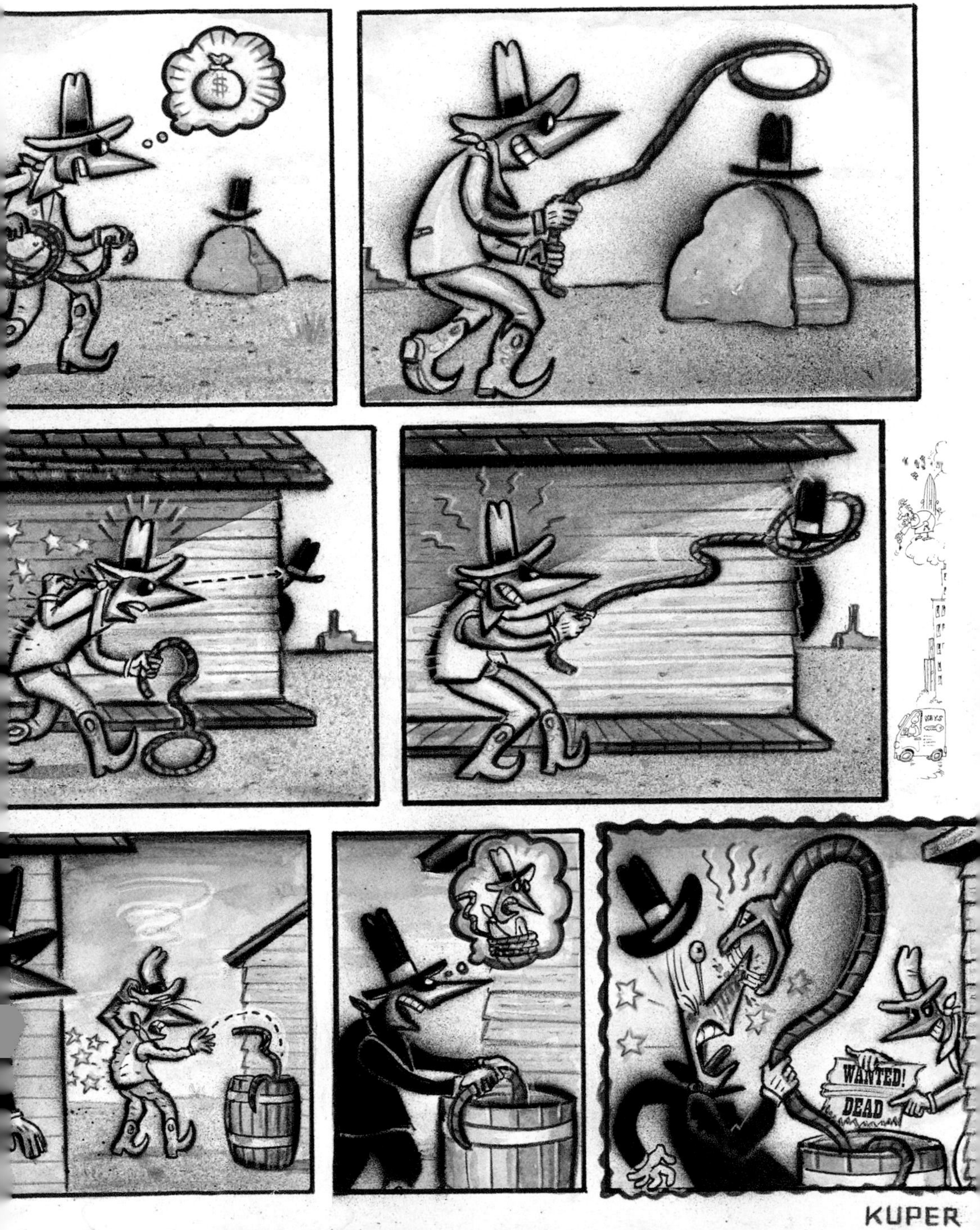
WANTED!
DEAD
KUPER

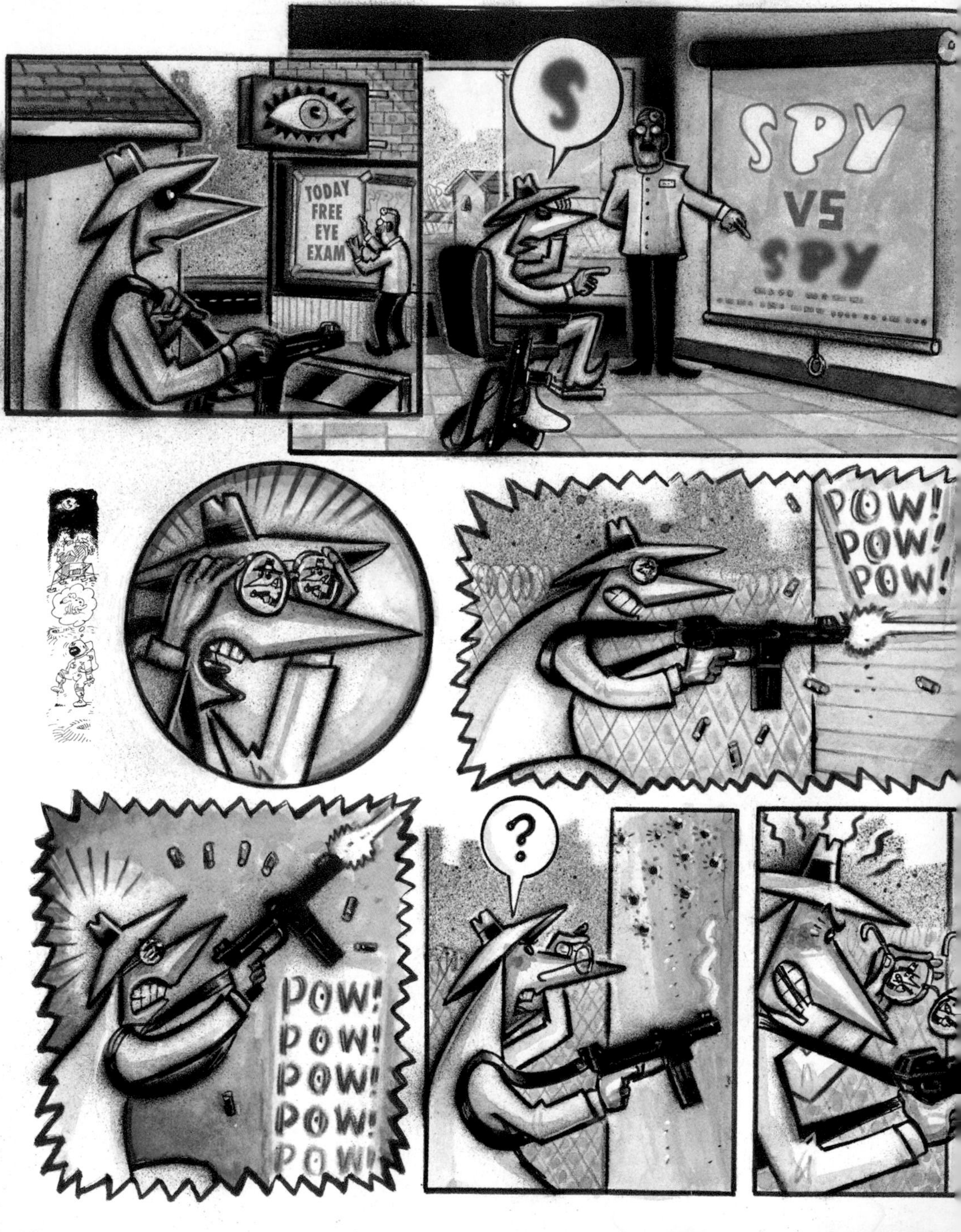
TODAY FREE EYE EXAM
S
SPY VS SPY
POW! POW! POW!
POW! POW! POW! POW! POW!
?

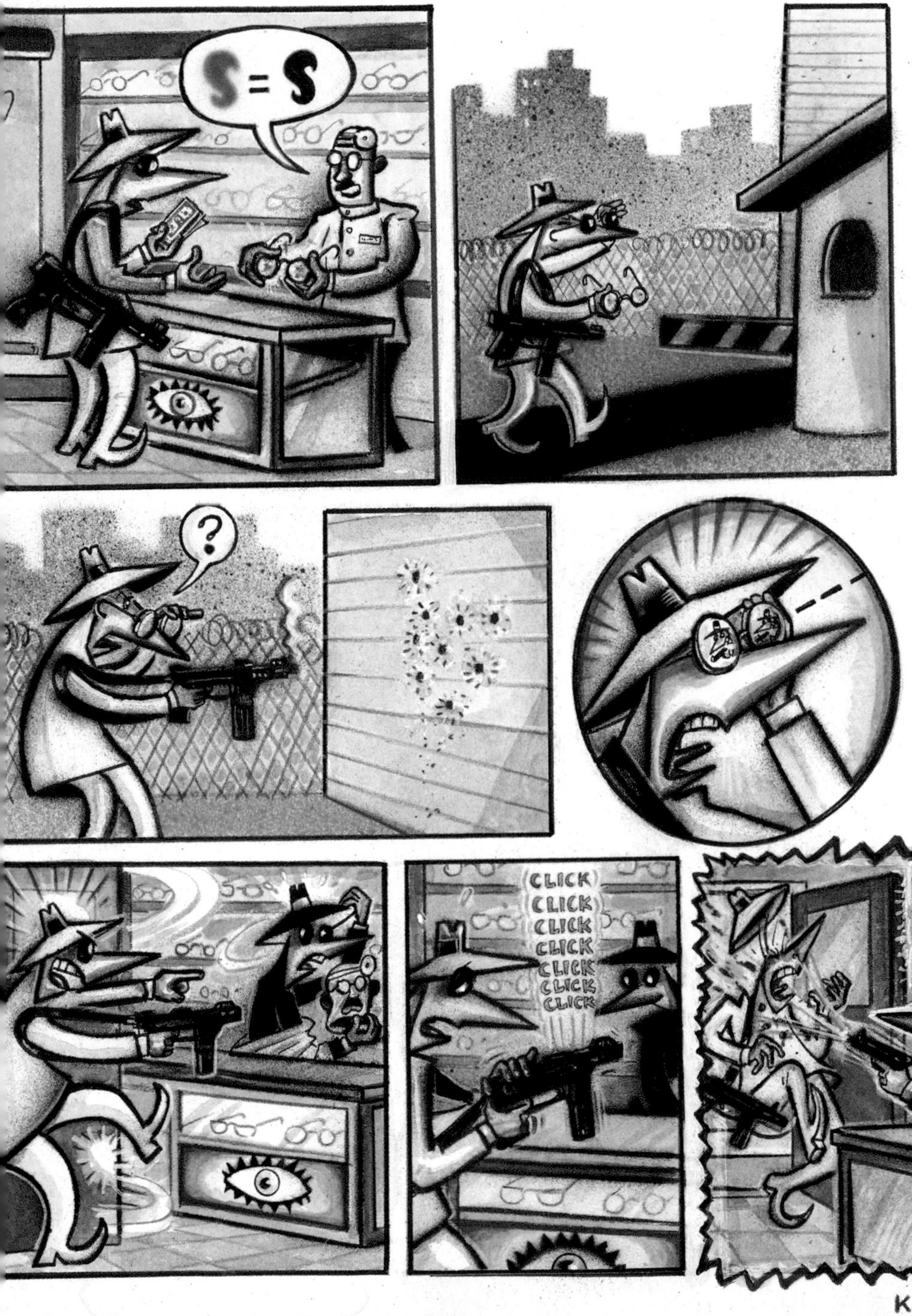
S = S
?
CLICK
CLICK
CLICK
CLICK
CLICK
CLICK
CLICK
POW!
POW!
POW!
KUPER

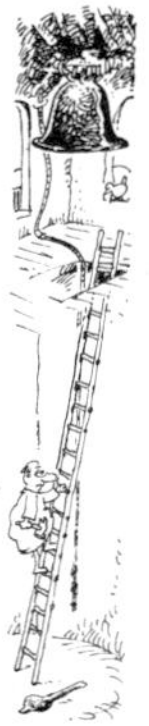

JOKE AND DAGGER DEPT.

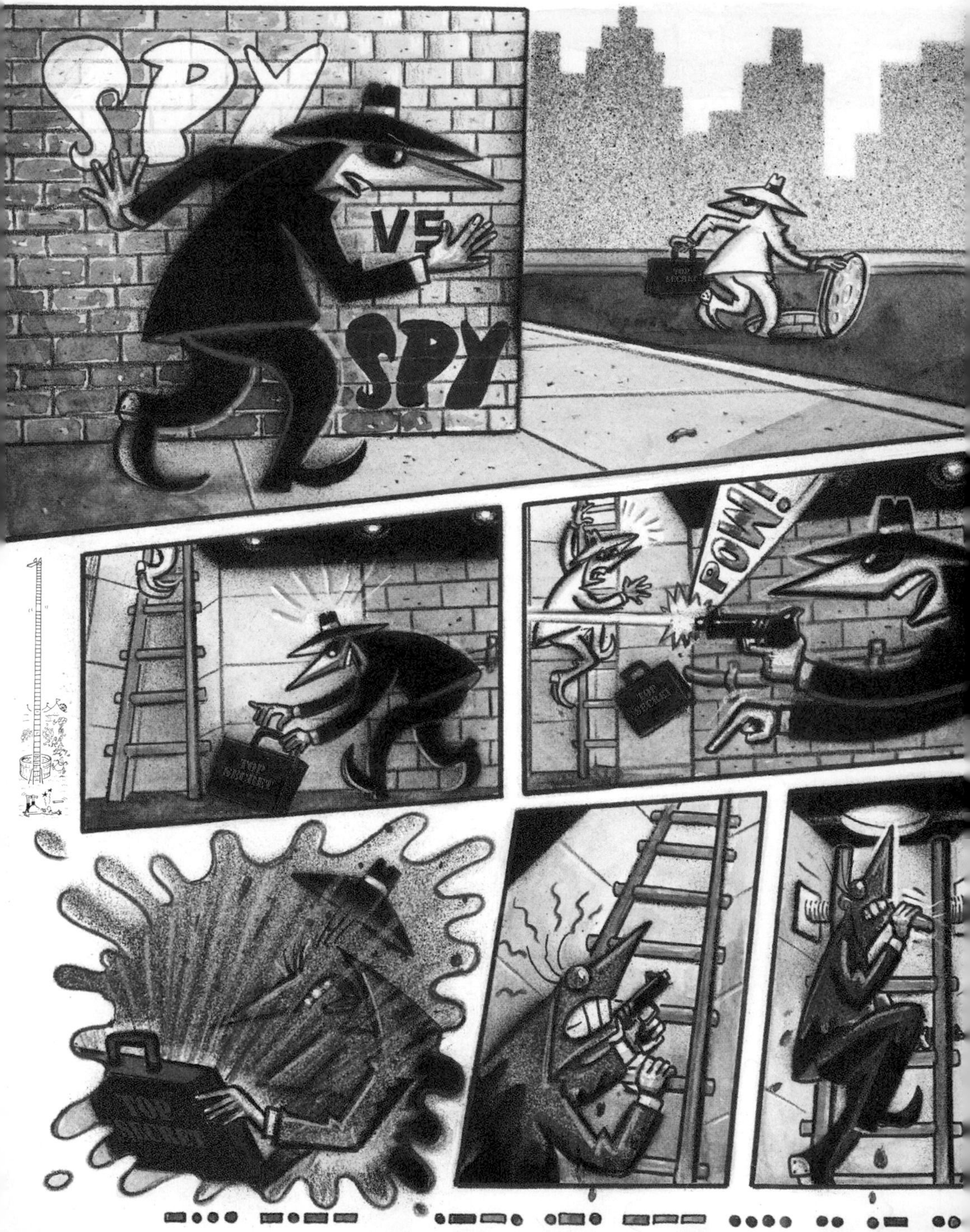
SPY
VS
SPY
TOP SECRET
POW!
TOP SECRET
TOP SECRET

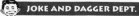

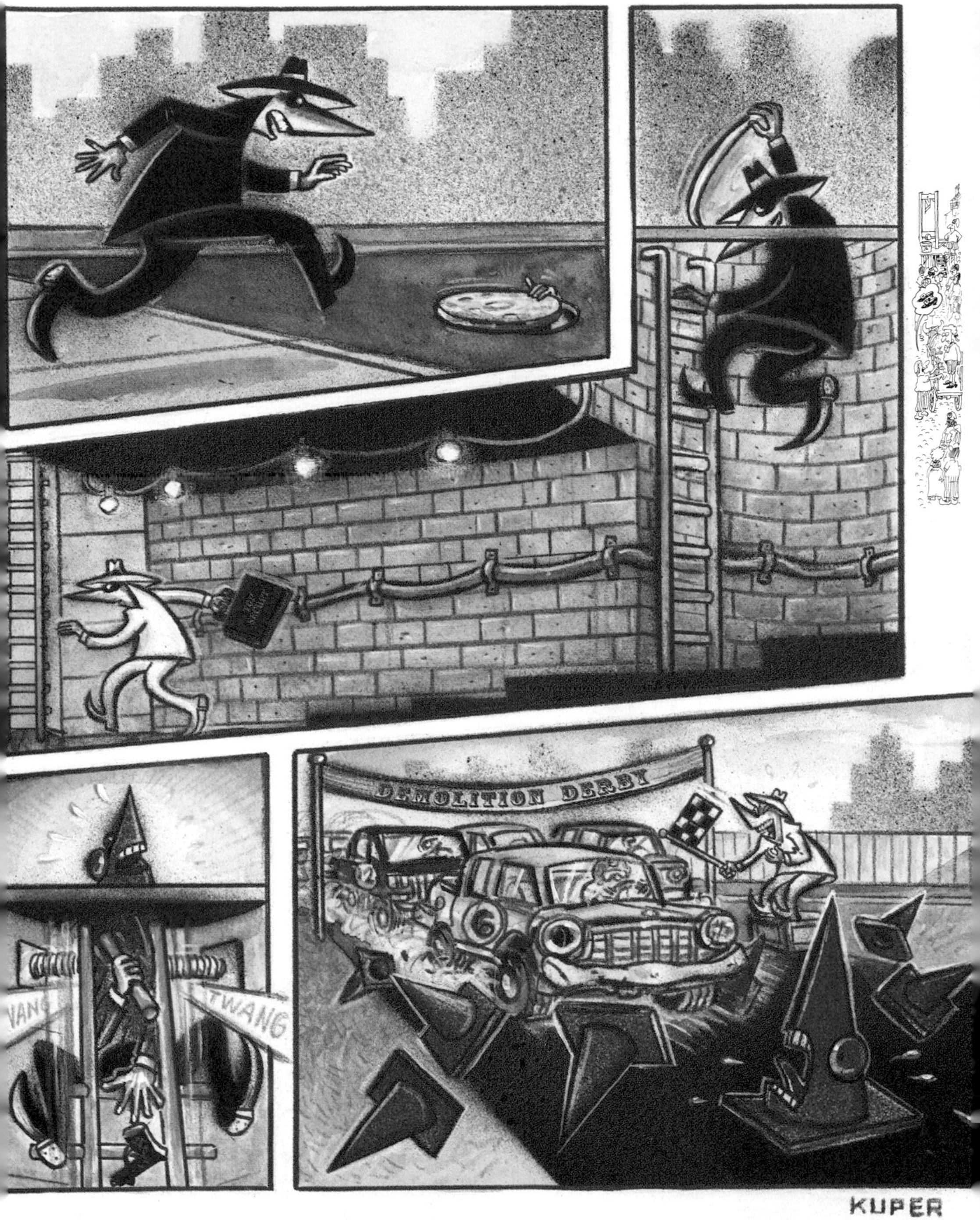
DEMOLITION DERBY
TWANG
KUPER

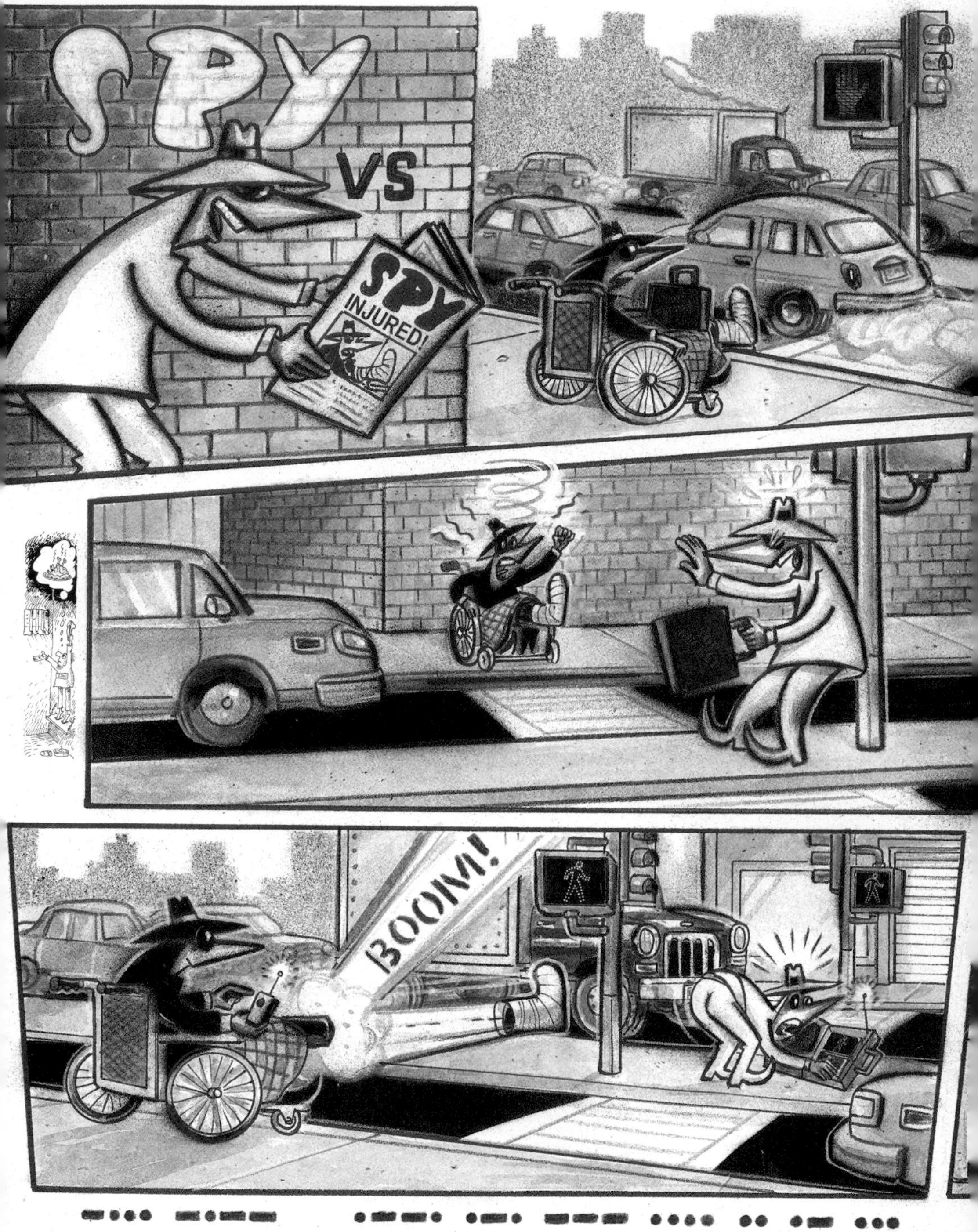
SPY
VS
SPY
INJURED!
BOOM!

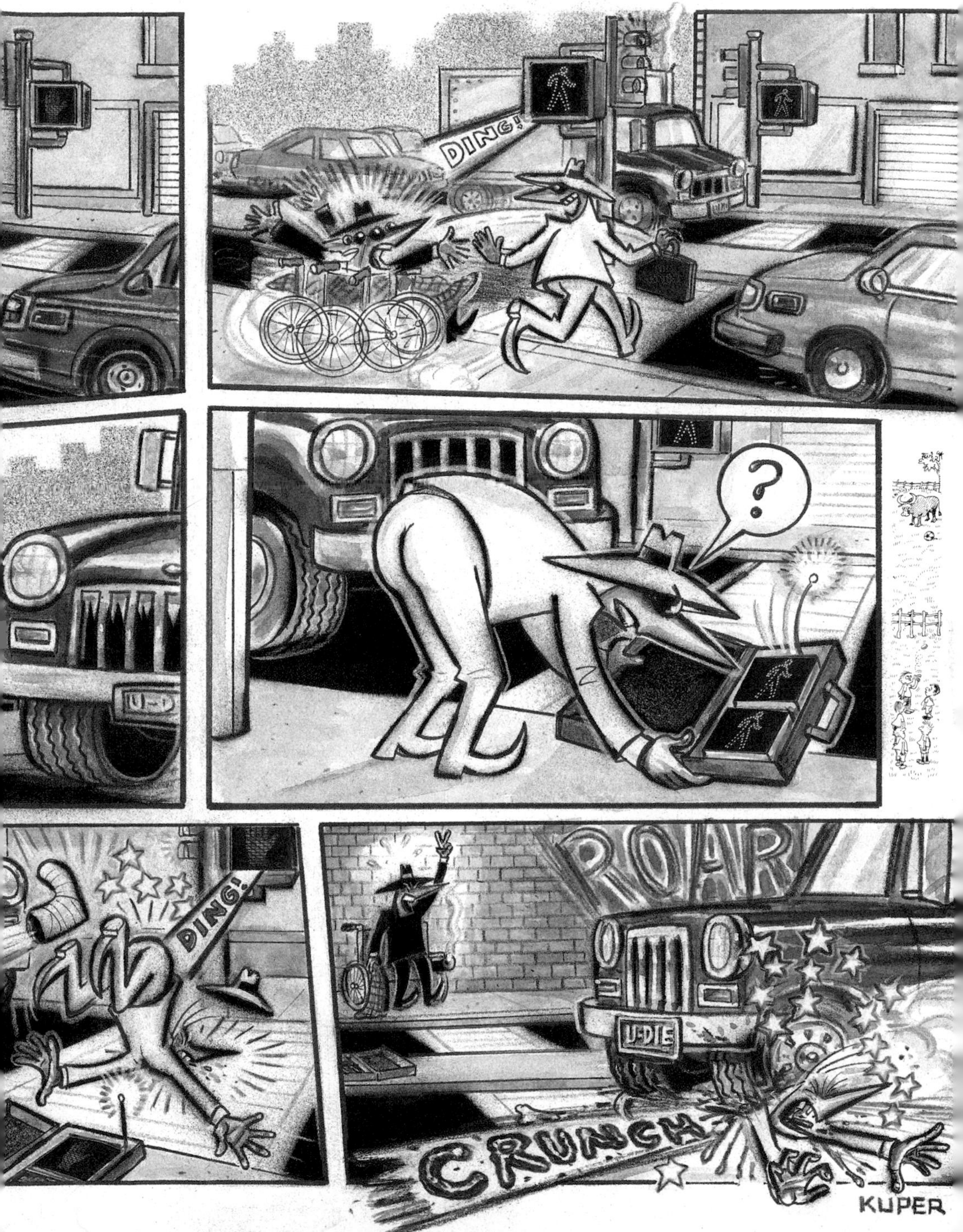
DING!
?
DING!
ROAR
U-DIE
CRUNCH
KUPER

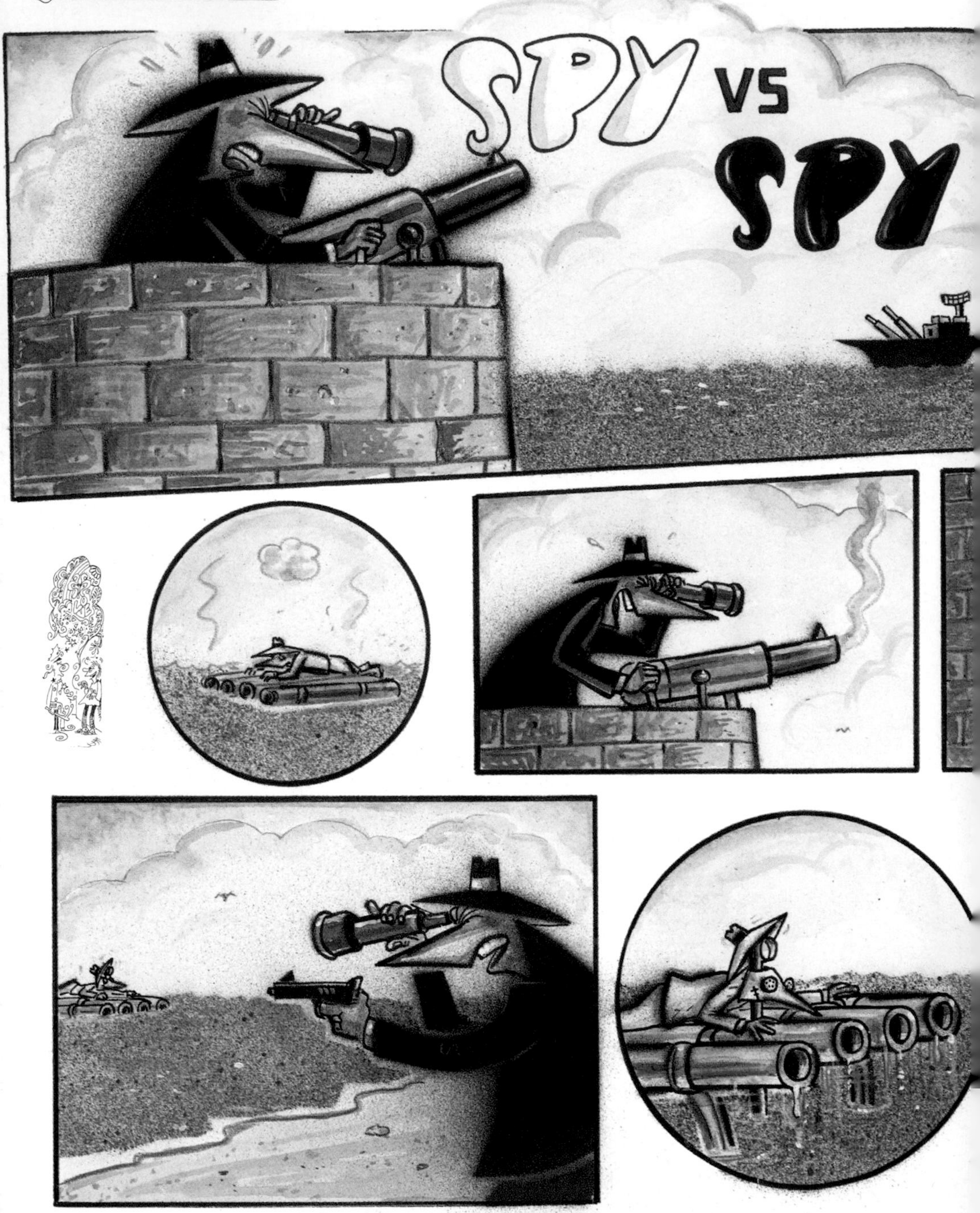
SPY VS SPY

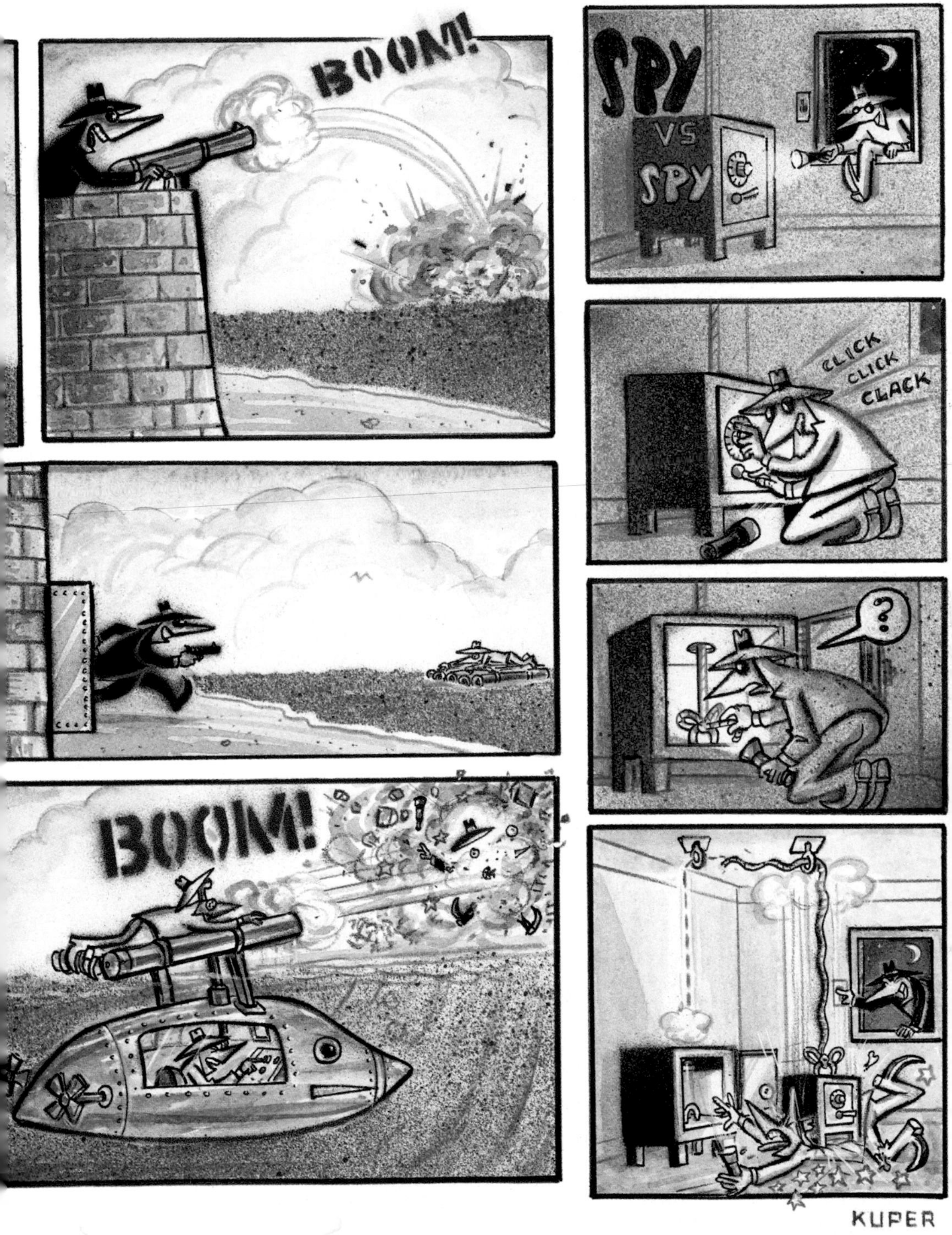
BOOM!
BOOM!
SPY VS SPY
CLICK
CLICK
CLACK
?
KUPER

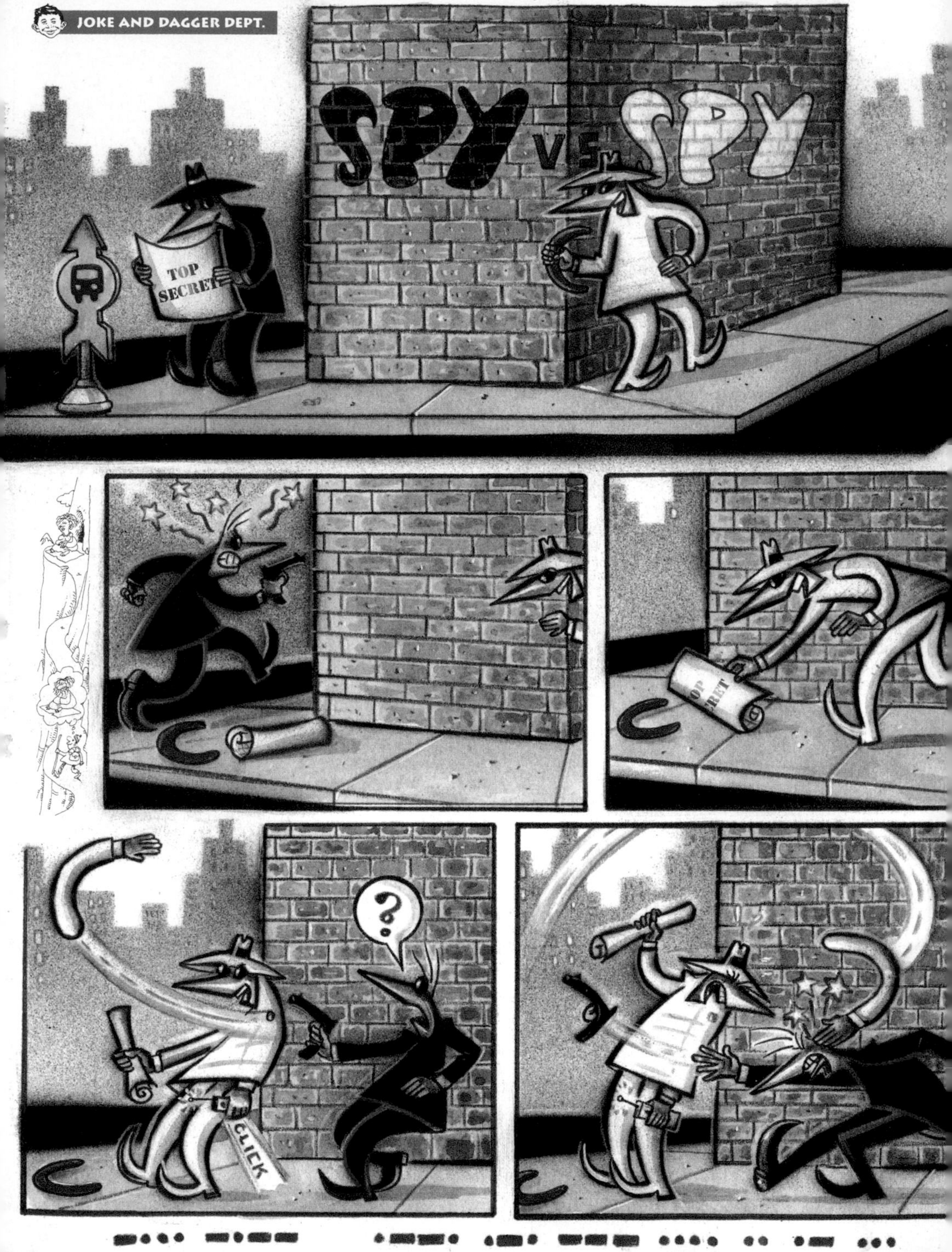
SPY vs SPY
TOP SECRET
?
CLICK

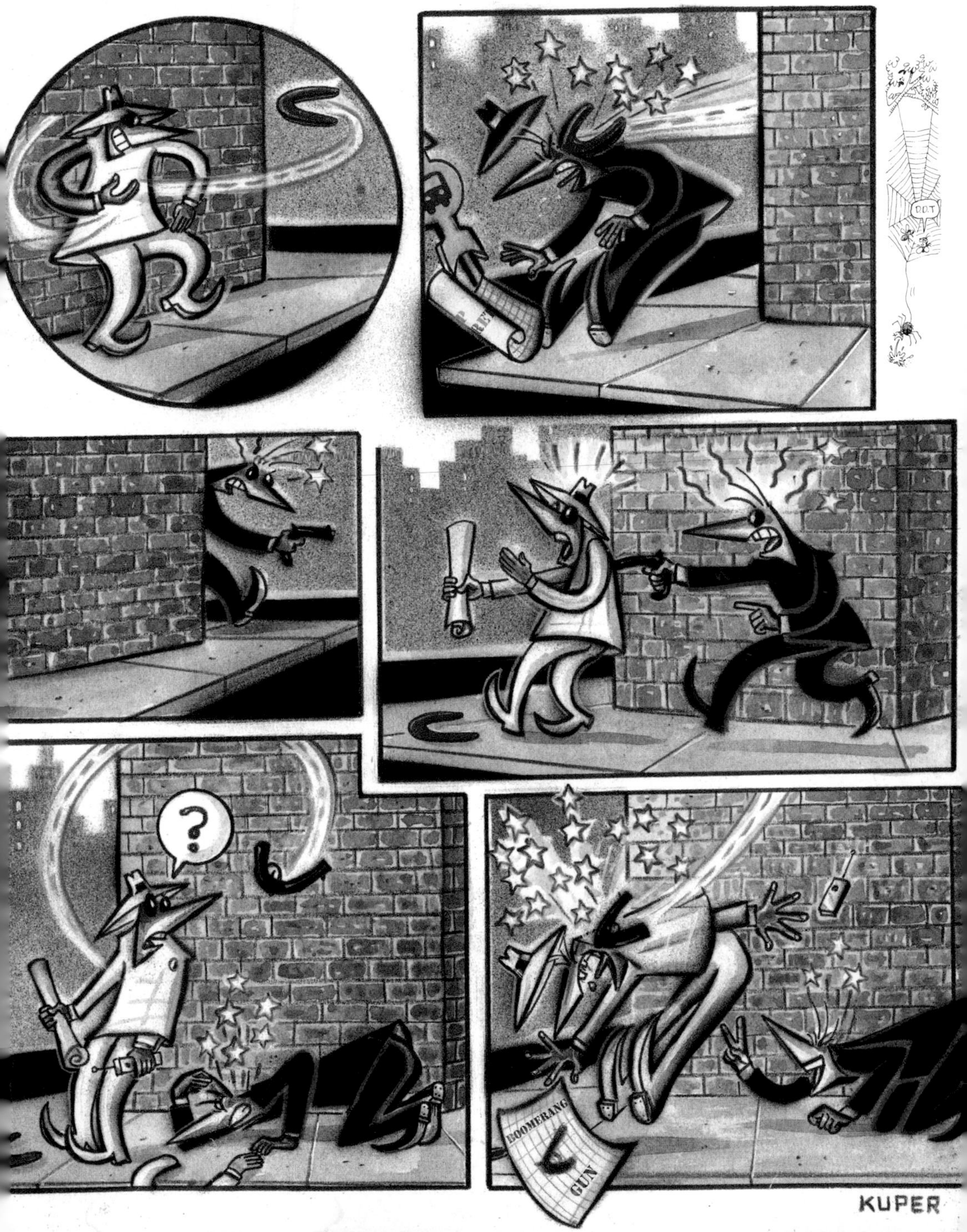
D.D.T
?
BOOMERANG
GUN
KUPER

More Misadventures from the Diabolical Duo of Double Cross and Deceit!

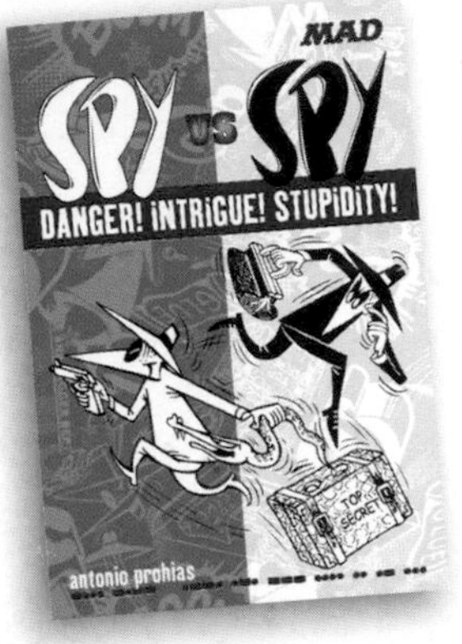
MAD
SPY vs SPY
DANGER! INTRIGUE! STUPIDITY!
TOP SECRET
antonio prohias

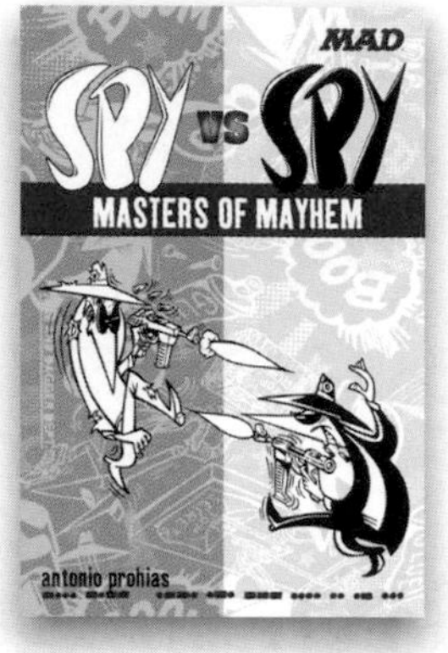
MAD
SPY vs SPY
MASTERS OF MAYHEM
antonio prohias

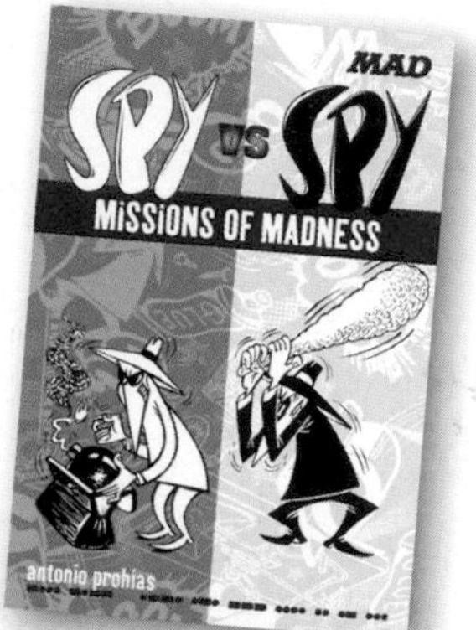
MAD
SPY vs SPY
MISSIONS OF MADNESS
antonio prohias

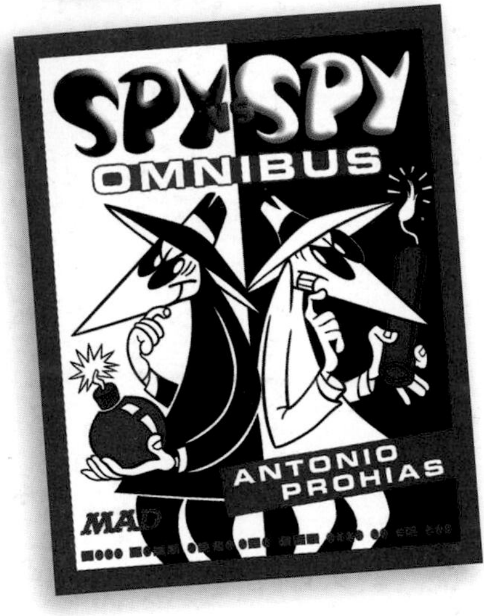
SPY vs SPY
OMNIBUS
ANTONIO PROHIAS
MAD

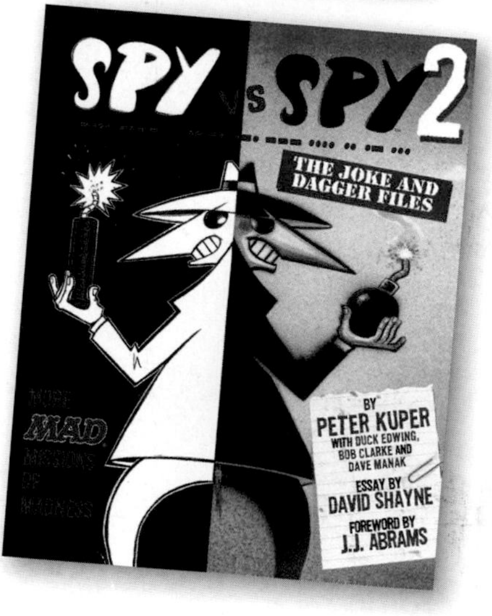
SPY vs SPY 2
THE JOKE AND DAGGER FILES
BY PETER KUPER
WITH DUCK EDWING, BOB CLARKE AND DAVE MANAK
ESSAY BY DAVID SHAYNE
FOREWORD BY J.J. ABRAMS